D0410888

PRAISE FOR CAROL ANN LEE

Roses From The Earth: The Biography of Anne Frank

'Excellent . . . serious, sensitive and scrupulous.'
Sunday Telegraph

'Vivid and shattering. A work of real
sympathy and imagination.'
Mail on Sunday

The Hidden Life of Otto Frank

'A tour-de-force of history and humanity.'
Reader's Digest

'Significant and fascinating.'
Financial Times

'Lee builds up a memorable portrait of a man
struggling out of the valley of death.'
Guardian

One of Your Own: The Life and Death of Myra Hindley

'A compelling read.'
Independent

'Scrupulously unsensational and as good a
biography of Hindley as we'll get.'
The Sunday Times

'Intelligent and impressively fair-minded.'
The Scotsman

Ruth Ellis: A Fine Day for a Hanging

'A forensically researched book that casts a haunting new light on the last woman to be hanged in Britain.'
Daily Mail

'Worthy of Truman Capote . . . the finest account of awaiting execution that I have ever read.'
Laurence Marks (Screenwriter)

About the Author

Carol Ann Lee was born in Wakefield, Yorkshire in 1969 and graduated from Manchester Metropolitan University. Three years later, her first book, *Roses from the Earth: The Biography of Anne Frank*, was published to great acclaim and has been published in fifteen countries to date. She went on to write several more bestselling books, six of which, including *Somebody's Mother, Somebody's Daughter*, have been optioned for television and film.

SOMEBODY'S MOTHER, SOMEBODY'S DAUGHTER

TRUE STORIES FROM VICTIMS AND SURVIVORS OF THE **YORKSHIRE RIPPER**

CAROL ANN LEE

Michael O'Mara Books Limited

First published in Great Britain in 2019 by
Michael O'Mara Books Limited
9 Lion Yard
Tremadoc Road
London SW4 7NQ

A CIP catalogue record for this book is available from
the British Library.

Papers used by Michael O'Mara Books Limited are natural,
recyclable products made from wood grown in sustainable forests.
The manufacturing processes conform to the environmental
regulations of the country of origin.

ISBN: 978-1-78929-039-4 in hardback print format
ISBN: 978-1-78929-130-8 in trade paperback print format
ISBN: 978-1-78243-925-7 in ebook format
ISBN: 978-1-78929-105-6 in audiobook format

1 2 3 4 5 6 7 8 9 10

Typeset by Ed Pickford

Every reasonable effort has been made to acknowledge all copyright
holders. Any errors or omissions that may have occurred are
inadvertent, and anyone with any copyright queries is invited
to write to the publisher, so that full acknowledgement may be
included in subsequent editions of the work.

Printed and bound by CPI Group (UK) Ltd, Croydon, CR0 4YY

www.mombooks.com

'Perhaps it's easier to see it as just another story, if you don't belong to the group of people the Ripper wanted to kill?'

Una, *Becoming Unbecoming* (2016)

CONTENTS

FOREWORD

I was an eighteen-year-old cub reporter when Peter Sutcliffe began his reign of terror – and it was a reign of terror. For five years, life for women in the north of England stopped. No woman went out alone after dark and we looked for the Ripper in every shadow, in every dark corner. But during those five years I learned all I needed to know about how not to treat women. Victims were divided into innocent and not innocent. All the detectives and most of the reporters were men, yet it was the ultimate crime against women. No real support was offered to family and survivors and a wild goose chase for a man with a North-East accent allowed Sutcliffe to go undetected for so long.

And yet, there was a strength among women which grew into a movement that was to change all of us for ever. The 'Reclaim the Night' campaign demanded an end to the suggested curfew on women when it was a man committing that most heinous of crimes. Female detectives no longer accepted their roles as coffee makers and filing clerks. And above all, the determination of those who survived and the families of those who didn't shone through as they demanded that the killer be brought to justice.

Now, almost four decades later, it is time to tell their stories. Too often Sutcliffe, who to this day revels in his notoriety, has been at the forefront of the headlines. Now it is time to remember and honour the women – thirteen murdered and seven who lived with life-changing injuries – who were all too often simply a list of names and photographs. Their stories, their dreams, and their lives are what should be remembered. And those they left behind.

Those five years taught me everything I needed to know as a journalist: never to judge, always to listen, and that *all* human life is sacred. I remember when Home Secretary Willie Whitelaw declared Sutcliffe would never be eligible for parole, Olive Smelt, who had been left for dead by the killer, looked at me and said: 'It's done, it's over. Never should his name be mentioned again.'

I commend this book to you as one step to try and redress the balance.

Christa Ackroyd

ACKNOWLEDGEMENTS

Many people helped in the research and writing of this book. I would first of all like to thank those who spoke to me but have asked not to be named. Survivors referred to the 'stigma' of the attacks, inflicted by the way police and press dealt with the case, and this continues to be felt by many of those most affected by Sutcliffe's crimes. One victim's relative felt unable to tell her children about the circumstances of their grandmother's death because of it, while another spoke on condition of strict anonymity, fearful of upsetting her mother, who had been orphaned at Sutcliffe's hands and kept silent ever since about it.

I am particularly grateful to Debra Sacks for talking to me about her sister Jayne MacDonald; to Geoff Beattie, for discussing his mother Irene Richardson; to Richard McCann for speaking to me about his mother Wilma McCann and sister Sonia; and to Mo Lea, a courageous woman who has used her considerable artistic skills to explore the attack she survived in 1980. I also thank journalist Christa Ackroyd, who interviewed most of those connected to this case over the years; her knowledge, compassion and integrity are inspirational. I'm grateful to Denise Cavanagh too, for discussing her experiences as a young policewoman, and to David Hinchliffe, for his insights into social work during the 1970s.

The staff of several archives were extremely helpful in finding source material and I would especially like to thank everyone at Leeds Central Library, Manchester Central Library, Sheffield City Archives, and the National Archives.

I must also thank *Radio Times* journalist Alison Graham and writers Nicola Upson and Mandy Morton for an intelligent and thought-provoking discussion regarding women and crime during the 2017 Felixstowe Book Festival. Many thanks too to Richard C. Cobb, whose forthcoming book *On the Trail of the Yorkshire Ripper* will be an insightful read.

I couldn't be more grateful to my brilliant literary agent, Robert Smith, for placing this book with the fantastic team at Michael O'Mara; I thank everyone there for their expertise, and especially my editor Gabriella Nemeth, whose patience and kindness are endless!

The original idea for this book came about years ago, when I read Joan Smith's searing chapter on the Yorkshire Ripper case in *Misogynies*. A more recent discussion with my friend, poet Valerie Anderson Gaskill, led to this book in its present form. Thank you so much, Val, for your encouragement.

I would also like to thank those people whom I tried to contact for interviews and regarding source material but was unable to speak to personally. I will gladly credit anyone I have missed in future editions of *Somebody's Mother, Somebody's Daughter*.

Finally, a heartfelt thanks to my friends and family for their support, especially my son River, and my mother, Doreen Lee, without whom this book could never have been written.

Carol Ann Lee

INTRODUCTION

Between 1975 and 1981 thirteen women in the north of England were murdered by Peter Sutcliffe; a further seven women are formally recognized as having survived his attacks. Over thirty-five years since he was sentenced to life imprisonment, scarcely a week goes by without some mention of him in the British media.

Most of us are familiar with Sutcliffe's face and tabloid title – the 'Yorkshire Ripper' – but would struggle to name his victims. While this is often the case with serial murders, the women who died at Sutcliffe's hands have suffered considerable posthumous denigration. Relegated to a monochrome grid of faces and stripped of individuality, they are usually defined by a single dynamic: 'good-time girls' or prostitutes, and those who were 'respectable'. With few exceptions, this is how they have been presented ever since the first confirmed Yorkshire Ripper murder, of Wilma McCann, in October 1975.

Unlike Sutcliffe, who is noteworthy only in terms of his criminality, each woman who died at his hands was more than the manner of her death, despite being defined by it publicly. Some had complex lives full of secrets, while others were newly independent, studying at university or embarking on a career. All had families and friends who mourned them deeply.

The women who lived are, as survivor Mo Lea phrases it, members of 'an exclusive club you don't want to be part of'. They faced gargantuan challenges in the years ahead: repeated surgery on injuries that left them with everything from memory loss to having to cut their own hair because salon workers were upset by their wounded skulls; temporarily losing custody of their children due to the psychological fallout of surviving attempted murder; being dismissed by the police as 'unreliable' witnesses or women of 'loose morals'; and even, in one instance of deplorable institutional racism, of being 'just this side of a gorilla'.[1]

While the media habitually fetishizes murderers, the disregard of these women may be due somewhat to the fact that all but two of the many books about the Yorkshire Ripper have been written by men who focus almost exclusively on the men involved in the case – from Sutcliffe and his father and brothers, to the all-male 'Ripper Squad'.[2] The *Guardian* recently noted the irony of how, due to the lack of women's authorship, 'the Ripper story has become a relentless examination of male identity, of violence perpetually in bloom'.[3]

Somebody's Mother, Somebody's Daughter is not a book about Peter Sutcliffe. Instead it aims to tell the stories of those women who came into his murderous orbit. The title is a rejoinder to Gordon Burn's convincing biography of Sutcliffe, *Somebody's Husband, Somebody's Son*, as well as being spoken by a detective urging the public's help in finding the Ripper. Although this book concentrates on those murders and attacks for which Sutcliffe is held judicially accountable, there can be little doubt that among the unsolved crimes in various constabularies are several committed by him.[4]

Above all, this book is a reminder that each of the women within its pages were individuals whose loss was and is keenly felt by those who loved them. They are a group only insofar as the man responsible for their deaths/attacks rendered it so, but in every way that matters, they were and are irreplaceable women in their own right.

1

ANNA

Tralee, the capital town of County Kerry in the south-west of Ireland, is situated on the Dingle Peninsula, famed for its wild Atlantic scenery. Anna Patricia Brosnan was born there on 21 March 1933, to Roman Catholic farmer Michael Brosnan and his wife.[1] All the Brosnan children – nine girls and three boys – were brought up in Tralee but keen to explore beyond it.

Fifteen-year-old Anna left home in 1948, joining her eldest sister, Helen, who had settled in the Yorkshire town of Keighley after the Second World War. Eleven miles north-west of Bradford, Keighley had a rich seam of Irish Roman Catholic immigration; those fleeing the Great Famine of the 1840s found work in the wool and cotton mills, and factories producing machinery. Anna was employed as a playing-cards sorter in Waddington's factory when she met textiles-accessories maker Roman Rogulskyj, six years her senior.[2] They shared a background of farming and Roman Catholicism, coupled with new lives in a different country; the Rogulskyjs were part of Keighley's large Ukranian community who had mostly arrived from Displaced Persons camps in Germany and Italy.

Anna and Roman were married on 19 February 1955 at St Anne's Church in Keighley, with Roman's father, Mychalo, as a witness. Anna was twenty-one. The marriage lasted eighteen years, ending in divorce in July 1973; there were no children. Roman swiftly wed again, remaining in Keighley with his second wife until his death in 1989. Despite her ash-blonde good looks and 'open, warm, almost childlike manner' Anna lost some of her confidence after the divorce.[3] Known as 'Irish Annie' in the town's pubs and cafés, she enjoyed working in Woolworths near her home on the sloping thoroughfare of Highfield Lane. Keighley was then in sharp economic decline: derelict mills and factories crumbled beside the River Worth, while brutal town planning swept away fine buildings, leaving boarded-up terraces and lacklustre pubs.

It was in one of these bars that Anna caught the eye of Geoffrey Hughes, who had recently moved into a terraced house on North Queen Street.[4] Much later, Anna learned that he had been discharged from a psychiatric hospital with a recommendation to 'keep away from women for five years'.[5] Geoff spent more time at Anna's home than his own, taking out his unpredictable temper on her. On one occasion he grasped her by the hair and plunged her head into a bucket of cold water. Still vulnerable after the failure of her marriage, she remained in the relationship.[6]

Two incidents in early summer 1975 further convinced Anna to stick with Geoff. Walking through Town Hall Square one afternoon, she was approached by a man near the Cenotaph, who pestered her to have a cup of tea with him. Anna refused and quickened her step. He stayed close behind as she crossed the road, and was a short distance away when she reached Highfield Lane. Resisting the urge to run home, Anna took different routes until she managed to shake him off. But he appeared again a few weeks later, in Wild's Coffee Bar where she used to work, and sat down opposite her. Anna recalled that he had 'racing' eyes and 'dainty' hands, thick dark hair and a springy beard.[7] She declined his offer of a drink and grew angry at his persistence. It was only when she warned him that the whole café would know what a creep he was unless he left her alone that he finally walked out.

Shortly afterwards, in one of his more generous moods, Geoff presented Anna with a colour television. She was delighted, but their incessant rows made her feel claustrophobic. On Friday 4 July 1975, Anna told Geoff she wanted to go out alone. His temper snapped and she ran crying into another room. He collected every pair of shoes she owned and hid them, before leaving the house himself.

It didn't take Anna long to find her footwear, jumbled together under the kitchen table. Still weeping, she pulled on a pair of green slingbacks and reached for her handbag, then stepped out into the warm evening air.

Intending to visit her sister, Anna stopped at a telephone box to let Geoff know she had outwitted him, but there was no reply from his home. Helen was not in either, so Anna headed for the bar of the Victoria Hotel. After a couple of drinks she caught the bus to Bradford, making her way to Bibby's, a lively West Indian club on Cornwall Terrace. She spent the evening with a couple of friends, telling them her troubles. They gave her a lift back to Keighley at midnight.

When Anna let herself into the house, she realized that Geoff had moved out. Feeling maudlin, she switched on the record player, singing along to her favourite Elvis Presley song, 'Crying in the Chapel' as she folded bed sheets left out to dry. Then she saw that Dumdum, her adored stray kitten, was missing. Convinced that Geoff had taken him, she grabbed her handbag again.

It was a ten-minute walk from Highfield Lane to North Queen Street. Anna cut through onto Mornington Street, crossed the main road and headed into Alice Street. The old Ritz cinema loomed on her right. North Queen Street was a row of mostly derelict houses with the odd ginnel. Preparing for a confrontation with Geoff, Anna was startled when a man's voice called to her from a doorway, asking if she 'fancied it'.

'Not on your life!' she retorted and hurried towards Geoff's home, where she banged her fist repeatedly on the door, waking an elderly neighbour.[8] Frustrated, Anna pulled off a shoe and struck the front room window. The glass shattered; she put her shoe back on and walked away.

A wide alleyway ran between the end of the terrace and the back of the cinema. As Anna passed it, the man who had propositioned her before emerged from the shadows, asking her to have sex with him. This time, she emphasized her refusal with an elbow to his ribs. A few more steps would have brought her to the open stretch of Alice Street, but Anna didn't make it. An unendurable pain burst into her skull and the world slipped into darkness.

At 2.20 a.m., a youth taking a short cut through the alley found Anna lying unconscious, face upwards in a pool of blood. Her clothing had been disturbed and the green slingbacks lay a short distance from her untouched handbag.

Shards of bone were removed from Anna's brain during a twelve-hour operation at Leeds General Infirmary. Although given the last rites, within hours she was recovering on a ward, head swathed in heavy bandages.

Forensic pathologist Dr Michael Green of St James University Hospital examined Anna's injuries. He found three crescent-shaped lacerations to her skull and fractures caused by a heavy object. There was defensive bruising to her hands and right forearm and peculiar marks on her abdomen: a graze about seven inches long with six or seven deep scratches above it, inflicted by her attacker before he had pulled her blouse back into position. There was no evidence of sexual interference.

'Woman in Hospital After Alley Attack' read Monday's report in the *Yorkshire Post*. 'Policewomen were waiting at the bedside of an injured woman in Leeds General Infirmary at the weekend. Mrs Anna Patricia Rogulskyj … has regained consciousness but is still very ill and the policewomen will remain at her bedside until she can give an account of what happened.'[9]

West Yorkshire Detective Superintendent Peter Perry headed the investigation, but there were few lines of enquiry. Anna was unable to remember anything after breaking the window, but was convinced that her attacker was local. Both Geoff and the youth who had found her were questioned and eliminated from the inquiry. Geoff's neighbour told detectives that Anna had broken the window between 1 a.m. and 2 a.m., and he had seen a man in his twenties or thirties, about five feet eight inches tall and wearing a checked jacket, around the time of the attack.[10] But this information led nowhere.

Anna's relationship with Geoff was over. Men would not feature in her life again, except for trusted friends and family, and those who could be admired from a safe distance; in her home, Anna displayed photographs of actor David Soul and BBC North television presenter Khalid Aziz alongside religious imagery.[11]

Having always taken pride in her appearance, Anna was distressed when her hair grew back steel grey. She stopped visiting her regular salon when a stylist was unable to hide her shock at the injuries to her skull. Leaving home became a challenge in itself; Anna kept to the edge of the pavement, panicking if anyone walked behind her. She fought hard not to lose sight of the woman she had been before the attack.

But then her assailant struck again.

2

OLIVE

Olive Smelt was eight years old when extraordinary events took place in her birthplace. It began on 16 November 1938, when two distraught female millworkers in Halifax burst into the cottage of a married couple, seeking refuge from a man who had struck them from behind with a heavy object. Both women were bleeding profusely but survived. On 21 November, another young woman was set upon as she walked home from work. Her name was Mary Sutcliffe, and a few days later she was attacked again by the same man who tore at her clothing.

Before the month was out, twelve people reported wounds inflicted by the 'Halifax Slasher'. Hysteria gripped the town as vigilante groups roamed the streets, suspects were beaten, businesses remained shut and the detective leading the investigation stoked the ferment by suggesting there were several assailants. On 29 November, Scotland Yard were called in, reaching a swift and unexpected conclusion: the Halifax Slasher did not exist. All but three of the victims admitted injuring themselves to gain attention; all but one of five people found guilty of mischief offences were jailed.

The story was consigned to history as an example of collective madness, and readers of the *Halifax Courier* were assured: 'There never was, nor is there likely to be, any danger to the general public.'[1] But a little under forty years later, a serial murderer struck twice in Halifax, and Olive was the sole survivor.

❖

Born in 1929 to Elsie Tempest, Olive was raised by her mother and grandparents in Halifax, eight miles south-west of Bradford. Originally one of Yorkshire's most architecturally impressive towns, post-war urban planners destroyed much of its industrial glory; the Burdock Way flyover dwarfed the Victorian Gothic elegance of North Bridge but improved road links to Bradford and Leeds. By 1975, the recession had rendered Halifax a shadow of its former self.

Olive was then a forty-six-year-old mother of three, married since 1948 to Harry Smelt, four years her senior. Home was an end of terrace house at 16 Woodside Mount on the slopes of Boothtown, overlooking Dean Clough, one of the world's largest carpet factories. Harry worked in a local rehabilitation centre, while Olive was an office cleaner for three companies. Their eldest daughter, Linda, was twenty-five and lived nearby with her husband, fifteen-year-old Julie was in her final school year, and Stephen was the youngest at nine. Olive described herself as 'happy-go-lucky, and the life and soul of every party', and Harry agreed that she was 'full of energy and enjoyed a night out'.[2]

On the evening of Friday 15 August 1975, Olive met her friend Muriel Falkingham at the White Horse in town. It had been a hot, thundery few days and that night was humid. The two women walked to the nearby Royal Oak and stood chatting at the crowded bar. Sipping sherry, Olive was unaware of a dark-haired, bearded man standing with his friend until he passed by, making a crude remark about her being 'on the game'. Never one to hold back, Olive set him straight.

Shortly before closing time, the two women accepted a lift from a couple of friends. Olive climbed out on Boothtown Road to buy a chip supper for Stephen and Harry; Julie was out with a friend. But the shop was in darkness and Olive headed home.

The brick chimney of Dean Clough rose like a beacon behind the terraced houses. Olive cut through ginnels and was within sight of home when the bearded man from the pub stepped out in front of her. 'He looked right into my eyes,' she remembered. 'I can hear his voice, a soft, nicely spoken voice saying, "The weather's let us down a bit, hasn't it?" Then nothing, a blank ...'[3]

Olive's life was saved by a neighbour arriving home: his car headlights disturbed her attacker, who had vanished by the time the man rushed to her aid. She lay face down on the cobbles, barely conscious, skirt about her waist and blood seeping from her head. Nothing had been stolen from her discarded handbag.

The neighbour took Olive into his home while another ran for Harry, who had dozed off after watching a pilot for *Kojak*. Julie was at home by then with a friend; after being told that Olive had suffered an accident, Harry asked the girls to keep an eye on Stephen, who had gone to bed.

Walking into his neighbour's kitchen, Harry gaped at the sight of his wife, tended by two paramedics. Blood coursed down Olive's face, saturating her white blouse. He was still in shock when they reached Halifax Infirmary, and more so when a doctor told him that Olive might not survive. She needed immediate surgery and the hospital had an obligation to inform the police about the attack. Detectives arrived to question Harry, who told them he had spent the evening at home, panelling the kitchen before watching television. At 5 a.m. he returned home as a suspect in the attempted murder of his wife.

He called on Linda, who listened in disbelief to the news that someone had tried to kill her mother. At home, he reassured Julie and Stephen that all would be well. The hospital rang as he was speaking: Olive was being transferred to the intensive care unit at Leeds General Infirmary. Harry made arrangements for Linda to look after her brother and sister while he bolted back to hospital.

In the neurological wing of Leeds General Infirmary, surgeons discussed relieving the pressure on Olive's brain. She had sustained two fractures to her skull. They could either operate, which carried a risk of greater injury, or hope that the pressure would decrease naturally, leaving no permanent damage. They decided on the latter. Harry left his wife to rest, returning home with her blood-soaked clothing in a carrier bag. He found Woodside Mount swarming with police, who were searching no. 16 and the surrounding area.

Linda showed him the front page of the *Yorkshire Post*: 'Battered Woman Found in Street.' In a daze, Harry read the article, which quoted a senior policeman: 'At this stage we believe she was attacked by an assailant with a blunt instrument. We are waiting to question her. It would appear that sex was not the motive.' The article also noted that police had been 'given the description of a man who spoke to someone else in the area shortly before the attack. He was aged about thirty, five feet ten inches, slightly built and had dark hair with some beard or growth on his face. He spoke with a foreign accent.'[4]

After handing in Olive's clothing for tests, Harry was quizzed by detectives for several hours about every aspect of his marriage, including whether he and Olive were faithful to each other and why she liked to meet friends without him. He vehemently denied trying to kill her, signing a thirty-page statement to that effect.

Dr Michael Green, the pathologist who had examined Anna Rogulskyj, also assessed Olive's injuries. He pondered whether the two depressed fractures to the top and back of her head might have been caused by a hammer, then rejected the idea. He studied the lacerations above her right eyelid and left eyebrow, and two abrasions above her buttocks. One mark was twelve inches long, the other four, and both were inflicted by a sharp instrument, prompting him to write to senior investigating officer, Detective Chief Inspector Dick Holland: 'It might be interesting to look again at the case of Mrs Rogulskyj, who was assaulted on 5 July, and compare the photograph of a wound on the abdomen with a wound on the back of Mrs Smelt.'[5] If the comparison was made, nothing came of it.

On Monday 18 August, a task force made house-to-house enquiries while detectives waited at Olive's bedside. She woke 'in a hospital bed, all covered in bandages, with two policemen at my side'.[6] Burly, bespectacled DCI Holland asked her to go over the incident. Olive described her attacker in terms similar to those mentioned by the press, with one notable exception: she was certain that he had a Yorkshire accent. The police seemed convinced her attacker was close to home. 'For weeks they accused Harry,' Olive recalled. 'One detective in particular would shout at me, "You know who attacked you, Olive. Tell us before he does it again and succeeds."'[7]

Detectives doubted her account of the attack. Olive told them that the first blow was struck immediately after the man had spoken to her, but she had been found several yards away from where she remembered being hit and there were no signs of her attacker having dragged her there. Nor could detectives understand why anyone should want to harm Olive: she was well-liked by all who knew her, as demonstrated by the abundance of cards and bouquets surrounding her hospital bed.

Still feeling as if her head was 'a crushed coconut shell', Olive was discharged after ten days.[8] She would never be free of the pains that plagued her afterwards, by turns piercing and dull, with a constant throb of discomfort. But apart from a few mobility problems, her physical recuperation was good. 'My injuries healed pretty quickly and the doctors said I had made a remarkable recovery,' Olive recalled. 'But the real damage wasn't on the outside – it was within me.'[9] She found herself 'terrified by every knock on the door, too frightened to go out because I knew the killer was out there. Sometimes I'd wake in the night, unable to breathe and once, when Harry touched my shoulder unexpectedly, I started screaming and couldn't stop.'[10]

The thought of venturing into town was anathema: 'I couldn't stand crowds anymore.'[11]

Imprisoned in her own home, Olive sank into depression: 'I felt life was pointless and would feel like screaming out ... Before the attack I used to enjoy housework and cooking, but afterwards I just did it to keep me going.'[12] She and Harry discussed moving away, but realized the trauma was emotional and as such, inescapable. 'It's impossible for me to ever put it behind me,' Olive declared.[13]

The most pressing barrier to her progress was knowing the attacker was still at liberty. DCI Holland found no persuasive evidence regarding the suspect or his means of transport, only rumours. At the end of August, the *Yorkshire Evening Post* announced that police wanted to question 'a man who was seen to run along a nearby street and climb over a cemetery wall. The man ran along Woodside View, Boothtown, Halifax, about the time of the attack – midnight on Friday – climbed on to the wall of the local cemetery and dropped over it by grabbing a branch of a tree. He was said to be 5ft 6in to 5ft 8in tall, of medium build, and with dark, collar-length hair. He was about thirty to thirty-five years old and was wearing dark clothing.'[14]

The lead proved false. Less than twenty-four hours before the article appeared, the man responsible for the attacks on Anna and Olive tried to kill again.

This time, his victim was a fourteen-year-old schoolgirl.

3

TRACY

The attempted murder of Tracy Browne received more regional press coverage than the attacks on Anna Rogulskyj and Olive Smelt. Her youth and the senseless ferocity of the incident in an idyllic rural spot generated greater interest.

Born in 1961, Tracy and her twin sister Mandy were always known by their middle names, as were their two older sisters. Parents Tony and Nora Browne provided them with a loving home at Upper Hayhills Farm, in the rolling hills above Silsden, with its blackened stone houses and disused textile mills along the Leeds and Liverpool Canal.

On Wednesday 27 August 1975, Tracy and Mandy visited friends on the other side of Silsden in Weatherhead Place, a thirty-minute walk from home. 'The village being so sleepy as it was, you just couldn't imagine anything bad happening,' Tracy explains. 'We were allowed half an hour later to get home. Normally it was about quarter past ten and we were allowed to be home for quarter to eleven. They were still fairly light nights as well. We started walking back, took a short cut through the park, which took about five or ten minutes off the journey. But I hung back to chat to my friends, whereas my sister, she carried on.'[1]

Realizing Mandy was out of sight, Tracy reluctantly left the park and headed up the steep lane. Resigned to being home later than her sister, Tracy sat down on a large stone for a few minutes to rest her feet, removing her sandals.

A man appeared from the lower reaches of the lane. Disconcertingly, he stood silently for a moment as he drew level with her. 'He had this beard, and afro-style hair and dark eyes. I remember his eyes being almost black,' Tracy recalls. 'He was about two feet away but directly in front of me. I looked at him but he just stared intensely down at me for a few seconds and then walked on without saying a word. I assumed he must be a local guy and I was too busy rubbing my sore feet to feel scared. After a few seconds, I set off again.'[2]

The bearded man was ahead, but his pace was slow. Tracy soon fell into step with him and he remarked evenly, 'There's nothing doing in Silsden, is there?'

'No, not really,' Tracy agreed.

'What's your name?'

'Tracy Browne. What's yours?'

'Tony Jennis.'[3]

His reply surprised her. Tracy had spent most of her holidays with a friend called Tony Jennison. The coincidence seemed remarkable. But the man was already speaking again.

'He asked, "Have you got a boyfriend?" and I told him I had and that he lived in Silsden,' Tracy recalls. 'I felt quite comfortable with him because he seemed such an unassuming, charming sort of guy. I said, "I've never seen you walking up here before. Where do you live?" He told me, "Up at Hole Farm", which is at the top of Bradley Road, about half a mile from my home. Our conversation tailed off into complete silence for a time but then he said, "My pal normally gives me a lift home but he's in the nick for drink-driving."'[4]

The man stopped twice to blow his nose, muttering about a summer cold, and once to fasten his shoelace. 'Other than that, he never took his hands out of his pockets,' Tracy states. 'We had walked together for almost a mile – for about thirty minutes – and I never once felt intimidated or in danger. Occasionally, I even waited for him to catch me up.'[5]

Dusk had fallen as they reached the turning to Tracy's home

in the hollow of the fields; light shone from its windows. She turned to thank the stranger for his company, but before she could speak, he lunged at her.

'The first blow sent me crashing down on my knees,' she recalls. 'I fell into the side of the road. I pleaded with him, "Please don't, please don't," and screamed for help. But he hit me five times and with so much force and energy that each blow was accompanied by a brutal grunting noise.'[6] Earlier that summer, she had watched Jimmy Connors lose his Wimbledon title; the sounds her attacker made reminded her of the tennis player delivering a serve. Then she thought of the man being hunted for killing heiress Lesley Whittle and shouted, 'Black Panther! Black Panther!' while trying to fend off the blows.

Like Olive, Tracy survived because of a passing motorist. At the rumble of car wheels, the assailant put one arm around Tracy's waist and the other under her legs, dropping her over a barbed wire fence. She heard him running off, his suede boots making a soft, insistent thud as he vanished down the lane.

Her world turned crimson: 'My vision had gone because I was so stunned from the attack and my eyes had filled with blood. I pulled myself up and slowly managed to stand up. I was very shaky and began staggering around the field, disorientated and still unable to see anything. I fell down several times but forced myself back up. I told myself I had to get home in case he came back to finish me off. That fear drove me on. I knocked on the door of a farmhouse but no one answered. I staggered around for another hundred yards, by which time I was covered from head to waist in blood.'[7]

Tracy stumbled across to a farmhand's caravan. It took all her strength to bring her fist down on the door.

'Oh, my God ...' Elderly Fred Hargreaves pulled himself together and helped her into his caravan. She was unable to speak coherently and shook uncontrollably. He led her home, but when Nora Browne opened the door it took her a moment

16

to understand what had happened to her daughter: 'I thought someone had thrown red paint over her. But it was blood … her jumper was squelching with blood.'[8]

Neurosurgeons at Chapel Allerton Hospital in Leeds operated on Tracy for five hours. In recovery, she gave detectives a detailed description of her attacker: 'I remembered his taupe-coloured V-neck jumper over a light blue open-necked shirt and dark brown trousers which had slit pockets at the front, rather than the side. I told the policeman he was 5ft 8in, had very dark, almost black Afro-type wrinkly hair and a full beard. I even mentioned the gap between his teeth and his insipid voice – a little man with a high-pitched voice. His accent I recognized as being local even though it wasn't strong.'[9]

Her story was immediately picked up by regional newspapers. 'Dragnet at Isolated Farm: Schoolgirl Attacked in Lonely Lane' read the headline in Thursday's *Telegraph and Argus*. The *Yorkshire Post* carried a comprehensive account about the attack by 'a dark stranger' who was 'aged about 20, 5ft 10in with dark curly hair, dark eyes, a dark straight moustache and separate beard. He was wearing a blue shirt and brown flared trousers.' The report noted: 'Police sealed off a few hundred yards between the farm and Bradley Road where the incident took place, for a thorough forensic examination. Det. Supt. Jim Hobson, deputy head of Bradford CID, said the girl had been visiting friends in Weatherhead Place, Silsden, and had left at about 10.30pm. Police are anxious to trace anyone who saw [Tracy] walking from Weatherhead Place along Howden Road, Kirkgate and Brigate to Bradley Road.'[10]

Further examination showed that Tracy had been struck five times about the skull with a ball-pein hammer. When her bandages were removed, she asked for a mirror and was aghast at her reflection: stitches rippled across her partially shaven head, her eyes were blackened and she had extensive bruising to her face. A fortnight after the bruises subsided, Tracy accompanied a plain-clothes WPC around local pubs in the hope of spotting her attacker. There was no sign of him.

Detective Superintendent James Hobson, with whom Tracy had spoken at length, took charge of the investigation. A number of items had been recovered near the crime scene, including a man's handkerchief, a wooden bracelet, and a stone from Bradley Road tip. Hobson was convinced the assailant was local; one suspect was questioned and searched but released without charge.

In addition to her verbal description of the attacker, Tracy worked with the police to produce a photofit. The likeness was published in the *Keighley News* and on posters throughout the Silsden area, prompting a witness to recall a man standing beside a white Ford car in Bradley Road at the relevant time. A second photofit was created based on the witness's description, but never publicly shown.

Hobson's enquiries were extensive, but Tracy's attack was not linked with those on Anna Rogulskyj and Olive Smelt. Yet there were similarities: all the victims were female, randomly accosted at night in residential areas; a blunt instrument had been used to inflict severe head injuries; the attacker was described as a bearded, dark-haired man; Olive and Tracy recalled a Yorkshire accent; Olive and Anna were cut beneath their clothing; and all three attacks had taken place within a matter of weeks and in a relatively confined area.

There was also evidence to suggest that the attacker had stalked his victims. Anna told detectives that her assailant had approached her twice prior to that night; Olive's attacker had been abusive in the pub only a couple of hours beforehand and may have tailed her home or had some idea where she lived; and Tracy's recollection of the similarity in names hinted at more than coincidence. She was certain 'Tony Jennis' had been watching her for weeks: 'He must have followed me home as he had worked out when I would turn into my drive and he attacked me just before we reached the gate.'[11]

After six weeks' convalescence and wearing a wig over her scars, Tracy returned to school. For some time she endured bullying and jibes about her father being the attacker, but put her energies into regaining full health: 'I had regular brain scans and was on drugs for two years to monitor any possible damage and prevent me suffering seizures. But I made a full recovery and I refused to dwell on things. I think I was helped because I had such a clear recall of my attacker that I knew I would recognize him straight away.'[12] She tried not to dwell on why she had been targeted and reconciled herself to having been simply 'in the wrong place at the wrong time'.[13]

Two months later, another young woman found herself in the same predicament. But unlike Tracy, Olive and Anna, Wilma McCann did not survive.

4

WILMA

History has not been kind to Wilma McCann. Made complicit in her own murder by the words of the Attorney General, Sir Michael Havers, described merely as 'a known prostitute' in the official post-trial investigation into the Ripper inquiry, and dismissed as a neglectful, alcoholic parent by commentators on the case, it fell to Wilma's mother and children to give her more dignity and substance in the public eye.

Wilma's parents, lorry driver John Newlands and his wife Elizabeth, had married during the war in Flotta, on the island of Orkney. They had eleven children: seven boys and four girls. Wilma was their sixth child, born on 1 July 1947 in Dumbarton. During the late 1950s, John Newlands worked as a plumber on the Isle of Skye, where the family lived for two years in a stone cottage on the eastern shore.

Something of the wild landscape was reflected in Wilma herself. 'She was always full of life and tried to live every day in her own dynamic way,' her mother Betty recalled. 'She was not a volatile girl, but she tended to get emotional very quickly – and then anybody within earshot knew about it.'[1] John and Betty were not particularly strict parents, although the teenage Newlands children were expected to work hard, and make-up was forbidden for the girls. Wilma, always a rebel, flouted the latter rule. Her father responded by burying her make-up bag in the garden.

Wilma often took care of her siblings while both parents worked. A young boy who lived next door to them on the island recalled her kindness, including the time when he had lain on an ant's nest and his hair became infested; Wilma took him indoors and washed them away. She attended the island school until work took the family to Inverness, where she remained an average pupil. One of her elder sisters found employment at the Gleneagles Hotel, an 850-acre shooting and golfing estate in Perthshire. Fifteen-year-old Wilma joined as a still-room assistant for two years. In 1964 she travelled to Leeds, where six of her brothers had settled.

As part of a nationwide programme, the city's slum housing and depleted industrial buildings were being razed to the ground, replaced by tower blocks, flats, council estates, flyovers and an extension of the M1. Pre-war immigrants moved out to more prosperous suburbs, leaving the streets to a new influx of workers, mostly from the West Indies and Pakistan. John Betjeman observed the creation of this 'Motorway City' in the documentary A Poet Goes North, musing, 'I am sure that most of the people here will wish themselves back in the old streets before long.' His pessimism was justified: community dislocation led to rising crime against a backdrop of dismal functionality, inadequate builds and a lack of green space.

Wilma's fresh start fell short of her expectations. Aged eighteen, she was arrested for shoplifting and an undisclosed offence, thought to be soliciting. Her arrest photograph appears in virtually every discussion of her murder, yet bore little resemblance to the mature woman: a striking strawberry blonde with green eyes. Wilma soon ran into more trouble, accruing four convictions for theft and disorderly conduct. Working as a hotel waitress provided stability until she met Londonderry-born Gerald McCann. They married in a Roman Catholic ceremony on 7 December 1968, two months after Wilma gave birth to their daughter Sonia Maree and moved into a council house at 65 Scott Hall Avenue, two miles north-east of Leeds city centre.

Scott Hall estate sprang up in the 1930s, a maze of red brick houses served by Scott Hall Road. No. 65 was the last in a terrace of four, with a small front garden and a large lawn at the back, behind which a path ran parallel with Prince Philip Playing Fields. Three more children followed in quick succession: Richard in 1969, Donna in 1970, and Angela in 1972. During that period, Wilma's relationship with her husband deteriorated, amid mutual infidelities. In his autobiography, Richard recalls his mother receiving psychiatric care for two nervous breakdowns caused by beatings and emotional abuse. On one occasion, Wilma fled with the children to Scotland, staying with relatives before returning to Leeds. She agreed to a divorce in February 1974, but failed to attend any solicitors' meetings and was distressed when Gerry began living with another woman.

Deeply unhappy and recovering from psychiatric care, Wilma remained in the house on Scott Hall Avenue with her four children. She was a fiercely protective mother, and when Richard was bullied by some older boys, she immediately marched round to their homes to give vent to her fury. 'When Mum "had a word" with you in her broad Scottish accent you knew all about it,' Richard confirms. 'She was what you might call a feisty woman. She wasn't scared of anyone.'[2] Wilma's best friend Caroline got to know her after they came to blows; Wilma had accused her of flirting with Gerry, but shook Caroline's hand afterwards, telling her, 'You're the only woman ever to stand up to me, because I'm the hardest woman in this town.'[3] Drink made Wilma belligerent; without it, she was calmer. She never raised a hand to her children, who remember her as a source of warmth and laughter, and she often went hungry to ensure that they were fed.

Yet even the most authoritative writer on the Yorkshire Ripper case describes her in purely negative terms: 'As a mother, Wilma was hopeless. She had degenerated into a terrible drunken state. The house, when police searched it, was filthy. She was sexually promiscuous and irresponsible and Gerry, a caring father, had become increasingly concerned.'[4] Wilma's son remembers it differently, however, and while her life in the months immediately before her death was chaotic, the problems she battled were part of the equation. Refusing financial assistance from Gerry, she taught Sonia and Richard crafts and sent them from door to door, selling their wares. It was a painfully deprived existence.

Wilma did rely increasingly on her eldest child, giving Sonia responsibilities far beyond her years. At night, she left her daughter to babysit while she headed for the bar of the Scott Hall Hotel, on the other side of the main road, or the Robin Hood pub on Vicar Lane. 'She liked to be out most weekends,' Richard confirms, 'and recently her weekends had begun on Thursdays. She used to go down to the city centre every Saturday as well. She told us it was to do some shopping, but from the way she applied her make-up and backcombed her hair, Sonia and I guessed she popped into a pub or two along the way.'[5]

Most of Wilma's boyfriends were heavy drinkers and violent. 'She was full of love and was so kind to us,' Sonia recalled. 'But all the men in mum's life were rotten.'[6] Sonia was six years old when one man raped her. He vanished from their lives as suddenly as he had appeared, and Sonia kept the abuse secret until adulthood. The only man Richard remembers had a temper that would explode without warning, raining blows on Wilma, who would scream for the children to run upstairs. The man once threatened Gerry with a hammer when he called to see his children; Gerry immediately took his son and daughters to his sister Katherine, who lived in another part of Leeds. Wilma turned up distraught the following day, begging for her children. A few days later, the same man destroyed all the Christmas presents Gerry had bought them. Wilma sat up through the night, trying to repair the girls' teddy bears and a plastic truck for Richard.

Some weeks before her death, Wilma began dating a long-distance lorry driver known to the children only as Tommy. A fellow Scot with black quiffed hair, Tommy was made in the same mould as her previous boyfriends. A row on 12 October 1975 culminated with neighbours finding Wilma in the back garden, agitated and severely beaten. Tommy had stormed out after terrorizing her with a knife.

Social services became involved and the children were placed on the 'at risk' register. Wilma sank further into depression when she heard that Gerry's girlfriend was pregnant. Never the tidiest of people, Wilma no longer had any interest in her home or surroundings. Unable to rouse her mother most mornings, Sonia would make breakfast and dress her sisters before accompanying Richard to school. Wilma suspected the neighbours of watching the house and reporting her movements to social workers. She began leaving by the back door, taking the path by the playing field to avoid prying eyes.

This routine was well established by Friday 29 October 1975. Early that evening, Sonia watched her mother applying make-up in a broken mirror propped above the kitchen sink, hands stained from the hair-dyeing kit she used without plastic gloves. She made a few adjustments to her outfit – pink blouse, white flares, an indigo bolero jacket and platform shoes – before ushering the children into their room.

Angela's cot stood beside the bed Sonia shared with Richard and Donna. Wilma kissed her children, adding coats on top of the blankets for warmth. She reminded Sonia not to let the little ones get out of bed and then she left, heels clicking quietly on the stairs. Sonia heard the back door close. Her mother's footsteps passed down the garden and grew fainter along the path, by the playing field.

At 9.30 p.m., two hours after leaving home, Wilma drank whisky and beer in the Old Royal Oak on Kirkgate, then stopped in at The Regent before crossing the street to The Scotsman. A fifteen-minute walk brought her to Room at the Top, a

nightclub pumping out Motown and reggae above commercial premises on North Street, near Sheepscar Junction. Wilma stayed until 1 a.m. Carrying a tray of chips with curry sauce, she edged through the crowd spilling out onto the pavement. Home lay over half an hour away on foot, along wide roads and empty, industrial streets.

Clutching the white plastic tray of food and shivering, she weaved deliberately into the path of thundering lorries and cars, hoping someone would give her a lift. One driver pulled over but when he saw how inebriated she was he put his foot down. Wilma climbed into a second lorry but got out just four hundred yards away when the driver changed his mind about a lift. A third driver slowed down but sped up when he realized she was drunk. At the junction of Meanwood Road and Barrack Street, a West Indian man wearing a trilby and donkey jacket took her a short distance in his red Avenger.

By 1.20 a.m., Wilma was still standing in the bitter cold, thumbing a lift. When a lime green Ford Capri with a black roof drew up against the kerb, she slipped gratefully into its warmth, pleased when the driver offered to drop her at Scott Hall Avenue. Her good Samaritan drove smoothly away from the city lights into suburban darkness.

'I remember the night being different because Angela was crying and my mum didn't come to her,' Richard recalls. 'I just remember it being surreal, not quite right – where is Mum? – and hearing Sonia telling Angela this story in the bedroom and then just finally, around five-thirty, Sonia waking me up and telling me that Mum hadn't come home and let's go look for her. Getting dressed and leaving the house, knowing we really shouldn't be doing that but because Mum wasn't there, what else could we do? And walking down that field at the back of the house, which Mum always told us to do, and feeling scared. It was pitch black and silent.'[7]

Richard and Sonia took the path past the mist-shrouded playing field. Glancing towards the wide expanse of grass, Sonia noticed 'a bundle, about twenty-five yards away. "Must be a Guy Fawkes some kids have made," I told myself as we turned away. "Right, let's go to the bus stop and wait for her. She'll be home soon."'[8]

They sat huddled together at the bus shelter on the main road: a tiny, red-haired boy with a brown duffle coat over his green pyjamas, and his sister in a long purple nightdress, her face pinched with cold and fretfulness. A yellow smudge of artificial lights blotted the dark sky above the city. 'Each bus came and went and she didn't appear,' Richard remembers. 'That fear that I felt, that anxiety, got worse.'[9]

At 6 a.m., the suburb began to stir. Lights went on in nearby houses and traffic started to build. Richard and Sonia walked home, glancing about for any sign of their mother but there was no one, just the milkman in a white, electric-powered van.

Alan Routledge continued his rounds, helped by his ten-year-old brother, Paul. At 7.40 a.m., Alan parked the van next to the main building on the playing field. Thick mist clung in the air, but he glimpsed something white as milk a few feet away on the slope. He stood a moment, then ran to the caretaker's bungalow, bringing his fist down on the door.[10]

John Bould listened in horror as Alan told him what he had seen. Peering over his garden fence, he felt a jolt of recognition as he gazed on Wilma's lifeless body: 'Both my wife and I knew her because she used to bring her kids to the nursery school. It was a terrible sight – she was lying on her back with her eyes staring, her clothes open, her body covered in blood. I told the milkman to get on the phone and dial 999.'[11]

Inside the bungalow, Margaret Bould drew back the curtains. 'I'll never forget the shock of what I saw,' she recalled. 'Those staring eyes just seemed to be looking in through the window at me. Ever since that morning I've tried to forget about the injuries I saw on her body – and the blood. What I couldn't get over – and still can't – is that we never heard anything. We always sleep with the window open and at the time we had a big South African ridgeback called Butch, who used to bark if anyone came near the house. It always used to wake me up. He didn't bark that night, yet this terrible thing was happening only a few feet from our window.'[12]

The playing field quickly became the scene of grim commotion. Two uniformed officers grappling with a privacy screen were too late to prevent a press photographer capturing an image of Wilma lying prone on the grass. One hundred yards away, her bewildered children ate a subdued breakfast, unaware that she was never coming home.

Detective Chief Superintendent Dennis Hoban arrived shortly before 8 a.m. Standing on rickety duckboards, he spoke to the police surgeon and established the dead woman's identity. At 9.25 a.m., Head of the Department of Forensic Medicine at Leeds University, pathologist Professor David Gee, crossed the grass to examine Wilma's body. She lay at a slight angle, feet pointing towards the car park. Her pink blouse and blue jacket had been torn open, and her bra pushed up. The white flares she favoured had been dragged past her knees to expose her pants, which bore a cheeky motif. Her platform shoes were still in place, and a rust-coloured handbag was attached to her left wrist by its strap. A button and a handful of coins lay in the grass nearby. The hair she had carefully backcombed the night before was thickly matted with blood.

Wilma had been stabbed repeatedly: once in the throat, twice below her right breast, three times below her left, and nine times in her lower abdomen. Blood had dried on her skin, bloomed on the right side of her blouse and stained the top of her trousers and the back of her right hand. One red trail ran along the top of her pants, which bore semen on the back. There was more semen on her trousers. Wilma had lain critically injured on her front while the killer masturbated; afterwards, he had turned her over and stabbed her to death.

The crime scene photographer completed his duties. Based on the drop in body temperature, Gee estimated that Wilma had died around midnight or shortly thereafter. An officer removed her shoes, trousers and handbag, packaging them for examination.

By 11.30 a.m., the mist had begun to lift but it remained overcast and there was a light breeze. Wilma's body was showing signs of rigor mortis. Wrapped in a plastic sheet, with bags over her head and hands to preserve any forensic evidence, she was carried into a windowless van and transported to the mortuary.

The activity near their home had alerted Wilma's children. On Sonia's instructions, Richard ran out to the front gate: 'It was light now and I could see that there was some sort of commotion going on at the end of Scott Hall Avenue. A couple of police cars were parked there and their flashing blue lights were attracting a crowd of onlookers, just a few yards from the route Sonia and I had walked earlier.'[13] He reported back to his sister, who grabbed his hand and headed for the cars. 'Some instinct told me that the scene we were walking towards had something to do with us,' Richard remembers.[14] A policeman bent to ask their names. 'Sonia and Richard McCann,' the small girl replied. The officer straightened up with a small intake of breath.

He walked them home, staying with them until a second officer arrived to lead the four children out to a waiting car. They sat quietly during a ten-minute journey that seemed to last for ever. Finally, the car turned up a steep hill in Meanwood and stopped before an imposing Victorian building with a sign that read 'Beckett's Park Children's Home'.

Professor Gee began the post-mortem at 2 p.m. with Detective Chief Superintendent Hoban present. The rest of Wilma's clothing had been removed for scrutiny and a fingerprint expert had examined her body. Gee made a vital discovery almost immediately. There were two lacerations to Wilma's head, one of which was fairly shallow, but the other had penetrated her scalp and fractured her skull. Two inches long, it had been made by a blunt object, either a hammer or an adjustable spanner. There were also fifteen stab wounds to her abdomen, chest and neck. Summarizing his four-hour examination, Gee declared that Wilma had died after being struck twice on the head, then stabbed with a weapon at least three inches long and sharp on one side.

At a press conference, Hoban described Wilma's murder as 'particularly savage and sadistic. The body was found less than a hundred and fifty yards from Mrs McCann's council house. We would like to speak to any person who might have seen her last night or yesterday afternoon. It is common knowledge she frequented local public houses and city centre public houses. We would like to see any relatives – we believe she has brothers living in the Leeds area.'[15] He appealed to Wilma's 'many boyfriends' to come forward before concluding: 'She was a quiet woman and had very little contact with neighbours.'[16]

Press and police converged on Scott Hall estate. News of Wilma's death filled the regional papers for days; the *Yorkshire Evening Post* led the way with a front page that blared: 'Murder In Fog: Savage and Sadistic Sex Attack on Leeds "Mother in Fear"'. Wilma's 1965 arrest photograph accompanied the article, in which a neighbour asserted that Wilma had 'wanted to get away from the area because she was frightened of a man who threatened her'.[17] Another recalled her habit of never using the front door: 'She would always go out the back way and walk down the edge of the playing field. I think it was because she didn't want people to know what time she was going out and coming home.'[18] The landlord of the Scott Hall Hotel on Sholebroke Mount mused: 'She last came in two Sundays ago. I haven't seen her since then. She was an attractive woman and had more than one boyfriend. Occasionally she came in with her brother.'[19]

Police with tracker dogs conducted an inch-by-inch search of the playing field after learning that one item was missing from Wilma's bag – a white clasp purse, which bore the word 'MUMIY', misspelled in Sonia's handwriting. Inside was £6 and a photograph of Tommy. Hoban announced to the press: 'This purse is now missing and we would urgently like to speak to anyone who feels they know anything about such a purse. It would now seem that, as well as the sexual assault, robbery may have been an additional motive for her death.'[20]

Aware that interest in Wilma's murder would wane without a breakthrough, Hoban decided to place her children temporarily in the media spotlight. They had learned of their mother's death at the Children's Home, where a policeman told them bluntly: 'Your mum has been taken to heaven. You won't be meeting her again.'[21] Shock and confusion stilled any tears, but later Richard reflected: 'My childhood ended that day.'[22]

Hoban set up a shoot at the Home with a *Yorkshire Evening Post* photographer, presenting the children with toys. 'Heartbreak Four Are Told "Mummy's Dead"' read the article, tugging at the heartstrings as Hoban had hoped: 'Four little children play happily together – unaware that their mother has been brutally stabbed to death. But the smiles in our picture were soon to be shattered. The children – now in a council home – were today told the heartbreaking news of their mother's murder … Mr J. W. Freeman, Leeds Director of Social Services, said, "We are just trying to keep the children in one of our homes, trying to do the best we can to comfort and protect them."'[23]

The following weekend, armed with sweets, Hoban spoke to the bewildered children, who told him about 'the various "uncles" their mother had brought home'.[24] Details of their mother's death were kept from them, but Richard recalls: 'We knew my mum had been attacked, we believed by a man – I don't know who said that but we just knew that she'd been attacked on the field at the back of the house. We didn't realize how she died, that came maybe two years later.'[25]

The children remained in care while their father was located and the paperwork for him to be given custody of them was completed. Wilma's family pleaded with the authorities to raise the children in Scotland, but their father's wishes had to be considered first. Wilma's brother Isaac and his wife Vicky visited the children regularly and took them home for weekends. Vicky made a point of showing them Wilma's photograph in the hall and instructing, 'Don't ever forget her, will you?'[26] Wilma's sister Lillian travelled up from her home in London, telling the press: 'No outsiders need offer homes to the kids. They are happy they are going to their dad, but the family would have had them.'[27]

Gerry took his children to the house in Leeds' Charlton Place where he lived with his girlfriend Pauline and baby daughter Cheryl. Reflecting on the decision to place them there, Richard states: 'I had a kind and loving mother, but even before she was murdered, violence had been a tangible part of my turbulent childhood. I was four years old when my abusive father left home, yet social services considered it was best that my sisters and me moved back in with him after our mum's death. One of the first things he did then was drown our pet dog in the bath, because the dog had annoyed him.'[28] He recalls other cruelties, including any mention of their mother being forbidden by their father, who 'became a very violent man when he was drinking. I remember him beating Sonia on one occasion at the bottom of the steps. He came back into the living room and he was panting as if he'd been in the boxing ring. Sonia went on to tell me later that he'd kicked her. He could be very violent. But he wasn't always like that, it was just in drink.'[29]

The police investigation into their mother's murder was based in an incident room at Brotherton House, the old headquarters of Leeds City Police. There were several positive sightings of Wilma on her last night alive; officers set up road blocks on the route she had taken from the Room at the Top, hoping to track down those lorry drivers who had interacted with her. The first lorry driver who gave her a lift contacted the police of his own accord, and another witness described the red Hillman Avenger driver, although he was never traced.

Two thousand posters were distributed featuring Wilma's face superimposed onto a WPC dressed in her clothing. A thorough search of her home recovered a large number of fingerprints, including one unidentifiable fragment. The toxicology report recorded 183 milligrams of alcohol, equivalent to around fourteen measures of spirits, in Wilma's blood. Examination of the semen found on her trousers and underwear revealed it belonged to a non-secretor, whose blood type wasn't secreted in their bodily fluids.

Police were cautious about revealing too much of Wilma's personal life, knowing that an implication of promiscuity could inhibit public sympathy. Hoban had already risked planting the idea that Wilma's death was a 'domestic incident' by mentioning that the killer appeared to harbour 'very personal feelings' towards her.[30] The national newspapers had paid little attention to Wilma's murder, but made the same point as the regional press in stating that Wilma was known to have 'several boyfriends'.[31]

Allegations of promiscuity led to rumours that Wilma had tried to resolve her money worries by selling sex, which quickly became accepted as fact by the press. Hearing his sister described on the local news as a prostitute prompted Isaac Newlands to telephone Yorkshire Television, insisting they were mistaken. Wilma's mother Betty told reporters that her daughter had 'liked having a good time but it is not fair what people have said about being a prostitute. Whatever she did was for enjoyment. She did not deserve to go this way. Not murdered.'[32] Yet 'the prostitute Wilma McCann' was how she came to be identified.

'It was hopeless trying to fight the slur against her character once the national press started repeating it,' Richard recalls. 'It didn't matter to me what Mum had done in that way, she was still my mum, but I knew that society looked down on prostitutes and I didn't want anyone looking down on her.'[33]

Enquiries revealed that in fact Wilma had a regular boyfriend. Detectives urged Tommy to come forward but he remained absent and they turned their attention to the red-light areas in Chapeltown, where violence had erupted the previous month. The Leeds district had a long history of police harassment and wrongful arrest among black teens; on Bonfire Night 1975, in response to a man being apprehended, hundreds of black youths rioted, hurling fireworks and attacking officers. Two policemen narrowly escaped death when their car was struck by a brick and hit a tree. Six youths put on trial the following July were acquitted of all charges.

By early new year over one hundred and thirty officers were involved in the investigation into Wilma's murder. Five thousand homes were visited and more than five hundred statements taken, with the results noted on more than three thousand index cards in the Brotherton House incident room.

On 21 January 1976, Wilma was laid to rest at Lawnswood Cemetery in Leeds. Her children were kept away but Richard had a recurring dream in which he tried to reach his mother, climbing the drawers of her bedside table where they floated in space. It was several years before he and his sisters were able to visit their mother's grave.

On the morning of Wilma's burial, a workman taking a short cut five miles away through derelict buildings in Sheepscar noticed a humped shape in a gap between two houses. Moving closer, he saw that it was a woman's body.

Wilma's murderer had killed again.

5

EMILY

Assumptions about the killer's motives began in earnest after the murder of Emily Jackson. Those views coloured the entire inquiry, leading to a set of judgements about each victim that undermined the evidence as it emerged, delaying the capture of the man responsible for the murders and attacks.

Born Emily Monica Wood in the West Yorkshire mining village of Hemsworth in March 1932, the second known victim came from a large, loving family of twelve children. Emily was in her teens when her parents moved to Armley, a mile to the west of Leeds, where there was more work; its skyline was a mass of smoking mill chimneys, church spires and seemingly infinite rows of terraced housing. Leeds Prison stood within its boundaries, a squat Victorian building of locally quarried stone. Ninety-three executions were carried out behind its castellated walls before abolition of the death penalty in 1965.

A bright, resourceful girl, slightly taller than average, with brown hair and hazel eyes, Emily first experienced grief when her twenty-year-old brother died of a heart defect while playing football. His family nickname, 'Smiler', passed on to her because she had the same optimistic nature. After leaving school, Emily worked in a local weaving factory and at nineteen she met roofer Sydney Jackson, two years her senior. They married on 2 January 1954, and parenthood soon followed, with Derek born in 1955 and Neil in 1958.

Violence marred Emily's marriage from the outset; on one occasion Sydney attacked her with a poker, breaking her collarbone.[1] When the abuse came to light in the wake of Emily's murder, he claimed her infidelities had driven him to it. Six years after their wedding, Emily left Sydney but he pleaded with her to return, and by 1961 they were living in a two-up, two-down house in Holbeck, inner city Leeds. Despite Sydney's promises, after the birth of their third son, Chris, the beatings began again and Emily walked out on her husband a second time. For a while she lived with a labourer named Mick and started divorce proceedings. But a chance encounter with Sydney led to their reconciliation and in autumn 1968 the Jacksons moved to Churwell.

Set between Leeds and the market town of Morley, Churwell was a village, but modernization marched through it nonetheless: the Jacksons' new home on Back Green was the only finished property on what was essentially a building site. Semi-detached, the house stood opposite the Methodist Chapel, where Emily enrolled Derek and Neil in Sunday School classes. The two brothers were unalike: Derek was tall and outgoing, with dreams of becoming a professional footballer, while Neil was smaller and quiet, regarding Derek as a mentor and best friend. A few months after the move, Emily gave birth to a daughter, who would always be known as Bubs rather than her given name, Angela.

Sydney craved his own roofing business, but couldn't afford to set one up. Emily's resourcefulness made it possible: she saved Embassy cigarette coupons, which could be exchanged for household goods, then sold them in bundles at a profit. 'S. & E. Jackson, Roofing Contractors' thus came into operation with a home office run by Emily. Because Sydney was illiterate she taught herself accounting, found clients and dealt with contractors. After passing her driving test, she became a familiar figure in Churwell, sitting at the wheel of their second-hand, dark-blue Commer van.

Life was more stable for the Jacksons, but in 1969, an appalling tragedy took place at the house on Back Green. Fourteen-year-old Derek was standing by the open back door when a sudden draught from the front door caused it to slam shut, taking him with it through the glass panel. Neil was nearby and witnessed multiple shards piercing his brother's body. Derek passed away from his injuries in hospital. His funeral was held in the chapel across the road and his ashes buried in Cottingley Hall Cemetery.

In the wake of their son's death, Sydney became withdrawn and monosyllabic, while Emily suppressed her grief to support him and their remaining children. She encouraged them to believe they should celebrate Derek's years and make the most of their own. 'We decided life was too short,' Sydney recalled. 'We would live for today and not bother about the future. I don't think my wife ever really got over it. We believed in having fun while we could.'[2]

They strove to provide their children with the best of everything, and it fell to Emily to fund luxuries. In addition to her duties with the roofing business, she started her own grocery delivery service, making holidays abroad possible and buying the first colour television in the area. Some of her schemes were unsuccessful: she bought pigs but couldn't bear to send them for slaughter, and she saved a pony from the knacker's yard to put it to work, but it became the neighbourhood pet.

With Neil at an age where he could be trusted to babysit his brother and sister, Emily and Sydney began socializing. They were regulars at Churwell's New Inn and at their old local in Armley, close to the homes of Emily's siblings and widowed father, who lived with his sister opposite Leeds Prison. By late 1973, Emily and her husband were also frequent patrons of the Gaiety, a new entertainment complex straddling Gipton beck on the junction of Roundhay Road and Gathorne Terrace. Its distinctive double-gabled roof housed five bars and a rotating dancefloor. It soon had an unenviable reputation, hosting portly comedians whose routines were too blue for television, with bored strippers grinding away during lunchtime shows and sex workers soliciting in the car park.

By the end of 1975, the roofing business had run into financial difficulties and Sydney was on the verge of bankruptcy. Despite having been a jealous husband most of his married life, when Emily suggested prostitution as the swiftest means of resolving their problems, he agreed. Under the pretence of visiting the bingo, after dropping Sydney at the Gaiety, forty-two-year-old Emily would drive to Chapeltown in search of clients. The old blue Commer van served a dual purpose, with roofing supplies, gas bottles and tins of sticky black bitumen pushed against the sides to accommodate a mattress.

Emily's solution staved off the immediate danger of losing the business and enabled them to buy the children Christmas presents. At seventeen, Neil worked alongside his father, but Chris and Angela were at Churwell Primary and still excited about Santa. After the usual Boxing Day gathering of Emily's relatives, she and Sydney saw in the new year at Holbeck's Crystal Palace pub and partied with friends. Two weeks into January, Britain's worst storm since the turn of the century brought down trees and power lines, causing flooding and widespread structural damage. The Jacksons were temporarily inundated with work.

Tuesday 20 January 1976 had been a long and tiring day for Sydney and Neil. That evening Emily prepared for work herself, slipping into a close-fitting blue-and-white-striped dress and white slingbacks. She dabbed her favourite scent, Coty L'Aimant, on her wrists and neck and grabbed her coat before leaving the house with Sydney at 6 p.m.

Gale force wind and rain shook the ladders overhead as Emily drove the van towards the city centre. Despite the weather, the Gaiety's bars were packed and Emily left Sydney nursing a pint while she looked for clients. At 7 p.m., she headed outside, recognizing nineteen-year-old Maria Sellars sitting on the low wall, waiting for a customer herself. The rain had eased and they chatted until Emily spotted a green Land Rover pulling up over the road and went across to it. Maria watched her climb into the vehicle before it vanished down Gledhow Row.

Sydney was accustomed to losing sight of his wife until closing time. After last orders, he strolled outside and saw the van parked where they had left it. Assuming Emily was either in the back with a client or had gone off with one, he took a taxi home and fell into bed, expecting her to return in the early hours. But when he woke the next morning, Emily's side of the bed was empty.

Her body was discovered at 8.10 a.m., half a mile from the Gaiety. Detective Chief Superintendent Dennis Hoban called the area where she was found 'the mucky end of town': a row of condemned houses on Manor Street Industrial Estate, facing the abandoned playground of Roundhay School, also scheduled for demolition.[3] A fire-damaged ginnel ran between two empty houses with rubbish filling the rear; in a doorway was the humped shape that caught a workman's attention.

Together with pathologist Professor David Gee and Forensic Scientist Ron Outtridge, Hoban picked his way down the ginnel, ducking against the wind and rain that threatened to destroy fragile evidence. The sight that greeted them left Hoban almost paralyzed with shock, despite his professionalism.

Emily lay on her back, right arm extended, right leg bent at the knee and hip, left arm and leg lying straight. Around her head were shallow pools and rivulets of blood. Her coat was in place, but the smart dress beneath was heavily bloodstained and rumpled around her waist. Tan-coloured, laddered tights had been pulled down over her left hip to expose her underwear. One shoe rested beside her right foot; the other lay near the wall. A plank of wood had been placed between her legs. Emily's wedding ring, which she had worn for more than twenty turbulent years, shone faintly in the half-light. Her handbag lay a few yards away. As wind howled down the ginnel, Gee made a swift examination and Hoban pointed out drag marks in the soil, the imprint of a boot near the entrance and small patches of dried blood nearby. Duckboards had been placed over a puddle swirling with blood.

During the post-mortem, Gee found two lacerations to Emily's head caused by a hammer or something similar. The uppermost injury had penetrated deeply enough to reveal a depressed fracture of the skull; the second depressed fracture was located at the back of her head. An area of soiling on Emily's thigh through her tights resembled the print found at the entrance to the ginnel. Both were made by a size seven Dunlop Warwick boot. Emily's bra had been pulled up over her breasts and she had been stabbed fifty-two times in all, perforating her heart front and back. The weapon had left cross-shaped impressions on her flesh.

Gee established that Emily had been struck on the head at the entrance to the ginnel before being dragged face down along the passage. Her killer had displaced her clothing to inflict the stab wounds, then turned her body over to stab her again, stamping on her thigh and leaving the plank between her legs. The pathologist could not be certain, but there was a strong possibility that Emily had been murdered by Wilma McCann's killer, judging from the similarities: lacerations to the head, caused by a blunt instrument; stab wounds inflicted while the victim lay face down, then again after the victim was turned onto her back; the displacement of clothing; and the use of a weapon resembling a cross-head Phillips screwdriver.

Gee also factored in the site of Emily's murder: less than four hundred yards from where Wilma had been seen thumbing a lift on her last night alive. After some discussion, Hoban and Gee agreed that in all probability the killer was a long-distance lorry driver, and if they didn't apprehend him soon, he would almost certainly kill again.

❖

Neil Jackson and his brother Chris were chatting in the kitchen of their home when their father appeared, flanked by two uniformed policemen. With Chris swiftly removed out of earshot into another room with Angela, Neil and Sydney were informed that a body had been found, believed to be Emily. A formal identification would be necessary. Both father and son agreed to accompany the officers to the police station.

One of the Jacksons' neighbours recalls Sydney turning up in a terrible state with his two youngest children. 'He asked if I would look after Christopher and Angela if he wasn't back when they came home from school,' the woman recalled. 'He said Emily had had an accident but when I asked how she was, he was so upset he couldn't tell me what was wrong.'[4]

Sydney confirmed to police that the woman in the mortuary was his wife. He was then led to an interview suite inside Millgarth Police Station, where Hoban had established an incident room. At six storeys high with glass stairwells on one side, the newly opened building dominated the nearby bus station and market. Sydney answered questions about his marriage, but volunteered nothing about Emily working as a prostitute, although rumours had already begun to stir. Preparing the ground for extracting himself from any blame, he intimated that she had been possessed of a sexual appetite he could not satisfy.

Neil recognized Hoban from a local television news appeal for information on Wilma McCann. He was bewildered by the questions put to him concerning his parents' marriage, his father's movements the previous evening, what his mother did for a living, whether she had bought herself any 'sexy clothes' recently, and if he thought his father capable of killing Emily.[5]

Hoban gave a televised interview from Millgarth, describing Emily as 'a woman who liked to go to public houses. She liked to go to bingo. She led a life of her own, really. We are anxious to contact any friends, lady friends or men friends, who may have seen her last night. She probably went to the Gaiety public house, which is a very popular pub in the area. We know the van she was in finished up in the Gaiety car park this morning.'[6] He gave no details of Emily's murder, stating simply that she had 'severe head injuries. There are other injuries I don't wish to elaborate on at this time.'[7]

Neil returned home before his father, arranging for his brother and sister to stay with an aunt; they had not been told that their mother was dead. Waving them off in a taxi, he turned back to the house to find an army of reporters, one of whom shouted above the exploding flashbulbs: 'This is a respectable neighbourhood, Mr Jackson. How long had your mother been working as a prostitute?'[8] He ran inside and locked the door, pulling all the curtains before sitting in the dark, his mind in turmoil.

By mid-evening, Sydney had admitted to detectives that Emily had been soliciting. Rather than explain his wife's desperation to save her family from financial ruin, he referred to his earlier comment about Emily's sexual appetite. Forty years after her murder, Sydney Jackson's explanation continues to be presented as the reason Emily embarked on sex work.

Allowed home that night, the following morning he awoke to newspapers ablaze with reports about his wife. The *Yorkshire Evening Post* declared: 'Woman Battered: "Killer May Strike Again" Warning', stating that Hoban had found links between Emily's murder and that of Wilma McCann. Hoban held another press conference, confirming that Emily had worked as a prostitute for the last few weeks of her life. The internal messaging system at Millgarth Police Station informed all West Yorkshire divisions and neighbouring forces that 'there are several indications that the person responsible for this crime may also have been responsible for the death of the prostitute Wilma McCann at Leeds on 29/30th October 1975. Motive appears to be hatred of prostitutes ...'[9] Hoban thus issued a warning through the press that 'while this man is at large, no prostitute is safe', adding that Emily would sometimes leave the Commer van at the Gaiety car park to 'go with clients in their own cars, when they would drive to some secluded place for sex. It was probably on one of these excursions that she met her killer.'[10]

Those who knew Emily found the revelation about her sex work as difficult to grasp as her murder. 'Never in a hundred years would I have thought Emily Jackson was on the game,' declared George Radnell, landlord of the Commercial on Elland Road.[11] Sydney's sister, taking care of Chris and Bubs at her home in Old Farnley, told reporters tearfully: 'It's time someone denied what is being said about Emily going into clubs and so on. She just wasn't that kind of person.'[12] It took years for Neil Jackson to deal with that aspect of his mother's life.

Sydney invited a *Yorkshire Evening Post* reporter into his home and wept: 'I know what people are saying but I didn't do it. There's nothing I want to say to the man who did do it. There's nothing I can say. But if he's done it once, he'll do it again. I just pray they'll catch him.'[13] He described his marriage as a happy one, putting a different spin on their early separation: 'We were parted for about two years eighteen years ago but I came back for the children's sake.' Asked if his wife had any enemies, Sydney shook his head. 'I can't think of any reason why anybody should want to kill her. She was well liked.'[14]

Hauled into Millgarth Police Station for further questioning, Sydney grew angry at being unable to work not only because of the emotional trauma but due to the Commer van being retained for forensic examination. Experts found four fingerprints in the van which they were unable to identify, plus another on a lemonade bottle in the rear, and a sixth on a betting slip in Emily's handbag.

Hoban eventually made an official announcement that Sydney was no longer regarded as a suspect in his wife's murder. A witness remembered seeing Emily walking along Spencer Place towards Roundhay Road at 9.45 p.m. on her last night alive. Hoban added publicly that Emily had been 'in the habit of patrolling the streets of Chapeltown for the purposes of prostitution'.[15] He appealed directly to women working the streets to come forward without fear of prosecution; those who did confirmed that the site of Emily's murder was often used as a place to take clients.

A task force of one hundred officers quizzed Chapeltown residents, while detectives armed with questionnaires visited the Gaiety. Maria Sellars told them about her last meeting with Emily and how she had vanished with a client in a Land Rover. Police issued a description of the driver and vehicle, together with an artist's impression, which was reproduced in the press. A man matching the description came forward of his own volition, explaining that he had been visiting Leeds from Essex and had spoken to prostitutes, but was emphatic that he hadn't paid for sex. He was eliminated from enquiries as two further leads proved futile: a dark-blue transit van with an 'L' registration spotted near the murder scene around 3.30 a.m. was never traced, and nor was a client of Emily's whom Sydney recalled being strange in some way.

Hoban had his team scour hardware shops in an effort to identify the weapon that had been used on Emily, but to no avail. He was convinced the wounds to her body were caused by a cross-head screwdriver, but tests failed to produce the same wound. Hoban eschewed the idea of trying to trace the killer by his footwear, but insisted that anyone brought into custody wearing similar boots and in possession of a workman's vehicle and tools should be thoroughly questioned.

A police van bearing a six-foot image of Emily toured Chapeltown, Roundhay Road and Harehills. Other police vehicles bearing the same image parked at busy road junctions, where officers questioned hundreds of individuals. Similar posters were displayed across the city and its suburbs. Neil Jackson recalls the pain of being confronted with those images: 'The worst thing was walking about and seeing photos of my mam on buses and walls or whatever. It shocks you. Really shocks you.'[16] Loudspeaker appeals were issued to crowds at rugby and football matches, bingo halls and cinemas. Hoban urged people to keep Emily in their thoughts, bearing in mind that she had been murdered with a ferocity which 'bordered on the maniacal' by a 'sadistic killer [who] may well be a sexual pervert'.[17]

Prostitution was now the common denominator in the murders as far as the police and press were concerned. The *Yorkshire Post* reported that sex workers in the 'gale-swept murder mile' of Chapeltown and Harehills appeared to have heeded police warnings and as a result, most of the people on the streets at night were uniformed police hunting the killer.[18] One girl told the press: 'Make no doubt about it, we are all worried. I can't get it out of my head that I could be next on his list. I could pick up a man in the street and how would I know he was the maniac knifeman until it was too late? Then someone would find my body in my flat.'[19] As part of their enquiries into Emily's murder, during the course of a year, police made in excess of 3,700 house-to-house visits, took 830 statements, checked 3,500 vehicles, and recorded the results on over 6,400 index cards.

Emily had been the glue that held her family together and without her, their home life collapsed. While Chris returned to live with his father, Neil joined the army and Angela remained with her aunt. Emily's relatives openly blamed Sydney for her sex work and held him responsible to some extent for her death. Emily had been her father's favourite, and shortly after her death he passed away. At his grandfather's funeral, Neil learned of the beatings his mother had endured while married to his father and why she had been drawn into prostitution. He regarded it as 'the bitterest pill I had to swallow', one which 'made me question everything about my past and, worse, left me disappointed in Mum'.[20] He remembers there being no counselling to help him or any form of specialist support:

'When Mum's death was first being investigated, the man in charge was Detective Chief Superintendent Dennis Hoban. He showed some genuine caring for the family and how we were coping. He kept us informed of what was happening. But after a while Mr Hoban was promoted and moved to Bradford and we were left on our own.'[21]

Emily was laid to rest alongside her son Derek, on a warm day in May 1976. Four months later her killer attacked again in Spencer Place, where she had last been seen alive.

6

MARCELLA

If there were no doubts regarding the killer's motives in the minds of the police, there was even less uncertainty about the victims themselves. Emily Jackson had worked in prostitution only for a matter of weeks when she died, but as far as Millgarth Police Station's telex machine was concerned, that was the most significant factor; she was an 'active prostitute', whose injuries resembled those inflicted upon 'the prostitute Wilma McCann'. Therefore, so police thinking went, both women had been murdered by the same man, who was driven by a 'hatred of prostitutes'.[1] Hoban addressed a press conference to confirm his understanding of the killer's motives, declaring: 'We are quite certain the man we are looking for hates prostitution. I am quite certain this stretches to women of rather loose morals who go to public houses and clubs, who are not necessarily prostitutes. The frenzied attack he has carried out on these women indicates this.'[2]

Hoban linked Emily's murder not only to that of Wilma McCann but also with the killing of forty-three-year-old Mary Judge in Leeds eight years earlier, an investigation in which he had been senior officer. Although media reports described Mary as married, there was no evidence of a husband; she lived with an elderly man as his housekeeper and had no family. Mary had convictions for soliciting, and was seen on the night of her death, 26 February 1968, with a man at the Regent Hotel on Kirkgate at 10.10 p.m. At 10.18 p.m., the Hull train rattled along the viaduct on its journey into central Leeds, and several passengers gazing out into the dark winter night saw a woman being attacked near Leeds Parish Church. The main witness was a young boy, who told police that a tall, slim man with dark hair had knocked a lady to the ground.

Mary's naked body was found on wasteland the next morning. Her clothes were strewn nearby, and 'a blunt instrument' had been used to destroy her skull.[3] The man she was seen with at the Regent Hotel was questioned and released without charge; there were no other suspects.

Hoban saw several parallels between Mary Judge, Emily Jackson and Wilma McCann: 'All three women followed a similar pattern of life, visiting pubs and clubs as prostitutes, although the Jackson and McCann killings are the only ones definitely linked. Besides her head wounds, Mrs Jackson was stabbed fifty times. In both cases, the obvious deep-seated hatred of prostitutes manifested itself in the many stab wounds.'[4] He added again, 'While this man, who shows every sign of being a psychopath, is at large, no prostitute is safe.'[5]

It was a story ripe for sensationalism, and the *Yorkshire Evening Post* led the way with a dramatic opener to an article about Leeds prostitution: 'Fear of a maniac Jack the Ripper killer today stalked the twilight world of hookers and good-time girls who ply for trade in the Chapeltown, Roundhay Road and Harehills area of Leeds. With two women having been brutally stabbed to death in the area in a matter of weeks, the girls are asking, "who is going to be his next victim?"'[6] *The Sun* promptly picked up the story, declaring: 'RIPPER HUNTED IN CALL GIRL MURDERS'. Neil Jackson was appalled when he saw the headlines: 'My mum had been murdered by someone named after the maniac who'd killed prostitutes in the East End of London in the nineteenth century … as I thought about all the drawings I'd seen of the Ripper victims in books I'd read as a kid, it brought home the terrible savagery of Mum's murder. This was worse still than the police description of her injuries or the smell of death just two days ago in the mortuary.'[7]

The casting of the contemporary killer as a reincarnated Jack the Ripper gathered momentum as the investigation progressed. Writer Joan Smith, then a young journalist covering the murders, observes: 'From this point on, both evidence and suspects would be judged according to the yardstick of how well they measured up to the theory.'[8] Hence the inclusion of Mary Judge in the list of women attacked by the new 'Ripper', and the exclusion of genuine victims Anna, Olive and Tracy.

In truth, a common thread *had* already emerged: all the victims were female. That was the unifying factor. None but Emily were active prostitutes and none of the attacks occurred in red-light districts. The survivors had provided noticeably similar descriptions of their assailant, whose accent marked him out as local. When Hoban gave evidence at the inquest into Wilma McCann's death some months later, he reiterated: 'There is little doubt in my mind that both offences relating to Mrs McCann and Mrs Jackson were committed by the same person – some psychopath with a deep hatred for this type of girl.'[9]

Betty Newlands reacted with pained fury at Hoban's description of her daughter: 'Wilma was not a prostitute and I hope and pray every day that the Ripper is caught, brought to trial and Wilma's name cleared. I can't get the horrible business out of my mind. I would not like any other mother to go through what I have experienced. That is another reason I hope this man is caught and brought to justice.'[10]

Although men filled the main positions of authority during the investigation, many female officers were involved in essential tasks, mostly administration, liaising with family members, recording witness statements and taking the role of murder victim in reconstructions. In the weeks that followed Emily's murder, female officers acted as decoys in Leeds red-light districts, shadowed by their male counterparts in a bid to catch the killer.

Women working the streets had been advised to take reasonable measures to protect themselves, but when a group of prostitutes began taking clients to a house in Bradford, police raided the property on grounds of it operating as a brothel. Some women moved further afield: residents of Forest Road in Nottingham complained that the local red-light district was overrun with prostitutes from Leeds and Derby, many of whom were sixteen years old, or younger.

Most Leeds-based sex workers gravitated to Chapeltown, home to the middle classes during the industrial revolution. Pogrom-fleeing Jews settled in the area at the turn of the century, but by the 1930s they had moved out to Moortown and Roundhay. Post-war Chapeltown offered a place to rebuild lives as displaced persons, Poles, Greeks, Ukranians, and Serbs arrived in the city. From 1948, the government's drive to recruit labour for a shortfall in the service industries saw an influx of West Indian families and ex-servicemen, who were joined in the late fifties by manual workers from Pakistan and the Punjab.

Among the West Indian families who made Chapeltown their home were ten-year-old Marcella Claxton and her mother. Born on St Kitts, Marcella's formative years were spent on an island paradise, but life was far from idyllic; her father's harsh and frequent discipline left her physically and emotionally scarred. Knowing there would be no peace for them on St Kitts, Marcella's mother left to make a new life for herself and her daughter in England.

Marcella struggled academically in Leeds. She was given an IQ grading of 50, but the evaluation was misrepresentative; with her troubled background, Marcella simply had difficulty expressing herself. But life in her adoptive city had its own problems. By the spring of 1976, Marcella was unemployed and pregnant with two children in foster care. Home was a terrace on Sholebroke Mount, a stone's throw from Wilma McCann's local, the Scott Hall Hotel. Chapeltown escaped regeneration: its once gracious terraces were being divided into substandard flats and its mansions left to rot. The economic slump inevitably fuelled crime and social problems, yet the neighbourhood retained a strong sense of community, with a vibrancy lacking in other areas. But in media terms Chapeltown was a 'Mecca of Vice' and the locus of moral panic, awash with muggers, prostitutes and pimps.[11]

On Saturday 8 May 1976, Marcella attended an all-night party a few streets from home. Shortly after 4 a.m., as she walked along Spencer Place, a car pulled up. Its driver offered her a lift. 'He was well spoken and smartly dressed and said he did not live in Leeds,' she recalls.[12]

The exact sequence of events that followed are imprecise, but Marcella has always been adamant that she was not soliciting, disputing those narratives that state otherwise. The solicitor who represented her during claims to the Criminal Injuries Compensation Board was equally vehement.

Marcella accepted the man's offer, which saved her a fifteen-minute walk, but rather than heading for Sholebroke Mount, he drove almost two miles north to Roundhay Park. Away from the main road, he parked a short distance onto Soldiers Field, a former parade ground opposite the luxurious block of flats on West Avenue. A thin row of trees led towards a low and windowless building used by visitors to the park as changing rooms during sporting fixtures.

Marcella climbed out of the car to urinate. As she crouched in the darkness, the man told her to undress fully. When she refused, he switched from being a genial stranger into 'the most terrifying person you can imagine', hitting her repeatedly with a heavy object.[13] 'His eyes were glazed and he didn't seem to have any control of himself,' Marcella recalls.[14] As she lay on the ground, moaning with pain and shock, the man masturbated over her. Afterwards, he pushed a £5 note into her hand and told her not to call the police. She heard his car reversing into the avenue before she lost consciousness.

An excruciating pain inside her skull brought Marcella round. She felt her way to a kneeling position and realized the grass was sodden with blood. Trembling violently, she used her pants to wipe her hair and face. 'Clots were coming out of my head,' she recalls. 'Big pieces ... My head was bleeding, and I was four months pregnant as well.'[15] Clutching the fabric to her skull, she stumbled across the park to a telephone box near the main road. She dialled the emergency services before sinking to the floor.

As she sat in the cramped space, still holding her pants to her head, she became aware that a white car was circling the park. 'It was the man that hurt me,' she remembers. 'He got out and began searching the spot where he had left me. He must have come back to finish me off. Thank God he didn't see me.'[16] She heard sirens in the distance and saw flashing lights, then drifted into unconsciousness again.

Surgeons at Leeds General Infirmary discovered eight lacerations to Marcella's skull, each wound approximately an inch long. She required extensive brain surgery and fifty-two stitches in her scalp.

While Marcella's attacker did not succeed in killing her, his brutality caused her to lose the baby she was carrying, a crime for which he would never be held legally responsible.

Detectives interviewed Marcella in hospital the following day. She told them that her attacker was a bearded white male with crinkly black hair, who drove a white car with red upholstery; he had said that he didn't live in Leeds. The police suggested that she was mistaken and her attacker was black. Marcella's response to the inherent racism in their insinuation was immediate: 'I said no black man would have done this to me.'[17]

Recovering from surgery made it difficult for Marcella to select the components for a photofit, but she persisted. The image she produced bore a strong resemblance to the photofit created by Tracy Browne, yet it was never made public. Her attack was not formally linked to the murders of Emily and Wilma, nor to the assaults on Anna, Olive and Tracy. It was not included in the 'Special Notices' issued to other forces, but instead treated as a one-off. An internal West Yorkshire Police document later noted: 'Although she had been struck about the head with an unknown instrument, there were factors which were dissimilar to previous "Ripper" attacks. Most significant was the absence of stabbing to the body and there was the motive of taking the money and running away.'[18]

After six days in hospital Marcella returned home with no support counselling. She had to find a way of living not only with the memory of her attack but the loss of her unborn child. Suffering with depression, she was told that the headaches, dizziness and occasional blackouts that plagued her would be permanent. 'It's like my brain is bursting and hitting the inside of my head, sometimes all day,' she explains.[19]

For months afterwards, she expected to see her assailant again: 'I am still in fear of my life. I think I can identify him and he must know that.'[20] During a night out with friends at the Gaiety she became paralyzed upon seeing a man she believed to be her attacker. By the time she had managed to alert her friends, the man had gone.

Marcella's attack was given far less press coverage than previous assaults. Police and reporters alike showed more interest the following year, when another young woman was taken to Soldiers Field and subjected to a similar ordeal. Marcella had moved away by then and it took time for detectives to trace her. They desperately needed her help, for unlike Marcella, the other woman did not survive.

7

IRENE

Possilpark in Glasgow hit the headlines in 2016 when its residents were found to have the lowest life expectancy in Britain due to chronic unemployment, poor housing and social neglect. Yet it was a thriving community until the fifties, built to house the workforce of Saracen Foundry, cast iron exporters to the British Empire.

Among the families who arrived from Glasgow's tenements after the war were the Osbornes. Munitions factory storeman John Osborne had been brought up in the Church of Scotland faith, while his wife Helen was from a strict Roman Catholic background. After their marriage, they raised seven daughters and three sons as Protestants in a frugal but loving household.

Irene, born at home on 28 March 1948, was a shy and sensitive girl. She cast off timidity in her early teens, and was frequently in trouble at Springburn Secondary School for smoking and playing truant. Tall and slim, with long brown hair, she was quick to laugh, loved pop music and wanted to travel. When Saracen Foundry closed in 1967, Possilpark went into decline and several of Irene's siblings moved across the border to England.

Seventeen-year old Irene headed for London, finding work as a chambermaid and waitress in a succession of hotels. She became a single mother in 1966 and cut off all contact with her family. Unable to cope alone, Irene put her daughter Lorraine into council care, where she was fostered at the age of eighteen months by Croydon antique dealers who adopted her two years later.

Irene contacted her sister Helen, who lived in Blackpool. She discovered that her father had passed away and the funeral had taken place without her because no one had known where she was living. Irene's life in Blackpool replicated her time in London: working as a chambermaid in a boarding house, she found herself pregnant and alone again at the age of twenty-one.

Irene switched jobs, becoming a cleaner on higher wages at Pontins Holiday Camp, overlooking the sand dunes. Blackpool's popularity as a seaside resort had waned since the introduction of budget air travel and package holidays abroad, but Pontins remained a cheap and cheerful alternative. Before her baby was due, Irene began a relationship with barman George Biggart Richardson, a twenty-eight-year-old divorcé and heavy drinker from her home town of Glasgow. They found lodgings together and discussed marriage, but on his terms. Under his direction, Irene gave her son up for adoption immediately after his birth in October 1969.

Eight months later, on 5 June 1970, George and Irene married at Blackpool registry office. By 1973 they were living in a house on Balmer Grove with their infant daughter, named Irene after her mother. George had little sympathy for his wife's post-natal depression. Alcohol diminished his patience further, resulting in regular beatings. A second daughter, Amanda, was born in summer 1975, but with no respite from the abuse and her own psychological problems, Irene fled to London, alone.

A few weeks after George reported his wife missing, Irene contacted him, asking him to bring the girls to her South Kensington address. They agreed to work at their marriage, finding a flat together near the Grosvenor Hotel where Irene was employed as a chambermaid. In April 1976, Irene vanished from their lives again. George returned to Blackpool and placed their daughters in council care.

Irene had found work at a different hotel in London, where

she met Greenwich-born former seaman Steven Bray. Described by the *Police Gazette* as '6ft tall, heavy build, fresh complexion, black hair, brown eyes [and] extensively tattooed', Bray was on the run after absconding during home leave from Lancaster Prison. Employed as a chef, he said nothing to Irene about having a wife in Hull, and she never mentioned George.

After six months, Bray was keen to move on before the police caught up with him. In October 1976, he and Irene settled in Leeds, where he worked as a doorman at Tiffany's nightclub in the Merrion Centre and she cleaned at the Residential Boys' Club, a YMCA hostel in Chapel Allerton. They had no fixed address, twice lodging in an attic room at a boarding house on the corner of Cowper Street and Chapeltown Road, and on another occasion renting a house on Sholebroke Avenue, a stone's throw from Marcella Claxton's home.

While living on Sholebroke Avenue, Irene became friendly with a neighbour, Mrs Marcella Walsh, confiding in her that she and Bray had set a date to marry at the registry office in Leeds. But when 22 January 1977 arrived, neither bride nor groom turned up. Both were unwilling to commit bigamy and Bray was already on a ferry to Ireland.

Afterwards, Irene failed to arrive for her shifts at the hostel, surprising warden Nellie Morrison, who thought her a pleasant and conscientious worker. 'Irene Bray' had previously asked Nellie for an advance on her wages 'to pay a large bill'.[1] Nellie could only let her have £1, but Irene had seemed grateful for it. In early February, she suddenly appeared at the hostel again, apologizing for not properly handing in her notice, but inisisting she had to get away from her partner. She took her work shoes and overalls then disappeared.

A few days later, a man turned up at the hostel demanding Irene's outstanding wages. Nellie gave him the money, but it later emerged that Irene had not received any of it. Clinically depressed, she was seen walking aimlessly about Chapeltown and slept in a public toilet for several nights. The landlord of the Cowper Street boarding house allowed her to take a ground-floor room rent free until a paying guest needed it.

Detective Chief Superintendent James Hobson later led the investigation into Irene's murder and reflected: 'In the last ten days of her life Irene Richardson was wandering about, without accommodation, practically penniless and hanging about street corners in the Chapeltown area. It may well be that she was mistaken for a prostitute because she had nowhere to go.'[2] He added that Irene 'got on well with the people she lived next to in rooming houses at four or five different addresses in Leeds. She seems to have been a jovial type of person and there is more and more evidence that she was trying to get work.'[3] Among the jobs Irene applied for was one as a nanny in a large property near Roundhay Park, giving her own address as 1 Cowper Street, Chapeltown, where she had a room.

On Saturday 5 February 1977, Irene appeared at the boarding house with sufficient funds for a single night. She seemed brighter, calling that evening on permanent resident Pam Barker. Her hair was freshly washed and she wore an outfit that suited her slim figure: yellow jacket and skirt, blue-and-white checked blouse, brown cardigan, brown knee-length boots and a long, Afghan-style coat. Delicate bangles hung from her wrists and she wore an imitation-gold watch.

Telling Pam that she was heading to Tiffany's in search of Bray, Irene left Cowper Street at 11.15 p.m. She headed for Marcella Walsh's home on Sholebroke Avenue and took away some small items she had stored with her, then set out for Tiffany's. The two-mile walk took her past the spot where Wilma was last seen thumbing a lift, and within a few feet of the condemned buildings where Emily's body was found. How far Irene walked that night will never be known, but her life was brought to a swift and pitiless end where Marcella Claxton had barely survived nine months earlier, on Soldiers Field.

❖

Forty-six-year-old chartered accountant John Bolton kept fit with a one-mile jog before breakfast every morning. His usual path from Gledhow Lane took him across Roundhay Park. He had just begun to work up a sweat that Sunday when he glimpsed a dark shape under the trees behind the sports pavilion.

'At first, I was not sure if it was a body,' he recalled. 'But as I got nearer I could see it was a woman lying on her side. I said something like, "Hello? What's the matter?" Her face was turned down towards the grass and covered by her hair. I brushed the hair to one side and then I saw the blood on her neck and her eyes were glazed and staring. She was obviously dead, so I ran to one of the houses and called the police.'[4]

Detective Chief Superintendent James Hobson had replaced Dennis Hoban as head of the Eastern Crime Area. He took charge of the investigation, but Hoban attended the scene that morning nonetheless. The two men were joined by Professor David Gee, who bent over the young woman on the grass. Irene's head was turned to the left, blood and debris matting her long hair. There were three injuries to her skull and blood staining her neck and cardigan. Lifting the coat where it had been thrown across her body, Gee saw the calf-length boots had been laid along the backs of her legs. The skirt and slip were bunched up around her waist and her tights had been removed from her right leg. She wore two pairs of pants because she had been menstruating; a tampon lay beside her body. The pants under her tights were in place, but the ones worn over them had been rolled into a ball with a sock, gathering debris inside the tights. Her jacket, cardigan and bra were undisturbed and her bangles were still around one wrist. On the other was her imitation-gold watch: behind the misted glass its hands had stopped at ten to nine.

The true extent of Irene's injuries became apparent when her body was rolled over. Her throat had been cut deeply enough to expose the larynx; her stomach had been slashed in three places. One of the gashes had cut through the abdominal wall, causing part of her intestines to spill out. A four-foot trail of blood led from her body towards the pavilion, where items from her handbag lay scattered: a cosmetics purse, lipstick, mortice key and a penny. Inside the bag were a packet of cigarettes and box of matches, bus tickets, thirty-five and a half pence, and details of the family who had advertised for a nanny.

A short distance away, the football teams due to play their Sunday fixture had arrived. They were told the match was cancelled, and why, before the area around the pavilion was cordoned off. Twenty uniformed officers conducted a fingertip search of the park while Irene's body was removed to the mortuary, where it was discovered that one of the head injuries had been inflicted with such force that a circular piece of skull had been driven into her brain. Vaginal swabs showed that intercourse had taken place at some point during the previous twenty-four hours. Semen stains on her tights and pants revealed that a second man had indulged in some form of sexual activity with her. He was a non-secretor; Wilma McCann's killer possessed the same genetic trait.

On the basis of Gee's findings, Hobson thought it probable that Irene had been 'prepared to resort to prostitution to get money', while acknowledging that she had no cautions or convictions for soliciting.[5]

The two men conferred on events leading to Irene's death. It seemed likely that she had accepted the offer of a lift from a stranger and was driven to Roundhay Park. Hobson believed she had agreed to sex and used the excuse of needing to urinate as a means of discreetly removing her tampon. She had then been struck on the head from behind. A jagged fracture suggested that the weapon, probably a hammer, had caught on a bone and her killer had prised it out before hitting her twice more. He had dragged Irene further onto the field and cut her throat before inflicting three gashes to her stomach. Gee pronounced himself satisfied that the killer of Wilma McCann and Emily Jackson had also murdered Irene Richardson.

❖

A telex issued from Millgarth Police Station to all West Yorkshire divisions and neighbouring forces requested that any apprehended men with bloodstained clothing should be questioned about Irene's murder. Hobson also ordered checks at all dry cleaners in Leeds.

Fingerprint experts were unable to identify a fragment of a print found on a bus ticket near the sports pavilion. House-to-house enquiries in the area, including a visit to DJ and television personality Jimmy Savile, who lived in a penthouse flat overlooking the scene, proved fruitless.

Detectives launched a mammoth undercover operation to identify tyre tracks left by the killer's vehicle. Preliminary checks revealed that the tyre brand was common to one hundred thousand vehicles in West Yorkshire. Details of those drivers requiring a home visit were recorded on a card index system. These were then filed at Millgarth Police Station with the registration number first, followed by the vehicle-keeper's name and address; there was no cross-referencing. The tyre tracking enquiry involved an enormous number of working hours and paperwork that came to an abrupt end when resources were needed elsewhere.

Before Irene's identity was released to the press, the *Yorkshire Evening Post* front page carried a photograph of the crime scene headed 'Lovers' Lane Murder of Mystery Woman', speculating whether her death could be linked to the 'unsolved "Jack the Ripper" murders of two Leeds women which terrorized prostitutes a little over a year ago'.[6] Hobson told reporters one day after the murder: 'The fact that all three women – McCann, Jackson, Richardson – were picked up in the same area, the fact that two of them were found dead on playing fields, and the fact that the injuries are very similar, makes a link between them. Mrs Richardson was not a known prostitute but we know she was depressed. She could have gone in a car with a man as a "punter" after she had visited Tiffany's. We are still trying to trace her movements that night.'[7] Yet Irene's killing was not officially linked to those of Emily and Wilma until May 1977, when a Special Notice was issued to all forces.

Media conjecture mounted nevertheless, with dramatic headlines querying: 'Link with "Jack the Ripper" Style Deaths? Police Chief Keeps Open Mind'; 'Jack the Ripper Murder Horror' and 'Police Investigating Jack the Ripper Style Killings in Leeds'.[8] The *Yorkshire Evening Post* further quoted Hobson: 'I have found no indication at this stage that Mrs Richardson had been acting as a prostitute. But our inquiries are being directed to see whether she had this mode of life.'[9] The same issue carried a brief interview with Pam Barker, who recalled that Irene 'only went out on Saturday nights and did not go drinking a lot, but had visited the Gaiety public house on occasion'.[10]

George Richardson had formally identified his estranged wife after an unmarked car collected him from Blackpool. He insisted to reporters: 'My wife was not a prostitute. She was sick ... She just could not settle down ... I went to work one day and when I came home she had gone. I never saw her again until last night [in the mortuary]. If I could find the man who did this to her, I would kill him and happily do time for it.'[11]

Irene's last love, Steven Bray, was still on the run and now suspected of killing her. Bray's wife told police that she hadn't seen her husband for three years or more. Hobson announced that he wanted to question Bray, adding again that there was 'no evidence at this stage to suggest [Irene] was a full-time or even an amateur prostitute. Her mode of life had been going down from the way she had been living before and she had little or no money.'[12] He confirmed that she had been involved with only two men in the last six years: George Richardson and Steven Bray.

Hobson was also keen to speak to Marcella Claxton about her attack on Soldiers Field. Detectives learned that she had moved away and enlisted the press as a means of tracing her. It worked: Marcella read the reports and contacted Hobson herself. After a lengthy meeting, he took her back to Soldiers Field but to her dismay, the assistance she gave resulted in Hobson's announcement to the press: 'At the time of the savage attack last year Marcella Claxton was working as a prostitute in the Chapeltown Road area. It now seems that West Avenue, Roundhay, the spot where Mrs Richardson's body was found, was a favourite spot for prostitutes to take clients.'[13]

Marcella underwent further anguish when Hobson dismissed the photofit she had compiled as 'not necessarily a description of the murderer'.[14] Instead of releasing the photofit, which subsequently proved to be an extraordinary likeness, he gave reporters his own description of it, omitting a crucial detail: the attacker's moustache and beard. The photofit only ever appeared in a confidential police report and a separate police circular.

Marcella told Hobson that her attacker drove a white car with red upholstery, but no association was made with evidence that on the night of Irene's murder, around 11.30 p.m., the driver of a white vehicle had pestered a woman in Chapeltown to accept a lift. The incident occurred in Nassau Place, running parallel with Chapeltown Road and intersecting Cowper Place.

Posters requesting information on Irene were distributed to retail outlets in Leeds and prominently displayed on Chapeltown Road. Hobson told another press conference: 'We are anxious to trace anyone who saw her after she left home in Cowper Street, Chapeltown at 11.15 p.m. on Saturday February 5. So far no one who saw her after 11.15 p.m. has come forward.'[15]

On 15 March, Steven Bray was apprehended in London and held at Leeds Prison for questioning. Satisfied that he had no connection with Irene's murder, detectives sanctioned his return to Lancaster Prison.

One month later, another woman died at the hands of Irene's killer.

8

PATRICIA

Thorpe Edge was the largest of several council estates built in Bradford after the Second World War. No. 39 Orchard Grove was a semi-detached house among mostly functional and cheerless flats, and had views over the countryside. It was home to the Atkinsons: laundry presser James and his wife Gladys, and their children Patricia, Barry and Anthony. A second daughter, Kathleen, died in infancy when Patricia was six years old.

Patricia left school in 1959 at fifteen, to train as a burler and mender. Once the wool capital of the world, Bradford's textile industry had gone into decline after the war, but Patricia's work at a mill in Greengates was highly skilled. In a quiet room away from the machines, it was her job to inspect finished bolts of cloth for imperfections and knots, repairing them to create a perfect length of material. At weekends she socialized in Lumb Lane's pubs and clubs. Taller than average and slim, she was far prettier than the single photograph of her issued publicly. She wore her long dark hair backcombed but loose, and was lively and good-natured.

Ramen Mitra, two years her senior, fell in love with Patricia immediately. His family were among the many immigrants to Bradford from India and Pakistan, keen to work and seeking a better life. Employed as a wool comber, he was known to everyone as Ray, and regarded as a true gentleman. He was devoted to Patricia, whom he called 'Tina' because he thought it suited her. Patricia's parents were deeply fond of him; he shared their home in Thorpe Edge before marrying their daughter at a registry office on 1 April 1961.

Five months later, Patricia's father died at the age of fifty and a year later her mother passed away aged only forty-three. Ray and Patricia left Thorpe Edge, settling in Girlington, west of the city centre. Three daughters were born in quick succession: Judy, Jill and Liza. Patricia adored her children, but at only twenty-two years old, she had been in a relationship with Ray for seven years and a mother for the past four. She began socializing alone, causing tensions in the marriage when rumours of her infidelity reached Ray.

In 1975, Patricia was cautioned for soliciting; the only published photograph of her dates from her arrest. Why she began working as a prostitute is unclear, but her marriage ended as a result. After the divorce in September 1976, Ray was granted custody of their daughters but never prevented Patricia from spending time with them. The senior investigating officer in her murder later mused: 'She led him a terrible life ... [He] did his best for her, did everything he could to help her. He wasn't that hard up, reasonably well off money-wise, but she was a bad girl. I thought about why she may have gone that way.'[1]

Patricia had given up soliciting after being cautioned but started drinking heavily. As she struggled financially, unwilling to exploit Ray's generosity, she returned to the streets, using her mother's maiden name and calling herself Tina Magee.

Ten days before her death, Patricia began renting a newly built flat on Manningham's Oak Avenue, about a mile and a half from the city centre. Around the corner was a bustling Asian market, held every Saturday on Oak Lane, with Lumb Lane just a ten-minute walk away. The complex where Patricia lived was already falling into disrepair, with poor plumbing and water gathering on the flat roof. The front aspect stood two storeys high; Patricia's flat was at the back where the land sloped and the complex rose to three storeys. Reached from a flight of steps on Oak Avenue, Flat 3 had a large bed-sitting room, tiny bathroom and kitchenette. The few bits of furniture had been chosen for practicality alone; there was nothing aesthetically pleasing about the main room. The only ornamental touches were two glass gondolas on the dressing table and a permanently empty vase.

Caretaker Jack Robinson knew Patricia only by sight, recalling that she was no trouble and always looked neat and attractive, usually wearing the same blue shirt, flared jeans, denim-coloured platform shoes and a short leather jacket. She had an expensive habit of taking a taxi from Oak Avenue to Lumb Lane, where the pubs she frequented most were those she knew from her teenage years: the Queens, the Flying Dutchman and the Perseverance.

A few weeks before her death, Patricia met heavy drinker Robert Henderson in one of the Lane's pubs. They spent Friday 22 April 1977 at her flat, drinking into the early hours. When he left that morning, Patricia freshened up, applying thick make-up and styling her hair before slipping into a white T-shirt and jumper, flared jeans and denim slingbacks. Slightly hungover, she put on her cropped black leather jacket, picked up her bag and headed outside.

Patricia's movements during the early part of the evening are unclear, but several witnesses saw her in the bar of the Carlisle Hotel, where the crowd was disgruntled because the stripper had failed to arrive. Patricia, inebriated, climbed onto the stage and proceeded to take off all her clothes. She was forcibly removed by the manager.

At 10.15 p.m., Patricia was seen drinking at the International Club on Lumb Lane. Three-quarters of an hour later, she retraced her steps and another sex worker spotted her on Church Street, weaving towards St Mary's Road. Patricia was heading home; her flat on Oak Avenue was just half a mile away. She arrived there before midnight, but not alone.

❖

Robert Henderson knocked on Patricia's door at 6.30 p.m. the following evening. When she didn't answer, he tried the handle and found it unlocked. Puzzled, he entered the flat slowly and saw Patricia lying in bed utterly still. Nearby, on the patterned carpet was a dark, spreading stain.

Henderson turned and ran for caretaker Jack Robinson, shouting that there had been a murder. Robinson opened the door expecting to find Henderson drunk and told him not to be 'so hysterical'.[2] He reluctantly agreed to visit Patricia's flat and recalled taking a step towards her bed: 'All I could see was the side of her head, an arm and blood on the pillow but I knew she was dead.'[3] He rang the police.

Detective Chief Superintendent John Domaille had been appointed head of Bradford CID only two months earlier. As Media and Community Relations Officer for West Yorkshire Police, he already had first-hand experience of the Ripper attacks; one glance at Patricia was enough to tell him that it was probably the same man. He looked around the room, where an invasive smell of burning filaments from the three-bar fire mingled with the reek of alcohol. Several items stood on the table: a can of Harmony hairspray, a box of Scottie tissues, hand cream, a large ashtray, some inexpensive perfume and a leather handbag. On the sideboard, next to a plastic tray, stood a pair of platform sandals. A denim bag lay on the floor in front of the table. Beside it was the pool of blood Henderson had almost stepped in.

As forensic experts crowded the room, Professor David Gee joined Domaille at Patricia's bedside. The young woman lay face down, head turned towards the wall, the awkward angle of her body hidden from view by the bedding. Gee lifted her head gently: Patricia's delicate features had been obliterated by the attack, with four severe wounds to her skull. When the bedcovers were drawn back, it was clear to see that the killer had arranged her body.

Patricia's tights were around her ankles. Her pants and jeans had been dragged down and the jeans had been pulled up again slightly. One shoe was in place, the other lay next to the electric fire. Her jumper was around her shoulders, while her T-shirt and bra had been lifted to expose her breasts. There were six stab wounds to her stomach, several odd surface wounds to her back, and a number of slashes along her left side. Patricia's thick, dark hair was blood-soaked, as was the pillow and bedsheets: she had bled to death.

Both men spotted the bloody imprint of a shoe on the bottom sheet. The cotton was crumpled, but it looked like a close match for the print left on Emily Jackson's thigh. Domaille took another good look around the room. The front legs of the wooden chair next to the bed bore bloodspots and on the carpet nearby was another large bloodstain. Patricia's favourite jacket lay on the floor with a substantial amount of blood on it.

There were no signs of a struggle as such, suggesting that Patricia had gone ahead into the flat followed by her killer, who struck her from behind a number of times. She had fallen to the floor, bleeding heavily, and must have lain there for several minutes before the attacker removed her leather jacket, discarding it by the wardrobe. He had then pulled down her jeans, tights and pants, causing her left shoe to fall off. He had struck another blow to her skull, then lifted her onto the unmade bed and delivered more blows. She would have lost a lot of blood even before he inflicted the stab wounds and other surface injuries. He had then arranged her body, piling the bedding on top, and departed.

Shortly before midnight, a windowless van arrived at Oak Avenue. Wrapped in protective plastic, Patricia's body was carried out and transferred to Bradford City Mortuary, where Ray Mitra confirmed her identity. Grief-stricken, he returned home to work out how to tell his three daughters, then aged eleven, thirteen and fifteen, that their mother had been murdered.

Professor Gee began the post-mortem at 1.30 a.m. Four large depressed fractures to Patricia's skull had been caused by a blunt object. Wounds above her pubic bone were potentially the result of stabbing with a screwdriver or chisel, while an irregular abrasion to the left side of her chest and other injuries were probably made by a large hammer. Toxicology results showed that she had consumed the equivalent of twenty measures of spirits. Vaginal swabs revealed traces of semen from sexual intercourse with her partner Robert Henderson several hours before death.

The media instantly linked Patricia's murder with the killings of Wilma, Emily and Irene. 'Yorks Woman Found Battered: Leeds Link Probe' read the headline in the *Yorkshire Evening Post*. The article continued: 'The body of divorcee Patricia Tina Atkinson, described by police as a prostitute, was found with severe head injuries. And the possibility of a link with three unsolved murders in Leeds was being discussed this afternoon at a top-level meeting of West Yorkshire police officers ... Mrs Atkinson, who also used the surnames Mitre and McGill [sic], left the Carlisle Hotel, Carlisle Terrace, Manningham at about 10.15 p.m. on Saturday. She is believed to have been the worse for drink.'[4] Detective Chief Superintendent James Hobson confirmed: 'Obviously I am very interested in the Bradford murder, in view of the fact that she is a prostitute.'[5]

Scenes of crime officers removed a diary from Patricia's flat. It contained many names, some of whom were thought to be clients. Domaille broke the news of the discovery to reporters, hoping to encourage anyone acquainted with Patricia to come forward: 'This was a brutal murder, a very brutal murder. The man we are looking for could be a maniac. The leads that we are following are that there are a number of people in the area that I know knew this lady. I have her diary. This lists a lot of people – names a lot of people – and I would like to see all those people, I shall be making inquiries to trace them. I shall treat as a matter of complete confidentiality any information that comes to me.'[6]

There was surprisingly little forensic evidence: all but nine of the fingerprints lifted from the flat were identified. Police concentrated their efforts on interviewing all 1,200 taxi drivers operating in Bradford and every woman convicted of prostitution in the area. Posters appealing for information on Patricia's movements in her final hours were displayed in English, Urdu and Punjabi, but nothing emerged.

Press interest evaporated quickly. The *Yorkshire Evening Post* covered Patricia's funeral at Scholemoor Cemetery on 27 June 1977 with a single photograph of her daughters at the grave. The rest of the page was filled with news of the latest murder: a pretty, sixteen-year-old blonde girl had been killed in Leeds, triggering a global surge of interest in the case.

9

JAYNE

The Bay City Rollers' popularity was on the wane by summer 1977, but sixteen-year-old Jayne Michelle MacDonald was still a fan and proud to have seen them live. Posters of the 'teen tartan sensations' adorned her bedroom walls and she bought their new releases religiously.

Born on 16 August 1960, Jayne was the daughter of British Rail worker Wilfred MacDonald and his wife Irene Sutcliffe, married since September 1959. It was the second marriage for them both; Irene's first produced two daughters, Carole and Janet, while Jayne was the eldest of Irene's three children with Wilf. Debra was a year younger than Jayne and Ian was born three months after Carole's marriage in September 1964, when Jayne was a bridesmaid. Two years later, Carole and her husband Victor settled in South Africa, while Janet remained living with her mother, stepfather and siblings.

The MacDonalds lived at 77 Scott Hall Avenue, six doors down from the McCanns. Jayne had regularly babysat for Wilma's children and helped out in the canteen of the Prince Philip Community Centre where they attended nursery. Most residents of the Scott Hall estate were familiar with her striking appearance and ready smile. 'She was so happy, always laughing and very happy-go-lucky,' Irene MacDonald said of her daughter. 'She just loved life. She went out every night either dancing or roller skating. Jayne was very bonny and had a very trim figure for her age, she drew boys.'[1] There had been one 'serious' relationship in Jayne's short life, which she ended after deciding she was too young to get involved.

Since leaving Allerton High School, Jayne had a full-time job as a sales assistant in the shoe department of Grandways supermarket on Roundhay Road. One woman recalls how local girls regarded Jayne with awe: 'She were right distinctive, Jayne. She had right long hair and she had the two blonde streaks which were in fashion at the time.'[2] Jayne's sister Debra smiles at this: 'That was her natural hair – it wasn't dyed, though lots of girls had it like that later. The whole front section of Jayne's hair was white blonde and the rest was darker. She was just beginning to realize how great it looked.'[3]

Debra remembers her early adolescence as extremely happy: 'My mum and dad were amazing parents, they gave us lots of love and they were very clever people too. If their circumstances had been different, they could both have done a great deal with their lives. Not that they didn't – but in a more career-orientated way.'[4]

Debra recalls Scott Hall as 'a good place to grow up. There was a proper sense of community that extended across to Chapeltown. Scott Hall was really an extension of Chapeltown. Outsiders think of the race riots from that period, but most of the residents got on really well. The big West Indian carnival had just got going too, and we absolutely loved that. Everyone, from all the streets and whatever their background, joined in. It was fantastic. There were some great parties. I loved living there.'[5]

Debra remembers Jayne as 'a really lovely big sister. She could be very stubborn – *so* stubborn – and she and Janet used to be horrible to each other sometimes, but only in that sisterly way. She really enjoyed getting me all dressed up and trying out new looks. I didn't mind, I thought it was fantastic. We socialized together too and had arranged to go out together that night, her last night. But she blew us out to go to her first works do. Everyone from Grandways was meeting in town and she didn't want to miss that.'[6]

Young, carefree and newly independent, Jayne listened to music in her bedroom as she decided what to wear on the evening of Saturday 25 June 1977. She settled on a blue-and-white halter-neck top, gingham skirt in the same colours, dark-brown tights and a pair of clog-fronted sandals. She added a grey gabardine jacket, then reached for her handbag. It contained a letter for Carole in Johannesburg that she had forgotten to post.

Jayne's mother worked until late, but her father was settled in his chair, watching television. His breath sounded ragged; a legacy of the chronic bronchitis that had put him on sick leave for five months. Jayne stooped to kiss his forehead. 'She was almost bursting with optimism and the sheer joy of life,' Wilf MacDonald recalled. 'She was so sweet and so clean as she bent down to kiss me goodbye. She was untouched and perfect, just like a flower.'[7] Then she was gone. He heard the latch on the garden gate snap and settled down deeper into his chair.

Hours later, he awoke in the same position, certain he had heard Jayne come in and that she had kissed him goodnight before going upstairs. Irene returned around midnight and together they locked up, thinking all four children were in their rooms.

When Jayne left, it was a beautiful summer's evening – warm and still, with a slight haze. Kids were everywhere: boys playing football or riding Chopper bikes; girls sitting on doorsteps poring over Farrah Fawcett's beauty secrets in *Jackie* magazine. Jayne called on neighbours Jack and Pat Bransberg as usual to let them know her plans for the night. Jack and Wilf had worked together at Leeds railway station; he and Pat were unofficial uncle and aunt to the MacDonald children and teased Jayne about spending all her wages on clothes. If she was going to stay at a girlfriend's she would ring them later, and they would let her parents know, since the MacDonalds didn't own a telephone. That night, Jayne told them she was meeting a friend at the Astoria on Roundhay Road first and promised to ring if she was going to be late home.

Instead of going to the Astoria as planned, Jayne met her new colleagues from Grandways at the Hofbrauhaus, a 'bierkeller' on the top floor of the Merrion Centre in town. She was underage but had no difficulty getting in and sat with her workmates at a long wooden table. The Bavarian band – a group of local lads in lederhosen and Tyrolean hats, singing 'oompapa' songs with exaggerated German accents – whipped up the already boisterous crowd.

Jayne stayed on soft drinks all night, flirting with Mark Jones, a good-looking lad of eighteen in a dark velvet jacket and flares. He recalled: 'We danced at the Hofbrauhaus. About 10.30 p.m. we walked into the city centre with a number of friends.'[8] Jayne wanted chips, so the two of them headed for a kiosk on Briggate and sat eating on a bench outside C&A. Jayne realized she had missed the last bus home; Mark lived on nearby Rigton Approach and said his sister would give Jayne a lift home 'but she didn't seem bothered either way'.[9] They set off towards York Road, but as they came in sight of his home, Mark realized his sister's car wasn't there. He offered to accompany Jayne as far as the hospital. They ended up in the garden of St James's nurses' home, kissing on the grass, and made arrangements to meet again before going their separate ways. 'I told her which way she could get home,' Mark remembered, 'and the last time I saw her was by the main gates of St James's.'[10]

It was 1 a.m. when Jayne started walking down Beckett Street towards the Dock Green pub. Two AA men spotted her at a taxi kiosk near the junction there. When her call for a cab went unanswered, she carried on walking.

Another witness placed Jayne in Bayswater Mount at 1.40 a.m., after which she emerged onto Roundhay Road. Her usual route home took her past the Gaiety, where Emily had spent time on her last night alive, and down Cowper Street, where

Irene Richardson had lived. A left turn took her into Reginald Street, where the street lights had been extinguished over two hours earlier, and Jayne walked on, into the darkness.

Church bells pealed across the city the following morning. It was another sunny day, and as Chapeltown stirred, three children rushed from their homes to Reginald Park, a large adventure playground between the tall Edwardian houses of Reginald Terrace and the rear gardens and sheds of Reginald Street. One of the children, a five-year-old boy, picked his way across the grass to explore the uneven ground near the high fencing on the right. Graffiti had been daubed in white paint across the timber slats: 'Jackie', 'Claude' and 'Gaz'. Along the foot of the fencing was an unfinished line: 'Bay City Roll—'.

Later that day, with some assistance, the boy made a statement: 'I saw a body on the ground, so I told the others. There was a brown bag about four strides away and I did not touch her. I told a man in Reginald Street about the lady. I told him the lady was dead. We went up to the shop and told a man there what we had seen.'[11]

Among the first on the scene were West Yorkshire's Assistant Chief Constable George Oldfield and Detective Superintendent Dick Holland. Detective Chief Superintendent James Hobson arrived in the expectation of leading another murder inquiry, but Oldfield took command, drafting in his own team. The three men made their way to the cordoned-off area with forensic scientists and pathologist Professor David Gee.

A trail of blood and scuffed debris ran from the sandy soil at the edge of Reginald Street to the park entrance. Beside the path, next to a bloodstained piece of paper, was Jayne's imitation-leather handbag. The men approached the fence, pausing at a spot out of sight of the street and filled with rubbish: empty bottles of pop, plastic trays, a length of half-rolled carpet and an old mattress.

Jayne lay face down, six feet from a derelict building, head resting on her left hand, right arm and legs extended, feet crossed. One of her sandals stood nearby. There was a hole in the left heel of her tights and the gingham skirt had been pushed up to her thighs. Her jacket was raised to shoulder height, exposing her lower back. Blood had dried in her hair, on her left hand and clothing, and had trickled down her upper body.

Gee examined Jayne's clothing. Her blue underskirt had been disturbed but her tights and pants were in place. Under her jacket, the blue-and-white top was dirty and had been bunched up, revealing a deep stab wound to her upper back. She wore no bra because of the halter-neck top.

When Gee gently turned her over, they all blanched slightly: below the rumpled fabric, embedded in a gaping wound between her chest and stomach was a broken bottle neck, its screw top still attached. There was also a second large stab mark, and several cuts and scratches. Below her body were two large pools of blood: one where the bottle had penetrated, the other near her head.

Officers searching Jayne's handbag found her address. Two constables were sent to break the news to her family, who were now aware that she hadn't arrived home. Wilf had noticed Jayne's empty bed when he took her a cup of tea; Irene had gone out for a Sunday paper. He assumed that Jayne was staying with a friend, but was exasperated that she hadn't let the Bransbergs know and was already running through what he would say to her when a knock came at the door.

'Are you the father of Jayne MacDonald?' asked one of the uniformed officers.

'Yes,' Wilf nodded, automatically adding, 'and I'll kill her when she comes home because she didn't phone last night.'[12]

The two officers exchanged a fleeting look.

Irene was chatting to a friend who lived a few doors down when the neighbour's son burst in: 'Uncle Wilf's crying! There's some big men – they could be policemen – and he's crying.' Afterwards, Irene reflected, 'I knew it could only be connected with Jayne.'[13]

On the sun-drenched playing field where Wilma McCann had been murdered, Jayne's twelve-year-old brother Ian was playing football. He turned his head as one of his mates raced across the park, shouting, 'Mackie, it's your lass ...'

The two police officers escorted Wilf to the formal identification of Jayne's body in the mortuary. 'It was her hair I can't get out of my mind,' he said afterwards. 'It had looked so blonde and soft a few hours before and now it was hard and caked with blood ... I just collapsed, there and then.'[14] Returning Wilf home, the officers called his doctor, who described the bereaved father's mental state as 'very bad. I have had to give him a sedative injection this morning because he has been in a state of complete collapse. This has been added to because of the fact that he had to go down and identify his daughter and see the terrible injuries she had suffered.'[15]

During the post-mortem, Professor Gee discovered three crescent-shaped lacerations to Jayne's scalp and depressed fractures to her skull. Slivers of bone had pierced her brain, while her heart, lungs and kidneys had been damaged by repeated stabbing. A long weapon with a thin blade had been thrust twenty times or more into the front and back wounds, considerably enlarging the front wound.

Afterwards, Gee outlined the sequence of events leading to Jayne's death: she had been hit from behind near the entrance to the playground and fallen unconscious immediately, dropping her handbag. The killer struck her again before cupping his hands under her armpits. He dragged her down the slope to the fence, unaware that a broken bottle had pierced her body. He stabbed her repeatedly on both sides of her body, then wiped his blade on her back, leaving long smears on her skin.

The telex message issued by Millgarth Police Station to all West Yorkshire forces informed them that Jayne had been 'subjected to violent blows about the head with a blunt instrument ... It would appear that the person responsible may also be responsible for the deaths of Wilma McCann at Leeds on the 29th/30th October 1975, Emily Jackson, Irene Richardson [and] Patricia Atkinson. Details of the injuries to the deceased Jayne Michelle MacDonald and the possible links with the deaths of McCann, Jackson, Richardson and Atkinson should not be disclosed to the press.' There was one final detail: 'There is no evidence that Jayne Michelle MacDonald was an active prostitute.'

Within hours, the *Yorkshire Post* were reporting Jayne's death under the headline, 'Ripper Riddle in Murder of Jayne, 16: Disco Girl Battered in City's Red-Light District' and informing readers that she 'could have been the fourth victim of a Jack the Ripper type killer in the "red light" district of Leeds'.[16] Assistant Chief Constable George Oldfield was quoted: 'There is a possibility that Jayne was killed by the same man we believe was responsible for the three other murders in the Chapeltown area. Until it is proved otherwise, these thoughts will be uppermost in our minds.'[17]

Oldfield appealed for 'the youth seen with the dead girl at the Hofbrauhaus' to make himself known.[18] Mark Jones contacted the police and was swiftly eliminated from the inquiry. Oldfield believed that approximately two hundred people had been out that night along Jayne's route home. Around fifty people were thought to have been in and around Reginald Street, while forty people had attended a West Indian club before leaving for a party in the adjacent street, Sholebroke Avenue, and the Chapeltown Community Centre in Reginald Terrace had hosted a darts match. But no one had anything useful to impart.

Two days after Jayne's murder, Oldfield announced potential links between her death and the previous killings. The *Yorkshire Post* speculated on the killer's motives, asking,

'Victims of a Burning Hatred?' and positing: 'The major difference between Jayne, who only left school at Easter, and the previous victims was that the others were known prostitutes operating in the Chapeltown area.'[19]

A similar sentiment regarding the differentiation of the victims had been expressed in the wake of Emily's murder, when one newspaper report on the city's 'Murder Mile' noted that it was not merely 'frightened prostitutes' avoiding certain streets but 'respectable women' too.[20] George Oldfield used the same adjective in describing Jayne: 'A respectable young working girl ... it seems quite likely that she was a chance victim of her assailant.'[21] Family friend Jack Bransberg pointedly informed reporters that Jayne was 'a sensible girl who knew right from wrong. She was not at all like some of the other girls who have been killed.'[22]

The national press picked up the story on 27 June. 'A Jack the Ripper killer with a hatred of prostitutes may have struck for the fifth time in twenty months – but killed by mistake,' declared the *Daily Express*.

> Police, who have launched a massive murder hunt, think that this time the killer picked his victim, pretty sixteen-year old Jayne MacDonald, at random ... Fair-haired Jayne, who was a shop assistant, was found battered to death at an adventure playground in a crumbling Leeds suburb which is the haunt of prostitutes ... Three prostitutes were battered, stabbed and mutilated within a three-mile radius of Leeds city centre. Another killing of a prostitute, ten miles away in Bradford, is also included in the 'Jack the Ripper' file, which police are studying.[23]

The *Yorkshire Post* reported the following day that police believed the killer was 'from West Yorkshire, certainly with good knowledge of Leeds and Bradford, and has possibly developed a psychological hang up about prostitutes, either at the hands of one or because his mother was one ... All the girls were "good time girls" except Jayne MacDonald, who could have been attacked by mistake.'[24]

Oldfield confirmed that his team were looking for 'a psychopathic killer who had a pathological hatred of women he believes are prostitutes ... We now have a clear picture in our minds of the type of man we are looking for.'[25]

The *Yorkshire Evening Post* carried a blazing editorial on their front page, titled 'An Open Message to the Ripper':

You have killed five times now.

In less than two years you have butchered five women in Leeds and Bradford.

Your motive, it's believed, is a dreadful hatred for prostitutes – a hate that drives you to slash and bludgeon your victims.

But, inevitably, that twisted passion went horribly wrong on Sunday night [sic – it was actually Saturday night/Sunday morning]. An innocent sixteen-year-old lass, a happy, respectable working-class girl from a decent Leeds family, crossed your path.

How did you feel yesterday when you learned that your bloodstained crusade had gone so horribly wrong? That your vengeful knife had found so innocent a target?

Sick in mind though you undoubtedly are, there must have been some remorse as you rid yourself of Jayne's bloodstains.

Is it not time for you to seek help, to call a halt to your slaughter, before another Jayne falls to your knife? ... If there are to be no more Jayne MacDonalds on your growing list of victims, now is the time to end your vengeance and seek help for yourself ...[26]

The language was inflammatory, expressing repugnance at the killer's 'dreadful hatred' for sex workers, yet suggesting a pious element to his compulsion, hence the 'passion' and 'crusade'. Nor was it the murder and mutilation of women per se that revealed him as 'sick in mind' but specifically the killing of 'innocent' victims from 'decent' families. National newspapers were in agreement, both then and latterly, with *The Times* ruminating on the hampering of police efforts to catch the killer, due to public 'apathy over the killing of prostitutes. Even the horrifying death in 1977 of Jayne MacDonald, an entirely respectable young shop assistant, scarcely improved the situation.'[27] Jayne's death *was* horrifying, but no more or less so than those of all the victims. Yet the *Sunday Mirror* stated unequivocally: 'There wasn't much sympathy for dead prostitutes. It is a high-risk business for girls whose hearts are as cold as their hands.'[28]

Feminist magazine *Spare Rib* was one of the few dissenting media voices, declaring deep disgust at those newspapers who saw fit to divide the victims and survivors: 'The "fallen" – prostitutes, even "fun-loving" housewives or students – are asking for it, deserve death, being out late on their own. The "pure" are granted respectability and concern, and we're told it's more worrying such a woman is killed.'[29] Public expressions of sympathy rang hollow with comments such as 'even prostitutes don't deserve to die like this'.[30] A spokeswoman for Leeds Rape Crisis Centre displayed greater insight into the killer than any detective when she described it as nonsense to think the Ripper had killed 'by mistake' because 'when you hate women as much as he must, any woman will do. Prostitutes are simply more vulnerable targets.'[31]

Victims' relatives were angry and resentful at the idea of their murdered loved ones being categorized into those fully deserving of sympathy and those less so. Emily Jackson's son Neil demanded after Jayne's death: 'What did it mean, an "innocent victim" this time? Was Mum a guilty victim then?'[32] Wilma McCann's son Richard grew up feeling painfully inadequate because of it: 'I felt like I was damaged goods. And I wasn't stupid. I knew the way these women were being portrayed as if they weren't good people and that did nothing for my self-esteem.'[33] He recalls one instance at the home of a friend, when the victims' faces flashed up on the television news, causing his friend's mother to make a spitting noise and sneer, 'They deserve everything they get.'[34]

One of the most vocal opponents to this prejudice was Jayne MacDonald's mother Irene, who asserted:

> I feel that if they had all been Sunday School teachers, the public would have come forward with clues and the man would have been found by now. But it is a sad fact that people just don't want to become involved with what happens in a red-light district. Men are ashamed of admitting they were anywhere near it. But many of them must be fathers too with daughters just like Jayne. I beg them to examine their consciences and ask how they would feel if it happened to their own daughter or wife. How can they be so selfish as to stay silent and turn the other way? The same applies to the killer's own family. He must have a mother – and maybe a wife and child as well. One of them must have a suspicion – if only a faint one.[35]

Jayne's sister Debra recalls: 'I do remember Mum and Dad feeling really angry about that – the division of the victims into good women and bad. It was terrible, and none of us saw it that way. The worst thing afterwards was the press. They were just never away from the house, following us to school – there was no let up. You'd be coming downstairs in the morning and the letterbox would fly up and a reporter would call, "Could we just have a word ...?" It was awful.'[36]

In an interview given a few days after her daughter's murder, Irene felt compelled to state that Jayne

> would never have accepted a lift in a car. She once got into a car she thought was a taxi, although it had no sign on.

The driver took her down the wrong roads and she asked what was wrong. He said he had lost the way and she would have to direct him to her home. She told me afterwards that she was never so relieved to get home. All the family have been frightened of this killer ever since Wilma McCann was murdered … Jayne was always careful about walking home on her own. She may have just decided to take a risk on Saturday night. She always told me not to worry and that she would always make sure there was someone with her if she had to walk home in the dark.[37]

Irene addressed her daughter's killer directly: 'How much longer can you go on? It is for your own good as well as everyone else's to step forward. Will you do it?'[38]

Jayne's eldest sister, Carole Skorpen, flew from South Africa to be with her family:

I got a message by telephone from a neighbour in Leeds to say that Jayne had been killed. I was shocked. I left Johannesburg at 6 p.m. South African time on Monday evening and arrived 'home' at midday on Tuesday. When I got to Heathrow Airport I just burst into tears. I had no English money and had to tell a porter what had happened. He was very kind and helped me. I've hardly eaten since I heard the news and was taking tranquillizers before I set off. Jayne used to write to me quite regularly. I understand she had a letter in her handbag, ready to post to me, when she was murdered. She was saving up to go on a holiday in Spain and I was encouraging her to come out and see us in South Africa and see a bit of the world before settling down.[39]

At Grandways supermarket, Jayne's colleagues had been stunned when manager Charles Wickert broke the news of her murder in a special meeting. He recalled feeling 'absolutely sickened' by her death, and that one girl who had been especially close to Jayne broke down completely and had to be sent home.[40] The relatives of other victims experienced fresh anguish in the wake of Jayne's murder. Wilma's mother, Betty Newlands, was distraught: 'I can't get it out of my mind and with each new murder the whole past history is raked up again. Often, I have Wilma's face looking at me from the TV screen.'[41] When his sister Sonia told him that Jayne used to babysit them at Scott Hall Avenue, Richard was frightened, wondering if the man had been stalking them ever since: 'I was convinced that the killer was watching the house from across the field and that he would come back and kill me.'[42]

Those who had survived attempts on their own lives viewed Jayne's murder as a reminder of what might have happened to them, and that the man responsible was still at large. Tracy Browne had been two years younger than Jayne at the time of her own attack; the news shattered the fragile shell of Tracy's determination to live without fear. She recalls: 'I was petrified, actually. I remember going to bed at night – I had to have the landing light on, had to have my bedroom light on, had to have my curtains open, breaking out in hot and cold sweats, and that took about six months to a full year to actually recover from that.'[43]

The public response to Oldfield's appeal for information was greater than it had been before, but fell short of his expectations. He urged people to be more proactive, warning: 'This killer will strike again and the public hold the key to the success or failure of the police inquiry. The public have the power to decide what sort of society they want. If they want murder and violence they will keep quiet. If they want a law-abiding society in which their womenfolk can move freely without fear of attack from the likes of the individual we are hunting, then they must give us their help.'[44]

The public were equally disappointed in the police failure to apprehend the killer. Pat Bransberg set up a campaign for the return of the death penalty, exhorting her neighbours to sign the petition. 'We're going to go round every house in Leeds if necessary,' she insisted. 'This kid never did anyone any harm in her life and when they catch her killer he won't get what he deserves.'[45]

A new lead emerged on 30 June, when a resident of Reginald Terrace informed detectives that she had heard 'a disturbance' in the playground on the night of Jayne's death. Oldfield recounted her evidence for the benefit of reporters: 'At 2 a.m. on Sunday she heard the sounds of banging and scuffling coming from the direction of the playground, and the voice of a man with a Scottish accent, mouthing obscenities. This would have been about the time that Jayne would have been in that area and about the time she met her death. We want to talk to this man as soon as possible.'[46] But no one came forward.

Detectives also questioned Chapeltown sex workers about their clients and set up static observations on vehicles passing through the district at night, noting registration numbers. Several initiatives aimed at improving relations between police and sex workers were implemented, partly to overcome the women's reluctance to speak, but their efforts were hampered by an erratic arrest policy and prison sentences for women convicted of soliciting. A further crackdown on street prostitution in Chapeltown saw more than one hundred and fifty women arrested and sixty-eight formal cautions issued.

Seven hundred homes were visited during house-to-house enquiries and three thousand statements taken. The paperwork generated by Jayne's murder was added to the files of the previous four, creating a major incident room on the top floor of Millgarth Police Station. In the meantime, any man brought into custody for a violent act was automatically questioned about his whereabouts on the night of Jayne's death. Roadblocks were put in place at the junction of Harehills Road and Beckett Street to question drivers familiar with the area. At the inquest into Jayne's murder, Professor David Gee stated that her death had been caused by 'shock and multiple injuries' that included a fractured skull, 'bruising and lacerations to the brain' and 'multiple stab wounds to her trunk'.[47] Proceedings were adjourned until 21 December 1977.

On 2 July, Oldfield announced that he had re-opened the file into the attack on Anna Rogulskyj, which bore 'certain similarities' to Jayne's murder. He told reporters that Anna 'liked the good life', an unmistakable euphemism for promiscuity. The *Yorkshire Evening Post* reiterated: 'Police believe the man who murdered the respectable Jayne and the four "good-time" girls is a psychopath with a pathological hatred for women he believes to be prostitutes.'[48] The resulting press and rumours locally left Anna appalled and increasingly reclusive.

Speculation mounted that a 'stockily-built, ginger-haired man with a deformed or scarred hand', who drove a Land Rover might be the killer, with two witnesses placing him in Manningham in March 1975 and Chapeltown in January 1976.[49] Another witness had seen a different man talking to Jayne shortly before her death, but efforts to trace him were unsuccessful. A Leeds taxi driver already under suspicion was questioned at length but there was nothing to tie him to the murder. The police reconstruction of Jayne's last walk proved equally fruitless. A freephone service was established in the incident room, but there was a certain amount of hostility between Chapeltown residents and the police, with local press fuelling the tension with critical articles that observed: 'As the all-too familiar battalion of uniformed and plain clothes policemen descended on the decaying district, a woman in a crowd of onlookers voiced the thoughts of the community, "Chapeltown is getting worse every day. When will it stop?"'[50]

The MacDonalds had applied for a new council house, finding it unbearable to remain in their home after Jayne's murder. They were offered a property in nearby Scott Hall Road; it was the shortest of transitions in terms of actual distance, but Irene felt it had helped them all: 'I couldn't even stand to pass Jayne's bedroom door at the other house. Little things bring back memories: seeing Jayne's Bay City Rollers gear when we were moving house; listening to the song "Raindrops Keep Falling", the tune played by one of Jayne's wind-up dolls; and hearing her favourite tune "The Flasher" on a neighbour's radio.' Irene acknowledged that she and Wilf were over-protective with their children in the wake of Jayne's death, and especially with fifteen-year-old Debra: 'We like her to stay in the area where we can see her all the time. We don't let her go out at night – and she should be beginning to enjoy life at her age. We make life hell for her, but there is always the feeling that whoever is responsible for what happened to Jayne lives locally. Going to the shops is a trial. People stop me and ask how I feel. I know they mean well but it brings it all back. They say they understand how we feel. But no one can know unless it has happened to them.'[51]

The MacDonalds had to wait six months to bury their daughter. On 20 December 1977, the funeral cortege made its way through a thick mist from Scott Hall Road to Harehills Cemetery. Jayne's twelve-year-old brother Ian was the only family member not present; his parents felt it would have been too much for him. Jayne's father created a headstone for her grave, carving a cross from the ladder of the bunk bed she had slept in as a child. It bore the inscription: 'R.I.P. Jayne Michelle MacDonald. Born 16.8.60. Died 26.6.77.'

10

MAUREEN

'A woman of loose morals' was how West Yorkshire Police ignominiously described Maureen Long in the wake of her attack, citing the fact that she was cohabiting with a man since separating from her husband and often enjoyed nights out alone.

Born Maureen Waterhouse in 1934, at the age of twenty she married Ronald Long. Maureen was small, slim and dark-haired. Quietly spoken but sociable, full of banter and warmth, Maureen began suffering from anxiety after the birth of her third child in 1966. She and her husband separated while Jacqueline was very young; elder daughter Denise had left school and son Ronald was in his mid-teens. A police report later stated that Maureen 'still held a good measure of affection' for her husband and the two would often socialize together.[1]

In 1974, Maureen met fifty-year-old Ken Smith at the Mecca Locarno Ballroom on Manningham Lane. Her two eldest children were already living independently when she and Jacqueline moved in with Ken at his neat terraced house on Donald Street in Farsley, a commuter 'village' in the borough of Pudsey, six miles west of Leeds and four miles east of Maureen's native Bradford. Farsley was home to several pubs, but Maureen loved to dance and was a regular at the Mecca where she and Ken had begun their relationship. Opened in September 1961, the Mecca was a mainstay of Bradford nightlife, with thousands of tiny bulbs set into the ceiling to resemble a starlit sky, a revolving stage and air-conditioned dancefloor.

Saturday 9 July 1977 was a sun-drenched day that drifted into a warm evening. Maureen changed into a long black dress, adding a pale-green crimplene jacket borrowed from Denise, and smart black stilettoes. She gave her naturally thick, wavy hair a quick spritz of hairspray before going downstairs to Ken and ten-year-old Jacqueline. Ken was accustomed to Maureen visiting the Mecca to meet up with friends, and knew that she would either stay with Denise, or with her ex-husband in Laisterdyke. 'I used to go with her,' Ken recalled later, 'but it has become too expensive.'[2] Kissing her partner and daughter goodnight, Maureen slipped her handbag over her shoulder and left shortly after 7 p.m.

In Bradford, she met up with her ex-husband Ronnie for a few drinks in a pub. At closing time, she left for the Mecca and he headed home to Birkshall Lane, expecting Maureen to turn up in the early hours.

The Mecca was heaving that night; a sea of tight denim and maxi dresses. While the 'filth and the fury' of the Sex Pistols played out in the press, dancefloor fillers at the club were strictly disco: Boney M, Hot Chocolate and Abba. '[Maureen] liked a drink to give her confidence,' Ken said afterwards, 'but she could drink a lot and I do not think she would have been drunk. But she has been taking some pills from the doctor for her nerves.'[3]

Maureen's recollection of events as the evening drew to a close were disjointed as a result of the attack. She remembered visiting the cloakroom around 2 a.m., then heading outside to find a taxi for the journey to Ronnie's home, but nothing after that. A hotdog salesman on the forecourt outside the Mecca saw her walking towards the city centre, but there were no further sightings of her until the following morning.

❖

Maureen came within yards of safety that night. Between Birkshall Lane where her ex-husband lived and nearby Mount Street was a sprawling patch of wasteland where horses from the adjoining gypsy camp wandered. Within an hour of leaving the club, Maureen's life began to ebb away on the uneven, rubbish-strewn ground. 'I remember trying to pick myself up,' she recalled. 'I kept falling and then I wondered what was wrong with me, and I kept falling back and, as I were trying to pull myself up, falling back again. Then I was screaming and I heard this dog barking ...'[4]

Scarcely a hundred yards away across Bowling Back Lane, security guard Frank Whitaker's Alsatian had heard a disturbance. Whitaker got up from his seat in the Tanks & Drums Factory and walked down to the unlit road to investigate. A car engine started up somewhere in the darkness; suddenly the vehicle appeared, racing up from the Mount Street incline with no lights. At the road end, the driver switched the headlamps onto full beam, then sped away. Whitaker heard nothing else, but noted that the time was 3.27 a.m. and the car had been white with a dark roof, possibly a Ford Cortina Mark II.

Hypothermia had begun to take hold of Maureen's body by dawn, causing her to shiver uncontrollably. Two women in the gypsy camp heard her moans and went in search of the sound. Neither woman could believe their eyes when they found her: blood poured from Maureen's savagely beaten skull and stab wounds in her chest, stomach and back. Her girdle, pants and tights were around her knees and her bra had been pulled down to her waist, exposing a long, vertical slash wound on her abdomen. She had been dragged fifteen yards or more from the cobbled street, resulting in innumerable grazes. An ambulance arrived soon after the women raised the alarm, swiftly followed by a mob of police cars.

As Maureen was driven to hospital, detectives Oldfield, Domaille and Holland made their way to the site of the attack. Bowling Back Lane was a long road dominated by warehouses, works units and empty ground; at one end was a Sikh temple, while the Farmyard pub with its bright yellow entrance door stood closer to the crime scene. When the detectives had finished their inspection of the area, forensic experts began searching for evidence. It emerged that Maureen's left shoe was missing, together with her large brown imitation-leather handbag.

At Bradford Royal Infirmary, Professor Gee examined Maureen's injuries in detail, observed by Oldfield and Holland. Her head had been partially shaven for surgery, revealing deep lacerations and a large, depressed fracture to her skull. One of the five stab wounds to her body had perforated her abdomen and liver, and she had three fractured ribs. While a police surgeon took intimate swabs, Gee remarked to his colleagues that Maureen was lucky to be alive, given the severity of her injuries. Oldfield spoke to her briefly in an attempt to learn more about her attacker, but she could only provide the most cursory information before being transferred to Leeds General Infirmary for specialist neurosurgery.

Oldfield told a press conference on 11 July 1977 that 'it is quite apparent now that we have a desperate and dangerous individual at large in this area. A person who is going to continue to strike until he is caught. I feel now that with the publicity which these cases have had, somebody somewhere must know who we are looking for. We need all the help we can get from the public and I would like them to bear in mind that the next victim could be a wife, sister, daughter or niece.'[5] He added that Maureen was 'fortunate to be alive' and there were detectives waiting at her bedside to learn more about her movements that night. He concluded: 'She is a woman who liked the good life.'[6]

The euphemism was immediately picked up by the *Yorkshire Post*, who built it into their front page lead story: 'Ripper Police at Woman's Bedside: "Good Life" Mother Battered and Left for Dead on Waste Ground After Night Out'.[7] The *Yorkshire Evening Post* was more restrained: 'A woman who cheated death may provide West Yorkshire detectives with a vital clue to the identity of a Jack the Ripper style killer. She is forty-two-year-old Mrs Maureen Long. But detectives at her hospital bedside may have to wait several days before they can interview her fully … Mrs Long survived a ferocious attack.'[8] However, the *Daily Mirror* highlighted Oldfield's phrase in their 'New Ripper Victim' article, stating: 'Mrs Long, who is separated from her husband, was said by police to "like the good life".'[9] The report was the first to use the killer's eventual moniker, announcing that Maureen 'believed to be the latest victim of the Yorkshire Ripper was lying gravely injured in hospital last night …'

Oldfield had taken charge of the investigation, setting up an incident room in Bradford and drafting in three hundred officers. Maureen's attack was linked to the murders of Wilma, Emily, Irene, Patricia and Jayne in a circular sent out to all regional forces. Oldfield set out to interview her after being informed that a second operation had gone well and that Maureen was prepared to speak to him after being returned to the neurosurgical unit at Leeds General Infirmary. He told reporters: 'I live in hope that she will be able to give us a lot more help – but what she has been able to tell us so far is very helpful.'[10]

Oldfield was less optimistic after their meeting, privately convinced that no one who had endured such trauma would be able to retain a reliable memory of events. Maureen's initial recall differed from accounts of the assailant given by other survivors; the description issued by the police after Oldfield had spoken to her outlined the attacker as being a white male, aged thirty-six or thirty-seven, with puffy cheeks, thick eyebrows, collar-length wiry blond hair, large hands and wearing a white shirt but otherwise dark clothing.

Frank Whitaker came forward to help identify the white Cortina Mark II with a black roof which he had seen leaving Mount Street for Bowling Back Lane around 3.15 a.m. on

Sunday 10 July. His testimony brought to an end police attempts to trace the tyre marks found at the scene of Irene Richardson's murder, since they were not a match for the car he recalled. Resources were funnelled instead into a search of all five thousand owners of Mark II Ford Cortinas, three thousand of whom were interviewed without generating further interest.

The continuing covert surveillance of drivers and vehicles in the Chapeltown area was extended to Manningham after the attempt on Maureen's life. Other lines of enquiry were also pursued: a search of the crime scene had unearthed an unidentified fingerprint on a small piece of china broken from a sink, while police officers arrived at the Mecca Ballroom one week after the attack, interviewing more than a thousand people in rooms set aside by the management for the purpose. Taxi drivers and their customers in Manningham were questioned, as were Maureen's neighbours in Donald Street and those of her ex-husband in Birkshall Lane. Police whittled down their suspects to a list of fifteen men, which included taxi driver Terry Hawkshaw, who bore a resemblance to Maureen's description of her attacker. Hawkshaw lived with his elderly mother at the centre of what the media called the 'Ripper Triangle' and was placed under surveillance for twenty-four hours. His home and car were exhaustively searched, and Oldfield subjected him to a rigorous interview, but nothing emerged with which they could hold him.

On 23 July, Home Secretary Merlyn Rees travelled to Leeds in order to discuss the case with detectives. Asked about his concern that the killer was still at large despite intense police activity, Rees replied tartly: 'I am no more concerned than the Chief Constable. Often piecing together evidence, considering it and analysing it does take time, unless someone is there with a camera when the murder is committed.'[11]

Maureen remained in hospital for nine weeks, fully conscious but on a ventilating machine to aid her breathing. After being discharged, she spent three weeks in a convalescent home before being deemed physically well enough to return to Ken and Jacqueline in Farsley. The psychological impact was lifelong and only just beginning, leaving Maureen unable to work, subsisting on £13 per week in social security benefits. It took an immense amount of courage for her to agree to assist the police in an undercover operation aimed at catching her attacker, but she did so immediately.

Over a period of three consecutive weekends, Maureen donned a black wig to hide the prominent scars on her skull, and accompanied Detective Sergeant Megan Winterburn around Bradford's many pubs and clubs. Wearing an old Afghan coat and heavy make-up, DS Winterburn essentially trailed Maureen from venue to venue while a male detective kept a discreet eye on them. She found Maureen pleasant and entertaining company, and was touched by how people responded to her with genuine concern and anger towards the man responsible for her injuries.

Although Maureen had described her attacker as fair-haired, during a turn with DS Winterburn on the dancefloor of the Mecca Ballroom, she suddenly stopped and stiffened. When Winterburn asked her to explain, Maureen pointed fearfully to a man with black wavy hair, believing him to be her attacker. 'Obviously, her subconscious had said, "the hair",' Winterburn recalled.[12] The man was questioned and eliminated from their enquiries.

Winterburn noticed that although Maureen 'made no bones about saying she was a Ripper victim and liked to show off her scars', the misconception that she was a sex worker had a profound effect that was in its way as damaging as the attack: 'She was mortified that people were saying she was a prostitute, which wasn't true. You had this very naïve and pleasant lady who was leading a normal life, with an active social life, labelled by the press as a prostitute. To have to explain this to your family, who were still coming to terms with you being attacked, must have been horrendous to her and her family.'[13]

Four years later, the man charged with examining the failures of the police investigation repeated the fallacy, even as he outlined its pernicious effect: 'Long, who admitted that she had acted as a prostitute, received serious injuries to her head from hammer blows and stab wounds to her abdomen and back, but fortunately recovered. Long's ability to describe her attacker was rendered more difficult because she was under the influence of drink at the time of the incident.'[14]

Lawrence Byford's report ended with the observation that although Maureen's attack had been openly linked to previous assaults and murders, hers 'did not excite much public sympathy, however ... probably as a result of the description of Long as a woman of loose morals'.

11

JEAN

In April 1978, investigative current affairs series *World in Action* aired 'There's No Place Like Hulme', revealing that residents of the vast Manchester housing estate were 'thirty times more likely to be mugged or murdered than the national average and three times more likely to show clinical symptoms of stress'.[1] The chairman of Manchester's housing committee admitted the estate was 'an absolute disaster' that 'should never have been built'.[2] A whopping 96.3 per cent of residents were desperate to be re-housed.

Six years earlier, city planners faced with the largest slum clearance project in Europe had sanctioned the construction of four colossal crescents and a series of low-rise 'decks' in which to house thirteen thousand people. The problems that surfaced within months were literally built into the fabric of the place due to urgency and inadequate supervision. Essential components were left out, defective ventilation bred unbridled damp and poor insulation made it easy for vermin to spread. There were few lifts, leaving parents lugging shopping and prams up several flights of stairs, while the high concrete balconies with low ledges were lethal for toddlers: in 1974 a five-year-old child died after falling from one.

Within a couple of years, Hulme had become a dystopian nightmare, isolated by its design and reputation as a drug-riddled playground for criminals; police circled the estate in panda cars but there were no 'bobbies on the beat' inside the complex. 'Hulme is a frightening place at night,' intoned the *World in Action* voiceover, 'and most women told us they never went out alone.'[3]

Among the women living there at the time was twenty-year-old Jean Bernadette Jordan, born on 11 December 1956 at Motherwell Maternity Hospital to unmarried hospital maid Catherine Jordan. Home was on The Neuk, a cul-de-sac of council houses in Wishaw, fourteen miles east of Glasgow, and the centre of Scotland's steel industry; the railway line that ran at the foot of the Jordans' garden rattled night and day with freight trains.

Shortly before her sixteenth birthday, Jean left Scotland without a word to anyone, boarding a train south with no idea where she was heading. Details are vague regarding the circumstances of her arrival in England; the first person she met became her partner, who subsequently gave two very different versions of their initial encounter.

According to Alan Royle's original story – as recounted to police, press and family – he spotted Jean wandering about Manchester's Victoria Station in October 1972. She was thin and pretty with long auburn hair and scarcely any belongings. He offered her a cigarette. Over a pot of tea, Jean told him that she had run away from home to start a new life in the first big city she liked the look of after crossing the border. Alan was twenty-one, a locally born chef with his own flat and invited Jean to stay with him.

Thirty years later, Alan Royle gave another account, more quantifiably true, although why he changed his story is unclear. In the later version, he and Jean met in London while he was working as a chef in a Kensington hotel. One year into their relationship and pregnant, Jean told him that she wasn't a receptionist as he thought, but was in fact a 'call girl', whose clients booked appointments by phone, visiting her at a place on Mayfair's Curzon Street or sent a car to collect her. Alan reflected: 'It didn't matter to me at all. I was hooked and I loved her, but, after she told me, she stopped it there and then, and said she wanted to move in with me. She said the only time she would ever do it again would be if her family was absolutely starving. We bought a flat and I started working for Mecca in the Empire, Leicester Square. Life was good and we were doing fine. We had to move around the country a bit then because of my job.'[4]

Their first child, named Alan after his father, was born in London a year after they met; James followed three years later, when they were living in Buckinghamshire. After Alan was made redundant 'life got very hard'.[5] They settled in Manchester, finding a tiny flat in Wythenshawe's Newall Green, eight miles south of the city centre. 'We were living in a rented place and were not getting on very well,' Alan admitted.[6] He was a fairly heavy drinker who would regularly engage in two- or three-day 'benders' with his old mates. His relationship with Jean became increasingly fraught, and she escaped by hitching a lift to Scotland from the nearby M56. After a couple of days with the relatives who were only too glad to welcome her back, she returned to her children, thinking about making another new life for herself with her sons.

Jean's desperation to start afresh convinced her to return to sex work. In 1976, renewed efforts to enforce the Street Offences Act virtually eradicated visible prostitution from the city centre. Women working in the sex trade headed for Moss Side and Whalley Range or Cheetham Hill, the city's equivalent of Chapeltown, with large houses and terraces converted into flats for poverty-stricken families and ethnic minorities battling unemployment and low wages. By 1977, Manchester's vice squad were frequent visitors.

Jean worked the streets of Moss Side mostly, hating every encounter but unable to find another job. Other women knew her as 'Scotch Jean' or 'Jean Royle', although she and Alan were not married. Sex worker Anna Holt was her closest friend; the two women often worked from another friend's city centre flat. During better weather they took clients to the disused allotments adjoining Southern Cemetery, three miles from the city centre.

In August 1977, Jean and her family left Newall Green for a flat in Lingbeck Crescent, Hulme. 'In an area dominated by ugly, barely habitable concrete council flats, Lingbeck Crescent and its neighbour, Gretney Walk, were the worst of all,' observed one local historian. 'Two blocks of low-rise, deck-access flats off Princess Road, they were infested with mice and rats, their lifts never worked and the dustbins were never emptied. The flats had bubbles of mould on the walls and the warped wood was often soaking.'[7]

The previous tenant of Jean's flat had died in tragic circumstances. Twenty-three-year-old Amina Thorne had turned to prostitution after her husband was sentenced to prison. In June 1977 her body was discovered at a roadside. Police traced her last client, a long-distance lorry driver from Austria; Amina's handbag was discovered in his cab. During a subsequent court case, a jury accepted the man's defence that Amina had died after jumping from the moving vehicle. He was fined £140, less than his week's wage. Amina's family and friends reacted with fury to the outcome, and her husband wept as he attended her funeral under escort.

Three months later, on the unseasonably warm evening of Saturday 1 October, Jean sat talking to Alan in the kitchen of their new home after putting the children to bed. The steady hum of traffic on Princess Road filtered through the open window. As their conversation petered out, she rose to pour a glass of lemonade for Alan, who told her that he was going out with his mates. Jean handed him the glass and went through to the living room. When Alan left, she was watching television, seemingly settled for the night.

Hours later, he returned to silence. The television was off, crackling faintly with static as he passed it, and the two boys were fast asleep. The bedroom he shared with Jean was empty, the blankets undisturbed. He stood for a moment, wondering whether she had gone out for the evening or if she had headed to Scotland again on a whim. He undressed and got into bed, thinking he'd have the answer by morning.

It was nine days before Alan found out what had happened to Jean. Monday 10 October 1977 was another dry, sunny day with a cool breeze across the allotments backing onto Southern Cemetery, the city's vast necropolis. Owned by Manchester Corporation and rented to private individuals, one section of the allotments had been fenced off to rot, the once neat rows of fruit and veg grown thick with weeds.

Twenty-three-year-old dairy worker Bruce Jones shared one of the existing allotments with his friend Jimmy Morrisey. They had spent the summer preparing the patch and were putting up a shed. Jones had found some bricks for a base in the old allotments, and collected them in a wheelbarrow while Jimmy set the bricks in place. On one of his trips that morning, Jones noticed a shape by a wooden shed within twenty feet of the cinder track: 'I saw what at first looked like a tailor's dummy. My initial thought was that I wondered who had thrown it there and why. But as I got closer the stench was awful. I soon realized that it was what remained of a woman.'[8] Certain the corpse hadn't been there the previous day, Jones glanced about fearfully. He spotted a man walking his terrier and shouted to him, then dashed across Princess Road to call the police.

Among the first to arrive was forty-four-year-old Detective Chief Superintendent Jack Ridgway, who took control of the investigation. Also in attendance were Home Office pathologist and lecturer in Forensic Medicine at Manchester University, Dr Reuben Woodcock, and fingerprint expert Detective Chief Inspector Tony Fletcher. None of them had ever encountered a crime scene like it.

Jean's face had been obliterated by eleven hammer blows to her head. She lay naked, head turned left, arms spread wide. A paint flake on her body matched the colour of an interior door leaning against the shed. 'She had been badly mutilated,' Fletcher recalled, 'and there was a coil of intestine wrapped round her waist. It was later established that death had been caused by head injuries consistent with having been struck a number of times with a hammer. An attempt had been made to sever the head, a fact that was never revealed to the press. It was obvious to the experienced eye that the incised wounds on the trunk had been inflicted a considerable time after death.'[9] Initially he thought perhaps someone had violated a recent grave, but Jean's clothing lay scattered in the long grass nearby: underwear, tights, blue polo-neck jumper, brown cotton skirt, blue cardigan, rust-coloured hooded coat and blue knee-length leather boots: 'Most of the top clothing was badly bloodstained and crawling with fully developed maggots. Under the privet hedge which separated the allotment from the pathway was a depression which was absolutely teeming with maggots.'[10]

The three men examined the scene, concluding that the young woman had died several days earlier; the killer had originally concealed his victim in the bloodstained hollow under the hedge, placing the door on top of her body. He had then returned to the scene, removing her clothing in order to inflict eight stab wounds to the chest, stomach and lower regions before attempting to decapitate her. The life cycle of the insects present soon enabled them to estimate a time of death as eight or nine days earlier. The second attack had taken place hours before she was discovered, with nothing nearby to identify her.

Ridgway established an incident room at Longsight Police Station. A swift records search failed to reveal any missing persons resembling the woman on the allotment. 'Who Is She?' asked the *Manchester Evening News* the following day, informing its readers that 'an attractive young woman' had been found 'savagely battered to death on a Manchester Corporation allotment. There was no clue on the naked corpse, which was discovered sprawled like a rag doll alongside a path running through the allotment. The woman, aged fifteen to thirty years old, was lying face down on the grass, shielded by low bushes from cars racing past on busy Princess Road.'[11] A later edition recounted how detectives had 'moved into Manchester's underworld in the hunt for the killer ... Inquiries are being made among prostitutes and the coloured community in Moss Side, in an attempt to identify the dead woman.'[12]

Alan Royle recognized Jean's clothing from the sketches that accompanied the article. He contacted the police, who collected him and the two boys from Hulme. While WPC Denise Cavanagh took the toddlers off in search of chocolate, Alan handed detectives a photograph of Jean taken at Belle Vue that summer. Asked why he had failed to report her disappearance, he replied that she occasionally visited her relatives in Motherwell on a whim. He asked to see Jean's body. Fletcher told him tactfully that it was better to remember her as he had last seen her; they expected to complete the identification process by matching her fingerprints with samples from the flat in Hulme. That proved more difficult than Fletcher had imagined; neither he nor a colleague were able to find Jean's prints at home. Items were packed into tea chests for scrutiny at the office, where they were eventually rewarded with a single fingerprint on the bottle of lemonade she had poured for Alan, who did all the cooking and most of the housework.

Speaking at length to detectives about his life with Jean, Alan recalled that the move to Manchester had put a strain on their relationship: 'She found friends – girlfriends, I thought – and would go out in the evenings with them, leaving me to look after the kids. Sometimes I would go out for a couple of days with the lads and leave her to it ... A week last Friday, on 1 October, I went out for a drink and when I came back she had gone. When she didn't come back on Saturday morning I wasn't too alarmed. I thought she'd taken one of her trips to Scotland again ... It wasn't until I read the paper with the description of the handbag and clothes that I started to worry.'[13] Detectives told him that Jean's handbag had not yet been found.

On 12 October, Ridgway informed the press that the murdered woman had been identified as 'Jean Royle' and 'there is absolutely nothing to suggest that Mrs Royle was a prostitute. It could be that while she was walking, some motorist stopped and offered her a lift and that she expected she might have been able to get a lift up to Scotland. She has hitchhiked on occasions before.'[14] Toxicology results showed a small amount of alcohol in her body, leading officers to make enquiries in the Princess Road and Moss Lane areas, in case she had gone to a pub with a friend before encountering the killer. 'She was not a woman who went out drinking regularly,' Ridgway declared. 'But she did on occasion go out for a drink with her husband or with a friend.'[15] He stressed again that 'there is absolutely no suggestion that this girl is a prostitute. Our information all points to her being a respectable woman.'[16]

Anna Holt contacted the police after reading the newspapers. At Longsight Police Station she nodded when shown a photograph: 'That's Scotch Jean. She's on the game – she worked the same patch as me. Poor Jean was not really cut out for it. She was guilty about her kids. Just recently she told me that she was going to give it all up, pack it all in, settle down to a decent home life again.'[17] She agreed to identify her friend in the mortuary.

Dr Reuben Woodcock carried out the autopsy with Ridgway present. Jean's head injuries varied in severity, with some clustered together and depressed fractures below. The hammer used to inflict them had been wielded with such force that four of Jean's upper teeth had been loosened, leaving fragments in her mouth. The slash wound to her body through which her intestine protruded was seven inches long and reached her backbone. The majority of stab wounds appeared to have been made in a left to right motion. No traces of semen were found in or on her body. Two vivid marks on Jean's neck showed the attempt at decapitation; Ridgway asked the pathologist to omit that detail from his report, hoping to retain it as evidence known only to the killer, making it easier to confirm whether a suspect was the culprit or not.

The head and stomach injuries reminded Woodcock of a recent slide presentation on the Ripper killings given at a conference in Wakefield by George Oldfield. Ridgway asked for the relevant intelligence report, which convinced him that Jean's death was another in the series. He called Oldfield to arrange a meeting, but found him stubbornly resistant to acknowledging Jean's murder as a Ripper killing. However, the *Manchester Evening News* reported:

> Police are keeping an open mind on the possibility that the killing is linked with Yorkshire's 'Jack the Ripper' murders in which a vicious attacker has claimed four lives, four of them vice girls ... Mr Ridgway, CID chief for Manchester central's crime area, was today back from a 90 minute conference with West Yorkshire detectives on the murders. He said, 'The Yorkshire killings involved prostitutes in some cases and ours involved an area where prostitutes are known to take their clients. But although there are many points of similarity between the cases, there are many points of dissimilarity. Neither the officers in West Yorkshire, nor ourselves, are in any way convinced that there is a connection between the two sets of murders.'[18]

As enquiries continued, sex workers who might have known Jean or her clients were promised immunity from prosecution in return for information, and detectives travelled to Motherwell hoping to learn more about Jean from her relatives. Witnesses placed her in Chorlton's Princess Hotel on the night she vanished, in the company of two men, one of whom was called Angus and hailed from Dundee. Both men were traced and eliminated from the inquiry. The last confirmed sighting of Jean was at 9.40 p.m. on 1 October.

On 13 October, the *Manchester Evening News* divulged one of the most chilling aspects of the murder. Under the headline 'Ghoul Stripped Body', the report revealed: 'Detectives hunting the killer of prostitute Jean Royle revealed today that the murderer wanted her body found. Scientific probes have shown that the killer had the fully-clothed body for nine days – then returned to strip it and drag it into the open.'[19] Ridgway was quoted: 'The body could not possibly have lain in that position for more than twenty-four hours. Some time after dark somebody has gone and moved the body.'[20]

Jean's missing handbag was found on Saturday 15 October 1977, after a city-wide poster campaign. One of the Southern Cemetery allotment holders noticed a green, imitation-leather handbag in the long grass under a wire fence that morning. Police officers had conducted a fingertip search of the area, stopping just short of the fence that separated old and new allotments. Ridgway immediately drove out to Southern Cemetery when informed of the discovery. It had been discarded sixty yards from where Jean had lain, with cosmetics, cigarettes and matches inside the main compartment, and a £5 note and £1 note in a small concealed compartment in an external side pocket. 'It appeared that the handbag had been searched,' recalled Fletcher, 'but whoever had done so had missed those two notes.'[21] Ridgway suddenly realized that after killing Jean, her murderer had rummaged through the handbag looking for the fiver he had handed over as a client and when he couldn't find it, he had flung the bag away. Later, it dawned upon him that the note was incriminating, forcing him to return to the allotments to search again. Unsuccessful a second time, he had flown into a rage, hence the frantic strewing of Jean's clothing about the place, and the vicious stab wounds.

Alan was shown the handbag and confirmed that it had belonged to Jean. Eighty Tactical Aid Group officers then scoured the allotments in vain for the murder weapon and any further evidence. Enquiries into the provenance of the £5 note revealed that it had been issued as a part of a batch dispensed in wage packets around the Shipley area shortly before Jean had disappeared. Staff at Shipley's Midland Bank narrowed the search to thirty-four firms which were visited in alphabetical order by detectives, who questioned six thousand people in total, sometimes twice. Ridgway was sure that the killer must have been interviewed and his name already in the system.

Paperwork from Jean's murder in Manchester was added to the burgeoning files at Millgarth Police Station, where Oldfield had decided to extend the covert surveillance of cars in red-light districts. In winter 1977, fourteen observation points were set up in Chapeltown, twelve in Manningham and seven in Huddersfield. Each evening, pairs of officers sat together in a vehicle jotting down registration numbers. It quickly became clear that there were far more men paying for sex than the police had estimated. To speed up the process of recording the number plates, officers were given pocket tape recorders.

On 31 May 1978, the inquest into Jean's death was held, formally acknowledging that she was a victim of the Ripper. Coroner Roderick Davies graphically described her murder as 'a rather revolting case where the killer had, either before or after death, ripped up the belly and pulled out the intestines. We can assume that she was not unconscious and that whoever committed this crime had ripped her up.'[22] Bruce Jones told the inquest about finding Jean's body; he began weeping when shown photographs of the murder scene. Davies read out a statement from Anna Holt in which she mentioned Jean's desire to stop sex work, and neighbour Mrs Patricia MacFarlane described Jean as a pleasant, quiet girl 'definitely not the sort to talk to strangers in the street'.[23] Another neighbour, Mrs Ruby Matthews, told the waiting press that Jean's flat had 'a double death jinx', referring to Amina Thorne's death. This led to dramatic headlines some months later following the death of a third sex worker on the estate when June McDonald, who had also worked the streets, jumped to her death from the tenth floor of Medlock Court, adjoining Lingbeck Crescent.[24]

Jean's funeral was held seven months later, on a rainy day in December 1978. The softly spoken Scottish girl who had longed for a settled life was laid to rest in the Roman Catholic section of Southern Cemetery on what would have been her twenty-first birthday.

12

MARYLYN

The Byford Report of 1981 observed that while Jean Jordan's murder had generated substantial interest, 'the fact that prostitutes continued to be the victims conditioned response from the public, and although five murders and a serious assault were at that time regarded as being within the series, there was no evidence of undue public concern'.

The misapprehension that the Yorkshire Ripper was 'a prostitute killer' resulted in an assumption that women not involved in sex work were safe unless they happened to be passing through an area associated with prostitution. The feminist movement was at its height in Britain during the mid-to-late 1970s; activists were vocal about all aspects of the Ripper investigation but declared war on police recommendations that women should stay indoors after dark to avoid reprising another 'mistake' murder like that of Jayne MacDonald. Arguing that women should not be expected to take responsibility for the Ripper's murderous urges, militant groups also pointed out the impracticality of the advice: many women were at work or college until after dark, especially in the winter months.

One month after Jean's murder, feminist activists organized the first 'Reclaim the Night' demonstrations in eleven British cities. Several hundred women turned out in each location to march, debate and brandish placards displaying their rage. Protestors in Leeds set out from Chapeltown, chosen according to one coordinator 'because it was the very place where a sixteen-year-old girl had been found dead earlier in that year: to make a commemoration for that young girl, to say: we have not forgotten you, and we will try to make a safer space for women, for the future'.[1] Curiously, there was no mention of other women who had been attacked or murdered, and the omission was repeated in Manchester, when Jean's name was glaringly absent from all the rhetoric. Historians suggest that militant feminist groups, along with other sections of the public, became far more incensed by the murders when police action curtailed the attacks on sex workers, making other women more vulnerable, and the lack of solidarity was due to prostitutes being regarded as pandering to men's sexual demands, 'letting the side down in the struggle against male dominance'.[2]

Twenty-five-year-old Marylyn Moore had one conviction for soliciting by 1977. Born in Leeds, she left home at fifteen and married a year later, giving birth to a son and daughter. After her divorce, Marylyn began 'hustling' as she called it, moving between Leeds, Bradford, London and Slough to avoid detection. At only five feet tall, she was petite but voluptuous, with red hair and an animated face. 'I didn't like doing it, but the benefits that you got then wasn't worth bringing your kids up,' Marylyn relates. 'You're always worried that you're going to get attacked or you're going to get mugged, or owt like that with a punter.'[3]

With her six-year-old son and one-year-old daughter temporarily in care, Marylyn had no fixed abode but stayed with a close friend whenever she was in Leeds. Fifty-one-year-old Peter Sucvic lived in 'the Bayswaters', among the tall red-brick, back-to-back terraces in Harehills, a short walk from the Gaiety. Once a thriving industrial district, Harehills had become another deprived community, where low rents attracted impoverished locals and immigrants who began their own businesses, shops and restaurants.

Sucvic later claimed to have had no idea that Marylyn worked as a prostitute; he assumed she was with friends when she went out or stayed away in Bradford, Halifax and further afield. On Wednesday 14 December 1977, Marylyn told Sucvic that her friend Beverley hadn't turned up as promised, so she was calling on her instead and expected to be home around 11 p.m. After visiting Beverley's house on Gathorne Terrace behind the Gaiety, Marylyn made her way to Chapeltown. The area around Spencer Place was, she recalls, 'the biggest "red" area, the hottest place'.[4]

It was a mild evening as she walked along Leopold Street. A man approached her for sex, but something about him made her turn him down. She became aware of a car cruising the area a little after 8 p.m. and retraced her route, heading down Spencer Place to meet it. When the car passed, she walked on to Leopold Street and caught up with the dark-haired, bearded driver, who was standing next to his vehicle and waving at someone. 'As I approached him, he asked me if I was doing business,' Marylyn remembers. 'I said yes. He didn't ask me how much, he said five pounds, so I said OK and I got into the car.'[5]

'Who were you waving at?' Marylyn asked, as the driver turned the car towards Chapeltown Road. He replied that he was visiting his sick girlfriend and knew two prostitutes, Gloria and Hilary. Marylyn asked his name: 'He told me Dave, and I told him to call me Susan. Then he took me to a place I already knew because I've been to that place many times before. He pulled up.'[6]

They had driven half a mile east, crossing Scott Hall Road to head down Buslingthorpe Lane. Derelict warehouses and factories lined the road, which curved to the right beside Brown's, a clothing manufacturer. The car trundled down the unmade track alongside the factory. 'There's a sort of car park there, just grass and mud, and that's where he stopped,' Marylyn recalls. 'I started unbuckling my right shoe, thinking we were going to stay in the front seat, but Dave said he wanted to go in the back of the car. It was a bit unusual, but I didn't mind because he seemed such a nice bloke. So I fastened my shoe and got out.'[7]

Forty-five-year-old Jimmy Pearson, who lived in a caravan in the nearby scrap metal dealer's yard, had noticed the vehicle. 'I was going out with my girlfriend,' he stated afterwards, 'and we both saw a red- or maroon-coloured car drive in. I saw figures which looked as though they were having a cuddle.'[8] Neither he nor his girlfriend paid any further attention.

A short distance away on the wooded slope to the right of Buslingthorpe Lane stood Scott Hall Farm. Above it, on the other side of the trees, were the playing fields where Wilma McCann had been murdered two years before.

Marylyn noticed her client bend to pick something up as he stepped out of the car before walking around the bonnet to stand behind her. 'I'd just got my hand on the handle of the rear door when he hit me,' she remembers. 'I didn't know what was happening. I didn't really feel the blow but I put my hands up over the back of my head for protection and he hit my thumb with the second blow. The third one really hurt and I began to go down. I could hear him screaming at me, "You dirty prostitute!" and the next thing I knew, I was lying on the ground and everything seemed to be a haze.'[9]

Marylyn's screams were heard by the occupant of Scott Hall Farm. With his dogs at his heels, he went out to the front garden, listening for the sound again. It was quiet and the dogs gave no indication that anything untoward was happening. He made a note of the time – 8.45 p.m. – before calling his dogs back into the house.

Marylyn lay bleeding profusely on the ground below the slope, her skull bursting with pain. She heard her attacker's footsteps advance to the driver's side of the car. The door slammed and the engine started up, followed by the back wheels skidding. She drifted into unconsciousness.

Time passed. Marylyn opened her eyes but a red veil obscured her vision as she pushed herself up from the ground.

She staggered towards the road, where a young couple stood chatting. After a moment's shock, they rushed to her aid, propping her between them for the walk to the nearest telephone box on Meanwood Road. Marylyn leaned weakly against a wall while the emergency services were called. Her friend Gloria happened to be passing by; after recovering from the sight of Marylyn covered in blood, she stayed until the ambulance came racing along the road.

At Leeds General Infirmary, Detective Chief Superintendent Hobson spoke to Marylyn before she was wheeled into theatre. He told a press conference the following day that she had been attacked 'in a spot which is a favourite haunt of prostitutes and their clients. I have spoken to the woman briefly in hospital but I am hoping to interview her more fully after she has had an operation. She is suffering from a fractured skull and injuries to her hand, sustained while she fought off her attacker.'[10]

Forensic experts descended on Buslingthorpe Lane to examine the cordoned crime scene. Professor David Gee arrived at the Infirmary, watching the final stages of the operation to save Marylyn's life. He had a quick look at her injuries when she was moved to a recovery ward. There appeared to be eight lacerations, each around two inches long to her head. A depressed fracture behind her left ear had pushed bones into her brain, requiring a further operation that involved elevating her skull bone to relieve the pressure. The lacerations to her head and another on the nape of her neck were oval in shape. There was a four-inch wound on her left thumb and hand, and heavy bruising to her right hand where she had tried to deflect the blows. Gee had no doubt that Marylyn had survived an attack by the Ripper.

Hobson was called to give evidence at Jayne MacDonald's inquest later that day. Her murder had occurred precisely half a mile from where Marylyn had stepped into the killer's car, and half a mile from where he had attacked her. In Hobson's absence, two detectives interviewed Marylyn as she lay heavily bandaged and groggy in her hospital bed. Fifty-six stitches held her scalp together. She was able to provide an encouragingly detailed description of her attacker, conveyed via Millgarth Police Station's telex machine to other forces: 'White male, 28 years. Five feet six inches. Stocky build, dark wavy hair, medium length beard with Jason King moustache. Wearing: yellow shirt, navy blue or black zip up anorak, blue jeans. Said his name was Dave. Had what is believed to be a Liverpool accent driving a dark coloured motor car with a well kept dark coloured upholstery, manual gearbox with some kind of box or similar object on window ledge in centre of vehicle.'[11]

The *Evening Post* ran the story 'Girl Attacked in Lovers' Lane' on their front page, reporting that detectives were 'keeping an open mind' on a possible link between Marylyn's attack and 'five 'Jack the Ripper' murders in Leeds and Bradford.[12] National press coverage was sparse, but on 19 December regional newspapers featured the photofit of Marylyn's assailant. The *Yorkshire Evening Post* announced: 'Here is the face of the man Leeds police want to interview in connection with the vicious attack in Leeds on Marilyn [sic] Moore,' reiterating that detectives were 'keeping an open mind on whether the attack is linked with the Jack the Ripper murders in Leeds and Bradford'.[13]

Police enquiries initially centred on Leopold Street in Chapeltown, since Hobson felt that 'this is where the key to this assault lies, in view of the fact that the man waved to someone there'.[14] Officers spoke to over two hundred sex workers, following the attacker's claim of being personally acquainted with prostitutes named Gloria and Hilary. The index at Millgarth was scoured for men called Dave or David; more than a thousand interviews were conducted and alibis for the night in question checked and recorded. At the crime scene, frogmen searched the waters of Meanwood Beck in the hope of locating the weapon used to inflict Marylyn's injuries, but found nothing.

The ongoing surveillance operation in Chapeltown had failed to log the registration number of the attacker's car. Detectives arranged for Marylyn to sit in a number of vehicles, hoping to narrow down the make. After ruling out several, she tried to be more precise about the car driven by her assailant, recalling that it had 'fins' on the back, was either dark-coloured or maroon and about the same size as a Morris Oxford, with two interior rear-view mirrors, and four doors. Her memory was later found to be mistaken.

A West Yorkshire Police report dated 13 January 1978 discussed tyre tracks left at the scene without making any reference to those found at Irene Richardson's murder scene. It was not until 14 March 1979 that further analysis linked the two, and the case that followed. The Byford Report of 1981 found that these omissions were 'an important contributory factor' in the failure to apprehend the killer at an earlier stage, since 'the vehicle tracks found at the Richardson, Moore and Millward scenes provided investigating officers with some hard factual evidence'.

Byford identified another significant error in processing the information generated by Marylyn's recalls of events: 'Although Moore's description of the car in which she had been picked up was accepted, the police placed less reliance on her description of her assailant.' A separate review of the Ripper investigation, conducted in 1981 by Colin Sampson, then Deputy Chief Constable, recognized the importance of Marylyn's photofit, stating that it was a remarkable likeness which should have provided the police with the turning point in their enquiries: 'If her photofit had been compared with those by other survivors, the similarity is so striking that it is beyond belief they would not all have been linked and considerable emphasis given to tracing the bearded man ... There was a failure during the investigation to link incidents with the series. The criteria were too narrowly drawn. An open mind should have been kept and the information, particularly the physical description, regularly assessed ... While publicity was given to the description of Miss Moore's attacker, little weight was given to this aspect during the investigation. Had this been done, and linked with others, the investigation might have been resolved much earlier.'[15] The implications of that observation are profound.

Yorkshire Chief Constable Ronald Gregory was forced to address the issue of the photofit in his memoirs, making a clumsy attempt to explain why so little credence had been placed upon it:

> Marilyn [sic] Moore's description was suspect. When she had been found, badly injured but still alive in December 1977, I prayed we at last had our breakthrough – a witness who had seen the Ripper face to face. Her recovery had been a medical miracle – her skull had been fractured and she had been stabbed eight times – but she proved an unreliable witness, or so we thought at the time. Three times she phoned us to say she had just seen the Ripper in a public house. Three times it proved a false alarm ... Moore had been drunk when attacked.[16]

Marylyn was not inebriated at the time of her attack, but she was summarily dismissed as an unreliable witness.

One person grasped the significance of Marylyn's photofit. Two years after her attack in Keighley, Tracy Browne spotted it: 'As the weeks and months went by I'd see in the papers every so often a girl being attacked. Another few months would go by and another girl would be attacked, or murdered. Then I saw this picture, exactly the same description that I'd given.'[17] Tracy showed the image to her mother, saying, 'That's the guy, the one who attacked me. It's obvious.'[18] Nora Browne immediately took her daughter to the local police station, where a young constable on desk duty listened to her explanation with a bored expression before sighing, 'We're all having fun and games today, aren't we?'[19] Nora was calmed down by a passing detective while Tracy filled in a form. There was no follow-up call or visit – nothing.

'They didn't take me seriously,' Tracy recalls. 'I don't know why, maybe it was my age. A lot of people didn't. If I told them I had been attacked by the Ripper they'd just dismiss me, so I didn't broadcast it.'[20] Nora tried another route, contacting her uncle Monty Featherman, a local magistrate and Hobson's personal friend, but nothing came of that either. Years later, Tony Browne reflected: 'If they had taken my daughter's account seriously – and released the photofit – some of the Ripper's victims would be alive.'[21] Tracy's photofit was left to languish on file, along with the one produced by Marcella Claxton. Marylyn's photofit was withdrawn from circulation.

The Christmas holidays provided Marylyn with an excuse to discharge herself from hospital. 'I still have a hole in the back of my head where he hit me and scars all over my scalp,' she told reporters months later. 'They shaved off all my hair and it has taken ages to get back to its old length. I left hospital just before New Year's Eve and went to stay with friends in High Wycombe. I couldn't stay in Leeds knowing that he might be in the same town.'[22]

Marylyn moved relentlessly from place to place, her once flame-red hair grown back brown. 'I can never forget that night,' she declared with a visible shudder. 'For the first few months all I could see when I closed my eyes was his face. Sometimes I wish he had killed me – it might almost have been better than the nightmares he has left me.'[23]

13

YVONNE

Yvonne Ann Pearson was born in Leeds on 2 February 1956 to warehouse foreman John Pearson and his wife Rose. Together with her three siblings, Yvonne was brought up as Roman Catholic and yearned for independence. At seventeen years old she left home to move into a city-centre flat, with little or no contact with her parents for two years. She claimed to have been travelling when she turned up on their doorstep again.

Her only serious relationship began around 1974, when she met a Jamaican-born man who was undecided about settling permanently in Leeds and had an open mind about their future together. 'We had an understanding that if either of us wanted someone else, that was OK,' her boyfriend later told the press. 'After all, I never put a ring on her finger.'[1] They lived with their two daughters in a terraced house at 4 Woodbury Road in the pleasant suburb of Heaton, two miles north-west of Bradford city centre.

With her partner unemployed, Yvonne had begun working as a prostitute to bring money into the home. She hated it, but was manipulated by her pimp into continuing. Chic and slim with a delicate face and thick platinum hair worn in a Purdey cut, she was streetwise and devoted to her children. Neighbours spoke very highly of her and were impressed by how beautifully she dressed her little daughters.

Toughening prostitution laws forced Yvonne to work away from the area. She travelled to London, meeting Skipton-born

Janie McIntosh, a high-earning call girl almost ten years older. Janie was divorced and without family, driving a silver sports car from her smart flat in Southampton to Shepherd's Market, where she had several wealthy clients. Janie took Yvonne under her wing, urging her to settle in the south, away from the Ripper as she had done. But Yvonne refused to leave her children for any length of time and her attempts to emulate Janie's working methods fell short, as a mutual friend named Avril recalled: 'She was always looking for the big time. So she'd go and give it a whirl in "the Smoke", doing business in some of the big West End hotels, but it never really worked for her. Don't get me wrong, she was always smart and looked good, but she was just an ordinary Yorkshire lass and she couldn't really compete with some of the toffee-nosed bitches who work the West End ... I think Yvonne was a bit out of her depth, though she never went short of money when she was down there, particularly when she managed to hit the Arab trade. But she'd always come to the Lane [*Lumb Lane*] in the end. This is where her mates were.'[2]

One of Yvonne's mates was Patricia Atkinson. The two of them had regularly socialized in the Lane's pubs until Patricia's murder in April 1977. Her death had a profound effect on Yvonne, who also changed her working habits. She no longer invited clients to Woodbury Road when the house was empty, and began carrying a pair of sharpened scissors in her handbag.

The year had further tragedies in store. Despite carrying the scissors, on one occasion Yvonne was badly beaten by a client who then sped away in his car. Shortly afterwards, she received two large fines for soliciting. On 1 November 1977, her friend Janie was stabbed to death in a bedroom on the fourth floor of the Posthouse Hotel in Bayswater Road. Guests admitted hearing screams that night, but assumed 'it was just someone having a good time'.[3] All hotel residents were questioned, along with sex workers in Southampton near Janie's flat, but there were no leads.

Unsurprisingly, Yvonne grew jittery after the second murder of a close friend, remarking to her babysitter, 'It would be just my luck to get knocked on the head.'[4] The fines she had received for soliciting put her in a Catch-22 situation: she had to work to clear those debts, and headed for Birmingham and London to avoid detection. She was arrested again one night in Manningham and faced a custodial sentence after being bailed to appear at Bradford's Magistrates' Court on Thursday 26 January 1978. Her partner ended their relationship and flew back to his family in the Caribbean, promising the children he would return after Christmas.

The strain of the past few months showed in Yvonne's appearance; she had lost a lot of weight and was painfully thin. Despite being in debt, she had set money aside to provide financial security for her daughters, the eldest of whom was two years old and the youngest only eighteen months. Friends agreed to look after the girls if she was sent to prison as she expected.

On Saturday 21 January 1978, Yvonne tried to keep herself occupied to stave off thoughts of the coming Thursday when she was due in court. She went grocery shopping with her daughters that morning, and in the afternoon called on a sixteen-year-old neighbour who was also a close friend, asking her to babysit the girls while she visited her mother in Leeds for a couple of hours.

At 4 p.m., Yvonne emerged from Woodbury Road clad head to toe in black: black polo-necked jumper, black trousers and black shoes. The only splashes of colour were the green stripes in her black woollen jacket, which she tugged tighter as she headed through the freezing streets towards town. She had never intended catching a train to Leeds; instead she walked to the Flying Dutchman, black clutch tucked under her arm.

A live reggae band entertained the pub as Yvonne played pool for a couple of hours with a friend, sipping pineapple juice. Just after 9 p.m. she headed for Lumb Lane and the junction with Picton Street. The Perseverance stood on the corner, one of Patricia's old haunts. A witness spotted Yvonne, at about 9.30 p.m., waving at an acquaintance on Church Street, coincidentally the last place that Patricia had been seen. Moments later, a vehicle backing out of Southfield Street almost collided with oncoming traffic in Lumb Lane. The driver of the car forced to brake spoke to Yvonne, who climbed into the passenger seat. She was never seen alive again.

Yvonne's babysitter was worried when she didn't appear as promised that evening; her curfew stipulated that she had to be home between the hours of 7 p.m. to 7 a.m. The girl put the door on the latch and bedded down with the two toddlers for the night. When there was no sign of Yvonne the following morning, she called the friends who had agreed to take care of the girls if their mother was sent to prison. They were deeply concerned, knowing that Yvonne would never have jumped bail and left her children. When she failed to arrive in time for a solicitor's appointment on Monday morning, they reported her as missing.

The police issued a notice to all regional forces:

Missing from home Yvonne Ann Pearson.

Although there is no evidence to suggest that harm may have befallen her, she has been missing since 1600 hours Saturday 21.1.78 after leaving an acquaintance looking after her two children (infants). She has not been in touch with home and this is said to be completely out of character.

On leaving home subject stated she intended to visit her mother at a Leeds address, and she would return before 1900 hours that day.

Enquiries reveal that subject has not been seen since Christmas 1977 by her mother.

Subject, a convicted prostitute, left home in possession of only train fare for Bradford to Leeds and stated that she expected her mother to provide her with some money.

Extensive enquiries in the Manningham area have failed to trace subject or any person who has seen her since she left home 21.1.78.

This woman is on bail to Bradford Magistrates Court, Thursday 26.1.78 to answer a charge of soliciting for prostitution at Manningham. Conditions of bail are a curfew between 1900hrs and 0700hrs daily.

Enquiries reveal that she intended to attend court on 26.1.78 and had made tentative enquiries to arrange for the custody of her children in the event of her losing liberty, which tends to indicate that she had no intention of absconding. It is also known that she failed to keep an appointment with her defending solicitor AM Monday 23.1.78.

Description:

Woman. White. Born 2.2.56. Five feet five inches tall, slim build, short dyed hair (platinum blonde), wearing black polo-necked jumper, black trousers, green and black wavy striped woollen jacket with wide sleeves, black shoes, no headgear and carried a small black handbag of the type which is carried under the arm (no handles).

It is emphasized that there is no evidence of foul play at this stage but all the circumstances give some cause for concern.

The press were not immediately informed about Yvonne's disappearance, but her neighbours talked of little else. 'She would not leave her children because she idolized them,' Margaret Kenny insisted. 'If she had been going away she would have taken her bank book and her family allowance book. All she had with her was a small handbag and only the price of two drinks.'[5] Another commented that Yvonne would have kept her court date, despite fearing the outcome: 'She had a lot of guts.

She faced up to things. She was easygoing and easily offended. She's the sort of person who plans things. She's one of those people who are punctual – that's why it's worrying. If she was going anywhere she would have taken her stuff with her.'[6]

One week later, West Yorkshire Police held a press conference to discuss Yvonne's disappearance. They disclosed that the last sighting of her had occurred where Patricia Atkinson was seen shortly before her death and there was a possibility that the same man might be responsible for Yvonne going missing.

Speculation was stilled on 3 February, when the body of another young woman was discovered in a timber yard in Huddersfield.[7] Reporters flocked to Dorset Terrace for a quote from Yvonne's parents in view of the latest news. Speaking from their home in Harehills, John Pearson declared:

My wife and I are going through hell waiting for Yvonne to get in touch. I have been told that she has been seen in a Leeds pub and that she has been seen in London. I cannot believe she is dead. I don't know why she has decided to disappear, although she was having domestic trouble. I don't want to know where she is living if she doesn't want to tell me. All I want to know is that she is safe. Both my wife Rose and I are horribly upset. I would just ask Yvonne to write to us, send a telegram, do anything to let us know she is ok. Please, just let us know you are alive.[8]

Reporters also spoke to Yvonne's former partner, who had returned from Jamaica to care for their children. He told them: 'I can't understand why anyone would want to kill her. She never harmed anyone.'[9]

Yvonne's body was discovered at noon on Easter Sunday, 26 March 1978. A youth taking a short cut through wasteground off Bradford's Arthington Street spotted something protruding from underneath an abandoned sofa and went across to investigate. Below the khaki-coloured velvet was a decomposing female hand.

Within minutes of the alarm being raised, the area was congested with police traffic. Situated behind Linfield Auto Ltd on Arthington Street, off Whetley Hill, the wasteground was surrounded by warehouses and factories. On the other side of the main road, the Woolpack usually did a brisk trade and consequently it was a fairly busy spot for people taking a short cut home. Local firms used the land to burn rubbish: bits of charred wood and twisted plastic poked through lumps of rubble.

Detective Chief Superintendent Trevor Lapish of Bradford CID ducked under the police tape to meet Detective Chief Superintendent Hobson, forensic scientist Russell Stockdale and a pathologist from St James's Hospital who was covering for Professor Gee on his weekend off. The four men sensed that the body below the sofa belonged to Yvonne Pearson.

The woman's slim right hand was marbled from the wrist. Beneath it rested a copy of the *Daily Mirror*, dated 21 February 1978. As the sofa was lifted, its wooden frame sagging, the woman's head came into view, extensively injured and bearing several holes. A small group of maggots clustered about her neck. The woman's left arm was raised above her head, caught in the sofa springs. Debris clung to her body, mostly grass, soil and horsehair stuffing. Her upper clothing had been lifted to expose her breasts. Stuck to the underside of her body were her trousers; the pants had been rolled down to mid-thigh, leaving her legs and feet bare. A small metal comb had been placed upright between her thighs. About twenty yards away lay a platform shoe and nearby were a length of wood, tights, a large stone, a condom and a purse. A small bottle of perfume and a handbag lay in another spot.

Assistant Chief Constable George Oldfield arrived later that afternoon, having already borrowed one hundred men from Lapish to investigate the Huddersfield murder. Continuity was deemed vital, and while the crime scene photographer got to work, someone succeeded in tracking down Professor Gee, whose car pulled into Arthington Street just before 6 p.m. After he had examined the woman's body in situ, her remains were conveyed to the mortuary.

Yvonne's fingerprints were held on the criminal database. After personal identification had confirmed who she was, Gee began the post-mortem, hampered by the body's advanced state of decomposition. Four hours later, he questioned Lapish's and Hobson's certainty that she had been murdered by the Ripper. The head trauma was more severe than in other victims; Yvonne's skull had been broken into seventeen pieces, as if crushed by a rock. To clarify the pattern of the fractures, her skull was rebuilt around a large ball of modelling clay.

After inflicting the head injuries, Yvonne's attacker had pushed a large ball of horsehair stuffing into her mouth, blocking her larynx. There were no immediate indications that a hammer had been used, nor were there any large wounds visible on her body or limbs. But her internal injuries – fractured ribs and a ruptured liver – indicated that the killer had kicked or jumped on her chest. It was impossible to ascertain whether her clothes had been disturbed before or after death. One peculiarity that was never resolved concerned the maggots, produced from a fly that usually feasted on cow dung and not associated with the area where she was found.

Yvonne's trousers bore streaks of mud on the back and were slightly torn; one shoe also bore mud smears, leading forensic expert Russell Stockdale to conclude that she had been dragged backwards, probably after losing consciousness. The newspaper found beneath her body was indicative of the killer having returned to the scene some while later, as he had with Jean Jordan and the young woman in Huddersfield. Lapish was inclined to believe that the Ripper wanted Yvonne to be found.

Despite Gee's doubts, when news of Yvonne's murder broke, it was greeted as a probable Ripper killing. The *Yorkshire Post* announced: 'Fears grew last night that the Ripper had killed his eighth victim – a missing prostitute whose body was found on wasteland on the fringe of Bradford's red-light area.'[10] Yvonne's parents were too distressed to speak to reporters, but John Pearson let it be known that no one in the family would tolerate the idea of his daughter working as a prostitute. Yvonne's neighbours were more realistic, with one close friend explaining: 'She was well thought of in the street. She only cared about her kids – too much. She didn't care, more or less, what people thought of her. She only went out on the game so she would have enough food and clothes for the children. She didn't do it for anything else, anyway. I have tried to persuade her to stop. She did say herself that she were afraid she might be the next one but she just had to go down to get food for the children.'[11]

Doubts about whether the murder weapon, thought to be either a hammer or a boulder, resulted in Yvonne's death being initially excluded from the Ripper series. The police telex machine described her murder as 'due to massive head injuries, possibly caused by a heavy blunt instrument. It is thought that death occurred some weeks ago ... It is probable that the clothing of the assailant will be heavily bloodstained and it is requested that laundries and dry cleaners be checked for the period from 21st January to 3rd February 1978 inclusive. It is thought from the pattern of the injuries that this death is not connected with the other circulated prostitute murders publicly referred to as the "Ripper Murders" ...'

Lapish informed the media that they were considering several possibilities:

This could have been a copycat type murder, someone trying to emulate the so-called Ripper or simply trying to throw us off his track by making it look like the other murders. We have not forgotten that within days of the 'Black Panther', Donald Neilson, being arrested, someone set out to try and beat his record. The Guisley student, Mark Rowntree, stabbed four people to death in eight days and was later jailed for life. Some people get unhinged at the thought of publicity. It may well be that we have such a person who, having seen the publicity, has decided to jump on the bandwagon. As a result of Professor Gee's post mortem, we are able to say that this murder is not in all probability one of the prostitute murders already under investigation. The injuries do not coincide.[12]

He confirmed his belief that the killer had returned after the murder to expose the body slightly: 'It is difficult to envisage that people came within yards of the settee and didn't see what I saw when I came to the site. It may be an animal pulled a hand or arm out.'[13]

On 28 March 1978, the *Daily Mirror* revealed:

A second Ripper may be on the prowl in Yorkshire. Police fear he may be a copycat killer jealous of the Ripper's notoriety – and determined to outscore him. And the rival Ripper may already have savagely butchered three women to death. This was the danger haunting detectives last night after they were told that prostitute Yvonne Pearson was not the Ripper's eighth victim. The mutilated body of the 22 year old mother was found on Sunday on a derelict site in the heart of Bradford's red-light district. It was at first believed that her murderer was the Ripper, who has killed – and mutilated – six prostitutes and a 16 year old shop girl over the last two years. But yesterday a pathologist told the police that her injuries were unlike those common to the Ripper's victims.[14]

The *Yorkshire Post* ended their report with a gloomy assertation that an 'epidemic of butchery' in the region had won Leeds and Bradford 'the unenviable titles of murder capitals of the country'.[15]

With the Bank Holiday at an end, enquiries began in earnest. Detectives questioned all those working in the vicinity of the murder scene, together with every known prostitute in Bradford. A task force had spent hours crawling across the wasteground, searching for the murder weapon. Efforts were made to establish the provenance of the ruined velvet sofa, which was thought to have been moved from its original location on the wasteground to where it had been found covering Yvonne's body. Her black handbag, discarded nearby, offered little useful information, other than that she was a member of a club also frequented by the young woman (Helen Rytka) who had been murdered in Huddersfield. The location of the handbag suggested that the killer might have escaped around the back of the garage, and the fact that he had moved a heavy sofa to cover his victim implied that he was reasonably fit, but neither consideration proved useful.

Yvonne's daughters were being looked after by their father, who raised them with loving care away from Woodbury Road. Their former home had been bricked up to prevent squatters invading it before demolition, but detectives forced entry to search the premises. They found Yvonne's gold-and-ivory pocket address book containing details of forty regular clients, most outside the county. Every man named within its pages was questioned, together with several prostitutes in the towns where Yvonne was known to have worked.

On 3 April, WPC Lena Markovic took the role of Yvonne in a reconstruction of her last hours. A crisis conference was held in Wakefield later that month; Yorkshire's Chief Constable, Ronald Gregory, announced that the Ripper inquiry had cost £1.5 million to date in overtime payments, transport and other facilities. Several officers had resigned from their posts, unable to cope with the pressure, while the crime rate in the region had increased by 17 per cent. Gregory's solution was to set up an elite squad of twelve men, headed by Detective Chief Superintendent John Domaille and based at Millgarth Police Station, tasked solely with catching the Ripper.

In April 1978, a twenty-three-year-old former sex worker appeared before Bradford magistrates to answer two charges of soliciting, which she admitted. After his client was given a three-month suspended sentence, Donna's solicitor told the court: 'She, like lots of other girls, has decided to quit since the death of her friends Tina Atkinson and Yvonne Pearson.'[16]

14

HELEN

The coroner at Helen Rytka's inquest described her murder as one of the 'utmost callousness and brutality. If the full details could be released they would shock even our modern, brutal society.'[1]

Born Elena Maria De Mattia on 3 March 1959 at St Mary's Hospital in Armley, she and her twin sister Rita Rosemary were presented with commemorative silver spoons, in keeping with hospital tradition. Their lives were anything but privileged, reflecting their own mother's childhood: Bernardina De Mattia had been placed in foster care for seven years following her father's death. In 1951, she left Italy for London, where she met Eric Rytka, newly arrived from Jamaica. Finding it difficult to secure long-term employment, they headed to Leeds, where Eric took several low-paid labouring jobs between long spells of unemployment. Their relationship was never stable, and when the twins were only four months old they were put into council care. Bernardina blamed poor living conditions, declaring after her daughter's murder: 'I have never had a big enough place for them. If I had a house I could have had all the children with me and all this might never have happened.'[2]

In September 1960, Bernardina and Eric became parents to a second set of twins, Antonio and Angela. Four years later, they brought Elena and Rita home to their council flat on Leopold Street in Chapeltown – the same street where Marylyn

Moore was picked up by the Ripper in 1977. 'It was a struggle but we were happy,' Bernardina recalled. 'I always made sure they were well clothed and well fed. I did my best and the main thing I gave them was love.'[3]

Raised a Roman Catholic in Venice, every Sunday Bernardina attended mass with her children at the Church of the Holy Rosary on Chapeltown Road. She enrolled Elena and Rita in Burmantofts' St Charles Roman Catholic Junior School where head teacher, Sister Joseph, thought them 'bright children, talented musically and artistically and good, all-round scholars. And they were essentially loving children. They were held back only by their difficult home background.'[4] Those who were later close to the twins described Rita as having been beaten by her mother.

Bernardina and Eric separated in 1969. Before marrying again the following year, Bernardina put all four children into care, professing to be 'heartbroken' by the decision.[5] She again cited inadequate housing as the cause but others recall her fiancé's aversion to becoming a stepfather. Responsibility for the two sets of twins passed to the Leeds Diocesan Rescue, Protection and Child Welfare Society, an organization working to 'rescue from circumstances or surroundings dangerous to faith or morals, boys and girls who have been baptized Roman Catholics'. They decided to keep the children together in the short term, finding places for them at St Teresa's Home on Thistle Hill in the leafy, genteel surroundings of Knaresborough, fifteen miles north of Leeds. It was a small Home, with only fifteen residents at a time, run by nuns and surrounded by large gardens that backed onto fields, with a main road nearby. All four Rytka children began attending St Mary's Roman Catholic Junior School, crossing the meandering River Nidd each day by bus to reach town.

'I used to go and see them regularly,' Bernardina stated years later. 'I used to worry about them. My only thought was that they would grow up all right. If I'd had a proper home they could have come back, but I never had.'[6] A foster home was found for Helen, as she was now known, and Rita, but the arrangement proved unsuitable and they returned to St Teresa's.

In early 1974, the *Yorkshire Post* ran a series of articles about fostering which caught Rita's attention. A talented young artist and writer, she penned a letter to the editor:

Dear Sir/Madam,
I am writing to you sending my views on fostering and adoption. I have read two of your articles on fostering and I think it is a marvellous idea. I am a child in care and have been for 12 years. If my twin sister and I got fostered out together it would be like winning £1,000 on the football pools. But money is not involved, LOVE is.

I have enclosed a poem called 'Lonely and Unloved' just to give you a good idea of what it is like to be lonely and unloved. I did not sit down for hours on end composing this poem, but I just wrote it down, changing only a few words to make it rhyme. I wrote it not from my head, but from my heart, because only from the heart can the feeling of loneliness be expressed and only from the heart can the feelings of being unloved lie deep within.

To get fostered out together means to us a place of love and care and it is then that you feel wanted, because someone somewhere realises what love really is and get fostered out is part of love itself. We can only wait, hope and pray to get fostered out together, but some day I hope we will.[7]

Yorkshire Post editor John Edwards was impressed. On 6 May 1974, the paper devoted an entire article to Rita and her siblings, calling them 'the Heartbreak Children'. The report summarized their situation:

Two sets of twins, all members of one family, highlight the tragedy of children in care who wait in vain to be adopted or fostered – the heartbreak of the hard-to-place children. Two are 15 year old twin sisters who have been in care for 12 years since their parents' marriage broke up. They have a twin brother and sister, aged 13, who are also with them in a children's home ... The twins have lived together in the home for five years and they do not want to be separated. The authorities are in difficulty – the older the children get, the harder it is to find foster parents for them.[8]

A poem written by Rita was printed in full:

> *Loneliness is to live in a world*
> *Where people do not care.*
> *Loneliness is to go outside*
> *To find no one is there, and*
> *You fall down in despair,*
> *Falling on your knees in prayer*
> *Asking God to rescue you,*
> *From this cruel snare,*
> *But no one comes*
> *No voice is heard.*
> *No one cares if I was lured,*
> *Lured into the deepest hole,*
> *Cast aside by those so cruel*
> *And treated like a mule.*
> *Yes!*
> *Loneliness is to live this way.*
> *Day after day.*
> *Yet I would pray*
> *So that some day,*
> *Love may find an open way,*
> *Unloved is to miss the love*

That all parents should give.
Yet they cast you aside
Put you out of their minds.
They put you in care.
There is no love there.
Yet the staff really care
Or they wouldn't be there.
Yet I know I shall die,
As my years drag by,
Oh, why was it me, Lord?
Why?[9]

Father Michael O'Reilly of the Leeds Diocesan Rescue, Protection and Child Welfare Society had already spoken about Helen and Rita to a couple in their forties on the foster-care register. The civil servant and his wife had recently bought a large, comfortable house in Dewsbury. Their names have been withheld, but the woman recalled Father O'Reilly making such 'an impassioned plea' on the girls' behalf that they agreed to foster them:

They came to us for their final two years before the local authority ceased to have responsibility for them at eighteen. They were very different, very unalike. Rita was very withdrawn and quiet. She said she had been beaten by her mother. It might have been the reason. Helen was the extrovert. It was always Helen who came to talk her problems over with me, never Rita. I would usually be cooking when they arrived from school and Helen would come and talk but Rita never did. Rita was the one who wrote the poem to the *Yorkshire Post*. She had a file of poetry and she painted. They both liked records.[10]

The girls had a bedroom each in the couple's detached house, and enjoyed the large garden, but it took both parties time to adjust. 'We had our ups and downs,' their foster mother recalled. 'It was a bit hard for us to get used to it at first, having two teenagers around when you have never had any children of your own. They would argue together but if we said anything to them they would gang up on us.'[11]

Helen and Rita began attending St John Fisher Roman Catholic Secondary School (now St John Fisher Catholic Voluntary Academy) on Dewsbury's Oxford Road. As part of the school's student exchange programme, two girls from Flensberg stayed with them for a while, and later Helen and Rita travelled to their visitors' home in northern Germany. 'They enjoyed every minute of it,' their foster mother recalled. 'They did not talk about anything else for weeks afterwards.'[12] The twins retained close bonds with their brother and sister, who remained at St Teresa's. On one occasion Antonio and Angela stayed at the house in Dewsbury, where the foster couple thought them 'lovely children, very pleasant and very outgoing'.[13]

The older twins left school in summer 1976. Although very different characters, they were physically almost identical, with large, expressive eyes, hair teased into cloud-like Afros, and willowy figures. 'Bright, artistic, introverted' Rita won a place at Batley Art and Design College, while Helen, 'open and vivacious', took a job at Bysel, a confectionery packaging plant in Heckmondwike, where Lion's Midget Gems were boxed.[14] It was monotonous work but she enjoyed the camaraderie; about forty women and several men worked at the factory. The manageress remembered her as an excellent team member: 'She was a lovely girl with a smashing figure, though she caused no jealousy. She could easily have got big-headed with her looks but she wasn't pushy or forward – she rarely bothered much with men, though she was friendly with them. She was a good, hard worker, quietly cheerful, but the most fantastic thing about her was her timekeeping. She was never late.'[15] Always conscientious, Helen paid her foster parents £3 board from her £20 weekly wage packet. At the weekend, she socialized with friends, persuading Rita to join them at the Pentagon disco in Mirfield's former town hall and at the Merrion Centre in Leeds. Both girls were passionate about music – pop, soul and reggae – and Rita was keen to explore her Afro-Caribbean heritage.

'They started going to Leeds with some West Indian boys,' their foster mother recalled, while her husband confirmed, 'They never had any special boyfriends, just ones which lasted a few weeks. More often than not they went out with a group of girls at weekends. Most week nights they stayed in. Neither of them could really afford to be going out every night.'[16] Helen had always sung along to the radio in their bedroom at St Teresa's and began to give serious thought to a career in the music industry. With no contacts and no means of making a decent demo tape, she took another route, performing at Cavernes discotheque on Great Horton Road in Bradford, and at Leeds Central, a basement club that hosted legendary soul and jazz funk nights.

For undisclosed reasons, Rita left her foster home and moved into the West Haven Hostel for Girls on Dewsbury's Huddersfield Road, where Helen called on her every day. Co-founder Sister Dolorosa was much loved by the girls in her care and remembered the twins talking about forming a pop duo: 'Their one dream was of becoming famous and they would have gone to any lengths to achieve this. They were both gullible [but] these girls were not promiscuous. They were young and ambitious.'[17]

Local authority responsibility for the girls ended when they reached eighteen, but they were advised to contact social workers if they needed help. St Teresa's Home had closed down, but the nuns relocated to Bradford with their charges, including Antonio and Angela. Leaving their foster parents, Helen and Rita asked the Diocesan Society for assistance with finding a flat near their siblings and moved to Manningham. Once Antonio and Angela were old enough to leave the nuns, all four siblings shared a flat in a high-rise block in the Bradford suburb of Laisterdyke. Helen had a seven-mile bus journey to work and Rita travelled a further mile to college.

Helen, Antonio and Angela had maintained contact with their mother and visited her occasionally in Leeds. Bernardina declared that Helen was 'always my favourite daughter. She would always come to talk to me and tell me her problems. She cared for me and I cared for her.'[18] Rita had no contact with her mother. During that autumn she became more withdrawn, eventually dropping out of college where she had been an excellent student. She then disappeared from the flat in Laisterdyke without telling anyone, leaving Helen distraught.

Bernardina recalled that Helen visited her one week before Christmas. She spoke about hoping to get a new job in a bakery but was extremely anxious about her twin. 'She kept asking, "Where is Rita?"' Bernardina stated, 'but I couldn't tell her because I didn't know where she was either. Elena was very close to Rita.'[19]

During the holidays, snow fell on the north, causing severe delays and cancellations with public transport. Helen's employer remembers that, despite the difficult conditions, Helen 'managed to get here – and on time too. Rather than go home to Bradford she had caught a bus as far as it went into Batley and then walked through the snowdrifts to her old foster home in Dewsbury. The following morning she did the journey in reverse. She was very conscientious.'[20]

Helen tracked Rita down over Christmas to a shabby bedsit at 13 Elmwood Avenue in Huddersfield, some forty miles from the flat they had shared in Laisterdyke. The town had enjoyed considerable prosperity in the nineteenth century as the hub of woollen textile production and its associated chemical and engineering works. The Highfields district, where Rita rented a room, was once the preserve of the wealthy. It remained a prestigious address until the redevelopment of Huddersfeld in the 1950s, when buildings were demolished to create an inner ring road and web of feeder routes. By the time Rita was living there, the area had become a deprived backwater, braced against the M62. The lintel stone above 13 Elmwood Avenue was inscribed 'Enderley', a reminder of prosperity long forgotten.

With no financial support from the authorities since giving up her college course, Rita had turned to prostitution, a path Helen refused to allow her to walk alone. Two weeks after finding Rita, she resigned from Bysel, abandoned any thought of working in a bakery, much less of becoming a pop star, and moved in with her sister. 'It came as a complete surprise,' a colleague recalled. 'She gave no reason. She just said that she was leaving to go and live with her sister in Huddersfield, said goodbye to everybody, picked up her money – and that was the last we saw of her.'[21] Nor did Helen mention finding Rita to their mother. Afterwards, Bernardina insisted, 'Elena didn't mention any problems. If she got into any difficulty after that, I wish she had come and told me. Whatever she got involved in, I would never have disowned her. I loved her and perhaps I would have been able to help.'[22]

Helen and Rita shared Flat 3, the former drawing room of 'Enderley'. Rita had given the place a fresh coat of paint and bought matching carpet and curtains in vivid orange swirls, but damp had already returned to mottle the walls. There was a shared bathroom down a stone-flagged hallway cold enough to store milk. For respite from their cheerless flat they visited Cleopatra's, a West Indian club on Huddersfield's Venn Street. The northern soul and reggae that attracted them was in the process of dying out, replaced by live punk bands, violence and solvent abuse.

The girls worked most evenings to pay their weekly £5 rent. The red-light district lay around Great Northern Street and Viaduct Street, both non-residential areas apart from two houses on the former. One belonged to an elderly couple and the other to market supervisor Fred Smith and his family. It was a bleak, uncompromising spot, half a mile from town. Warehouses, builders' merchants and a timber yard stood on the main stretch. Nearby were two markets, one retail, the other cattle, as well as an abattoir and bus depot. The Leeds–Manchester railway ran along the viaduct, forty yards from the road. After darkness it was more isolated, with sex workers walking up and down the streets, waiting for clients in cars or on foot, copulating in the derelict arches while trains thundered by overhead.

Helen and Rita had a spot outside the public lavatories at the market end of Great Northern Street, opposite the junction with Hillhouse Lane. For their own safety, they tried to accept clients at the same time when possible, allowing the man twenty minutes before returning to the toilet block. Helen had scarcely begun working there when she came to the attention of local police. Told to expect a caution if she was caught soliciting again, she felt helpless, seeing no immediate alternative.

Early 1978 brought a cold snap that endured day after day. By mid-month, gale-force winds had created deep drifts of snow on high ground and grey piles of slush in the streets. On the last day of January, Helen and Rita stayed huddled in bed until 1.30 p.m. to keep warm. Shunning the expense of the gas fire, they dressed swiftly. Helen pulled on tight denim flares and a black polo neck, rearranging the chain of the delicate silver cross she always wore over the rolled collar. She added gold stud earrings and a bangle before doing her hair and make-up.

After sipping mugs of tea, the girls prepared their only proper meal of the day: an economical version of Jamaican pepperpot stew. As they ate at the table, a radio in one of the upstairs flats warbled the bagpipe intro of 'Mull of Kintyre', then at the end of a long run at the top of the charts. At 5.30 p.m., the girls shared tea and biscuits while snowflakes melted against the window. At 8.30 p.m., Helen pulled on her favourite fake-fur jacket and they left the flat.

The unlit hillside path that led down to the market was slippy underfoot. All day, the area reverberated with the shouts of Punjabi and Urdu tradesmen but at night it was quiet, with only the muffled snap of canvas awnings breaching the silence. Half an hour after arriving on Great Northern Street, the girls were spotted by Gwen Smith, the market supervisor's wife, as she walked home with her son. She watched them pityingly for a moment: two very slender teenage girls, plainly chilled to the bone as they tottered either side of the road, looking for punters to whom they meant nothing but a function.

Their first clients were two chauffeurs who had left their bosses enjoying a directors' dinner at the George Hotel. They each agreed a price of £5, waiting while the men made use of the nearby toilets before leaving separately with them for the short journey to the car park of Huddersfield Town Football Club. Helen was the first to arrive back at the public lavatories; she left with another client before Rita was dropped off at 9.30 p.m. It was bitterly cold. When a white sports car pulled up, Rita directed the driver to Elmwood Avenue, unwilling to have sex in the open. When he had gone, she stayed at the flat, expecting Helen to appear at any moment.

Rita sat up all night. When dawn broke behind the curtains there was still no sign of Helen. She couldn't bring herself to call the police, knowing Helen was already on a warning. But when her sister failed to turn up as that day and then the next wore on, Rita's anxiety outstripped her fear and she reported Helen as missing.

The police search around the Great Northern Street area began on the morning of Friday 3 February 1978. A call was put through to Garrard's timber yard, given its reputation for night activity. Foreman Melvyn Clelland agreed to allow the police access to search the premises 'on a serious matter'. Two days earlier, one of the lads had found a pair of bloodstained pants in the yard and nailed them to a packing case, but Clelland thought nothing of it. He assumed that the police were looking for Lester Chapman, a young boy missing from home.

The dog handler arrived just after 2 p.m. A light rain fell as Clelland showed the uniformed officer around the main building: a vast warehouse made of corrugated metal, with a carpet company next door. They walked through the yard, where stacks of sawn timber piled nine feet high smelled strongly in the rain. At the back of the yard, beside the steep railway embankment, was a disused toilet block, where the Alsatian suddenly leapt forward on its lead. The dog had scented something behind a heap of timber stored between a cabin and fence. Edging forward, the police officer craned his neck, then drew back sharply.

Instructing Clelland to wait by the cabin, the dog handler returned to his van for tape and polythene sheeting, sealing off the area. Within minutes, sirens wailed from the main road and half an hour later, blazing arc lights had been set up, the rain slanting down like black needles in the beam.

Professor David Gee and a female colleague from the University of Leeds headed towards the cabin, meeting forensic scientist Ron Outtridge, Detective Chief Superintendent John Domaille, Assistant Chief Constable George Oldfield and fingerprint expert Detective Chief Inspector Peter Swann. Gee peered into the gap between cabin and fence, where Helen's body had been wedged into a space eighteen inches wide between the wall and planks of timber. A sheet of corrugated asbestos partially hid her from view. Nonetheless, Gee could see that she was naked apart from a black jumper and bra, which had been pulled up over her chin, and a pair of socks. Her arms were raised above her head, covered by cloth or paper; a piece of blue material was wrapped around her left arm. In the hollow of her neck glinted a silver cross, minus its chain. There was a large laceration to her forehead, another wound to the back of her head and three stab marks to her chest. The skin on her thigh bore ridges, as if something had pressed against it.

It took considerable effort to lift Helen's body out from its hiding place. Mortuary attendants at Huddersfield Royal Infirmary cleaned her face in preparation for the formal identification process. With two police officers hovering in the background, Rita entered the room, gazing down on the sister she regarded not simply as her twin, but an extension of herself.

At the rainswept timber yard, lights were carried to areas the pathologist wanted to inspect. A small amount of blood lay on the debris beneath the spot where Helen's body had been pinioned, but a larger patch of blood behind another stack of timber towards the back of the main warehouse led Gee to believe that she had been killed there.

A task force arrived the following day. Their search unearthed a thin metal bangle, single gold stud earring, a button, some coins and a used condom near the crime scene. Helen's slingback shoes lay on one side of the fence beside the embankment, her jeans and fake-fur jacket on the other. It also emerged that one of the timber yard employees had found a handbag two days earlier.

The police telex machine conveyed the news to regional forces:

At 3.10pm on Friday, 3 February 1978, the naked body of Helen Rytka born 3/3/59, a half-caste Jamaican woman was found partially concealed in a timber yard off Great Northern Street, Huddersfield.

The body had severe injuries to the head with a blunt instrument and stab wounds to the body. Neither instrument has been found. It has not yet been established whether the deceased had been subject to sexual interference.

The deceased, who was an active prostitute, had only lived in Huddersfield for the past two months but it is known that she took clients to the woodyard where her body was found. She formerly lived in Bradford.

She was reported missing from home on the 2nd February 1978 having been seen by her sister, also an active prostitute, at 21.10 hours on Tuesday 31st January 1978 in Great Northern Street Huddersfield, at which time she was seen to get into a dark blue coloured saloon car, possibly an Audi 100ls driven by a white male about 35 years of age and of smart appearance.

Attention is drawn to previous offences of murder of prostitutes which have occurred in the West Yorkshire Metropolitan area since 22/7/75.[23]

George Oldfield took charge of the investigation, assisted by Detective Chief Superintendent Domaille. At the incident room in Huddersfield, Oldfield spent a long while talking to Rita Rytka, after which he gave a short statement to the press, informing them that Helen had been found with severe head injuries, and 'at the moment we cannot rule out the possibility of a link with the so-called Ripper murders. We are awaiting the outcome of the post mortem examination being carried out by Professor David Gee. The woman had some signs of body injuries, including cuts. Naturally, in view of what has happened in the past, we treat all deaths of women with suspicion from the outset, particularly when bodies are found in the open.'[24]

The *Yorkshire Evening Post* was swift to interpret Oldfield's words: 'Vivacious good time girl Helen Rytka (18) – who only recently moved to Huddersfield to live with her twin sister – is believed to be the seventh victim of Yorkshire's Jack the Ripper murderer.'[25] The *Yorkshire Post* declared that the killer had a 'death toll' equal to that of his Victorian namesake: 'History was made in Huddersfield last night when the latest Ripper victim was discovered brutally murdered in a garage. The man, who has maintained a reign of terror over the red-light area of Leeds for more than two years, with a series of frenzied stabbings and batterings, has now murdered as many women as his never-to-be-detected predecessor, Jack the Ripper.'[26] In an overview of the killings, Jayne MacDonald's death was described as 'the most tragic' while Helen was branded 'one of life's losers'.[27]

Professor Gee carried out the post-mortem on Saturday 4 February 1978. When the mortuary attendants removed Helen's jumper and bra, the silver chain that held the tiny cross fell out. Mud, debris and several small hairs lay on the surface of her skin and inside her mouth was a single pubic hair. Six lacerations had been inflicted on her head with a hammer; below some were the familiar semi-circular fractures to the skull. A long-bladed knife had caused stab wounds that had penetrated her heart, lungs, aorta, stomach and liver. The weapon had been inserted at least thirteen times into two of the wounds. The indentations in her thigh and lack of blood where her body had been discovered suggested a hard object had been pressed against her skin after the murder had taken place elsewhere. Outtridge proposed that she could have lain under a plastic sheet for several hours before being moved to the cabin. The killer had returned to his victim, but in this instance he had done so to conceal her more effectively.

For the purpose of a reconstruction, Rita accompanied detectives to clothes shops for items similar to those worn by her sister. Posters showing Helen's face superimposed on Rita's body were distributed throughout West Yorkshire, with two hundred copies printed in Urdu and Punjabi, headed 'Sympathetic Murder' to confirm Helen's death as an unprovoked attack.

Rita gave in her notice at Elmwood Avenue. She returned to her siblings in Laisterdyke, under constant police guard in case the killer should attempt to contact her. For several days she made the fifteen-mile journey to Huddersfield to confer with detectives. Oldfield urged reluctant witnesses to come forward voluntarily, given that 'it could be in their best interests for them to do so, to avoid embarrassment in the future, especially if we have to make inquiries to trace them, which we will be obliged to do'.[28] The two chauffeurs contacted the police about their meeting with the twins, informing detectives that another man at the urinals in Great Northern Street that night had asked if he was in the right place for prostitutes. They told him that he was but the two girls outside were booked. The man's two-tone Ford Granada had been parked near the toilet block. All three men were subsequently eliminated from enquiries.

On 7 February, West Yorkshire Police set up a freephone service, putting callers straight through to the incident room in Castlegate, where magnified maps of the region covered the walls, marked with key timings. Oldfield was particularly keen for sightings of Helen after 9.30 p.m., and the time gap between her being dropped back at Great Northern Street by the chauffeur and meeting the killer.

Officers were also eager to trace three cars: a dark-coloured Morris Oxford Farina saloon, a Ford Cortina Mark I and a white Datsun 160/180B. The Cortina and Datsun were tracked down and ruled out; the Farina had been seen by the toilets on Great Northern Street and its owner was already wanted in connection with the attack on Marylyn Moore. Most Farina owners were traced and eliminated, but not all.

On 9 February, Oldfield was a guest on Jimmy Young's BBC Radio 2 show. He implored women to speak up if they had any suspicions about their menfolk. 'I'm hoping that the broadcast will have done a lot of good,' he confirmed afterwards. 'The Ripper is someone's neighbour and he is also someone's husband or son. It may be that someone who has been listening might have their memories jogged about some suspicious person or event.'[29]

That same day the *Yorkshire Post* ran an interview with Bernardina, who posed with family photographs and letters from Helen. 'I was very distressed when I heard she had been living as a prostitute,' she asserted. 'She was not that kind of girl at all. She was a good girl. She only went to live in Huddersfield two or three weeks before she was killed, and I don't know what could have made her do what she did. Everyone thinks she was a prostitute but it's not true. She wasn't like that at all …

Despite this tragedy I still have faith and I am praying that this man who took my daughter's life will be caught. I have had a hard life and so have my children. We still have a chance but Elena is gone'.[30] The Deputy Director of Leeds Social Services agreed: 'From our knowledge of the girls it would appear quite surprising that they became prostitutes.'[31] But Sister Dolorosa acknowledged how easy it was for young girls to get into difficulties without anyone to guide them: 'The heartbreaking thing about this tragedy is that girls like Rita and Helen have to leave our care when they are eighteen and many of them are not ready to face the world on their own.'[32]

The world's media wanted to interview Rita. She appeared on Yorkshire Television's *Calendar*, telling viewers: 'I could have lost nothing dearer than Helen. Nothing closer to my life could have gone than Helen. For his own sake and the public's sake he should hand himself over. The public will appreciate he has done that. If anyone is withholding information they should, for their own sake, come forward and give that information which is so vital to find him. I knew the Ripper was in West Yorkshire but you don't expect it to happen to you. It just happened to Helen.'[33] Asked how she was coping with her sister's death, Rita replied: 'I am still young. I have my whole life ahead of me. I have to survive.'[34]

Reporters doubled their efforts to speak to her. Rita agreed to write a poem in her sister's memory, which was printed in the *Sunday Mirror*. One verse stood out:

> *In innocence she lived,*
> *In innocence she tried,*
> *In innocence she walked the streets*
> *Simply to survive,*
> *In innocence she died.*[35]

Sensing an opportunity for invaluable publicity, Oldfield persuaded Rita to take part in a press conference on 12 February, until Leeds Diocesan Rescue, Protection and Child Welfare Society stepped in. The organization instructed Dewsbury-based solicitor Thomas Disken to inform West Yorkshire Police that they would not be party to her exploitation. Oldfield argued that her appearance could result in vital evidence that might change the course of the investigation. After protracted wrangling, Disken and a female friend accompanied Rita as she entered a conference room packed with journalists. Dressed in jeans and a sweater, and clutching a white handkerchief, she read a statement written on a page torn from an exercise book: 'Helen was a very happy girl and her main ambition in life was to sing. The circumstances did not allow her to fulfil that ambition. She was very close to me. No loss could be greater than hers. I hope the public will not forget her. I am helping the police all I can and I hope anyone who has information will show sympathy and come forward.'[36] .

A few witnesses responded, including one man who had driven along Great Northern Street twice between 9.25 p.m. and 9.30 p.m. and remembered seeing Helen by the toilet block. Oldfield also declared that there had been a 'magnificent response' to the £5,000 reward offered by the *Yorkshire Post* and the *Evening Post* for information leading to the Ripper's conviction; local businessmen contributed another £5,000 and appeals were launched to boost the total to at least £20,000.[37] By 14 February, around three thousand people had been interviewed in connection with Helen's murder. Regional newspapers reported that in the wake of her death, 'Huddersfield's good-time girls have gone to ground', with Great Northern Street almost deserted apart from police officers carrying out spot checks on motorists.[38] The nominal indexes and vehicle indexes from the previous murders and Maureen's attack were amalgamated into the system at Millgarth. But nothing emerged to move the investigation substantially forward, although the Byford Report later observed that Helen's murder 'did invoke public sympathy and was well covered by the press. The fact that the victim, an attractive girl with a twin sister, was also an orphan, produced some public response so that police appeals for assistance produced an improved flow of information.'

Rita Rytka's nineteenth birthday fell on Friday 3 March 1978. Helen's absence had a presence of its own in the flat where her twin sister sat for the entire day, staring out at the shining wet rooftops of Laisterdyke. The following Monday, Rita took the stand at the inquest into Helen's death, describing their last day together. After adjourning proceedings for the statutory year, Kirklees coroner Philip Gill advised anyone shielding the killer that while they might have 'some mental anguish or reservations about coming forward, unless this person is apprehended there is the greatest possible likelihood that he will commit another similar offence and we will have another death on our hands'.[39]

Helen was buried in Bradford's Scholemoor Cemetery on Thursday 9 March 1978. A requiem mass was held at St Anthony's Church in Clayton, conducted by Canon John Murphy, administrator of Leeds Diocesan Rescue, Protection and Child Welfare Society. Assisting him was Father Michael Killen, who had heard the twins' first confessions at Knaresborough. There were around thirty mourners, including Helen's sisters and brother, her mother, and a handful of colleagues from the Bysel factory. Bernardina placed a wreath on her grave which read: 'To my dearest daughter Elena, with everlasting memories, from Mother and family.'[40]

15

VERA

Apart from her murder, very little is known about Vera Evelyn Millward. Her surviving relatives, including her sons and daughters, have never spoken about her publicly.

Vera's life began and ended in violence, that much is certain. She was born in the Spanish capital of Madrid on 26 August 1937, in the midst of a civil war. Two years later, the city was under siege; Vera's first memory was of the ear-splitting bombardment and gunfire from execution squads as thousands of Republican prisoners were rounded up by the Nationalists. Years of hunger followed the sealing of the French and Portuguese borders. Vera was eight years old when the war ended, and still in her teens when she joined the thousands of Spanish men and women leaving to work abroad.

After her death, Vera was often referred to as divorced, but she never married, although she wore a ring on her wedding finger. In the mid-1950s, while living in her adoptive city of Manchester, she met Yusef Sultan, eleven years her senior. A gentle, compassionate man, he had worked as a chef since arriving in Britain from India. Their relationship broke down when the last of their five children turned fifteen and Vera left home to work the streets of Hulme and Moss Side. What led to that decision is unclear, but she came to the attention of the police using the names Anne Brown and Mary Barton.

While Yusef devoted himself to their children, Vera settled into a relationship with Jamaican-born Cyrenous Birkett, eight years her senior, and had two children with him: a son, born in 1969 while they were temporarily living in London, and a daughter, born in Manchester three years later. Home was a council flat at 8 Grenham Avenue in Hulme.

By November 1973, Vera had five convictions for soliciting. A young neighbour named Janie recalled: 'I used to work the streets at the same time as Vera. Our beat was the Moss Lane/ Denmark Road area.'[1] The two streets were separated by Whitworth Park, described by one historian as 'a parading ground for prostitutes'.[2] They shared their patch with Jean, who confirmed: 'I did know Vera. She was all right. She was only in it because she had kids to keep. She was car trade, Vera, although she had a "special", I remember, someone who used to meet her regular, in a big car.'[3] Police later traced this man, who told them he had known Vera for five years and that he paid her to spend every Tuesday night with him but for company, rather than sex. Occasionally, he gave her small gifts of food to take home.

Other than her arrangement with him, Vera was not thought to be working at the time of her death. Since the birth of her last child, she had suffered periods of chronic ill health, with three major operations in her final two years, including the removal of one lung. Crippling stomach pains plagued her every day and she had a tendency to drag her right foot when weary. One neighbour described her as 'a quiet, frail person who always seemed to be ill'.[4] Her partner Cy confirmed: 'She used to be a prostitute, but since the operations she had given all that up. She was a sick woman.'[5] Another girl who worked on Denmark Road agreed: 'We haven't seen her down here for some time. I thought she had given up street walking.'[6]

Although she was no longer soliciting, in the last few weeks of her life, without further explanation, Vera told her friends Janie and Jean that she didn't think she had long to live.

At the beginning of April 1978, West Yorkshire's Chief Constable, Ronald Gregory, gathered a group of twelve experienced senior detectives to investigate why the Ripper inquiry had so far failed to capture the killer. Based in their own offices at Millgarth, the Special Homicide Investigation Team (colloquially known as the SHIT squad) was led by Detective Chief Superintendent John Domaille. His team began reviewing the files of those murders and attacks attributed to the Ripper, and examining those which had been rejected from the series.

Later that month, Marylyn Moore and Maureen Long agreed to be questioned under hypnosis in a bid to recall more about their own attacks. Marylyn's sessions with Dr Philip Snaith, senior lecturer in psychiatry at Leeds University, led to the issuing of a new photofit which was fundamentally the same but showed her attacker with longer hair. Detectives appeared to lose faith in Marylyn when she twice contacted them to say she had spotted her assailant. Both men were eliminated from enquiries, but the first bore a striking resemblance to the second photofit.

Renewed police efforts against street prostitution divided senior officers on the wisdom of the approach. Chief Constable Ronald Gregory told *The Times*: 'I would not be against legalized prostitution but not in its present form. I think these girls are exploited and the prostitute industry as it is today, I am against. In a different form, I think it could be regularized. It could be legalized, I think, in some way. That would eliminate a lot of these vicious attacks.'[7] Taken within the context of a national campaign to reform prostitution laws, his comments caused outrage. Meanwhile, substantial resources were funnelled into logging cars in red-light districts.

Among those areas not yet included in the scheme was Manchester, where Vera Millward spent an uncomfortable evening on Tuesday 16 May 1978. When she left home at 10 p.m. complaining of severe stomach pains, her partner assumed she was heading to hospital for an emergency supply of painkillers, as she had in the past.

Vera bought two packets of Benson & Hedges from the nearest shop, then walked back to the flat to wait outside for her Tuesday date. She wore a checked blue and brown coat over a cardigan and yellow floral shift dress, with blue canvas shoes. She smoked a couple of cigarettes and glanced up the street, expecting the Mercedes to appear with its lights flashing as usual. When it didn't arrive, she began walking.

At 11.15 p.m., a man walking with his son through the grounds of Manchester Royal Infirmary heard a scream pierce the air: three cries for help that were abruptly silenced. He stood rooted to the spot, but when no further sounds came, he assumed the cries had come from within the hospital and went on his way.

At 8 a.m. the following morning, two vans pulled into a small walled compound adjacent to the hospital's private wing. A Rochdale landscaping company had been tasked with redesigning an area of wasteground in Livingstone Street where it met April Street. Jim McGuigan, one of six labourers, began unloading tools. Something caught his eye: an object near the collapsed wall fenced off with wire mesh. At first he thought it was a doll, but a closer look revealed otherwise. He shouted for his workmates. A nurse heading to her shift heard the commotion and called over a doctor, although no one needed to be told that the woman lying by the fence was dead.

Vera lay face down on her right side, arms folded beneath her body, legs slightly bent, shoes removed and placed neatly on top. A piece of paper covered her head and her coat was thrown over her torso. Neither her tights nor her bra had been removed but her underskirt and yellow dress were pushed up, exposing a large wound in her stomach through which her intestines protruded. She had been repeatedly stabbed through a wound on her back and struck on the head three times with a hammer. There was a puncture to her bruised right eyelid.

Grazes on her body and scuff marks in the gravel showed where she had been dragged twelve feet from the entrance of the compound to the fence. Four yards away, tyre marks indicated that a car had accelerated away at speed.

Led by Detective Chief Superintendent Jack Ridgway, the team who had investigated Jean Jordan's murder arrived. Detective Chief Inspector Tony Fletcher recalled: 'I was told that the body of a woman had been found in circumstances which left little doubt that she was the ninth victim of the Yorkshire Ripper.'[8] They were all familiar with the compound as a spot favoured by sex workers and their clients, despite it being largely floodlit at night. Near the tyre marks was a pool of blood containing hair and brain tissue; splashes of blood led back to where Vera lay. While twenty uniformed officers wearing overalls conducted an inch-by-inch search of the area, policewoman Denise Cavanagh stood guard over Vera's body. Staff and patients were questioned, but no one had seen anything untoward.

An officer from the Vice Squad recognized Vera when her body arrived at the mortuary. He knew her as Vivienne Brown but a fingerprint check against the criminal database identified her real name. Detectives contacted Cy Birkett, who arrived a short while later to view her body. 'It was a terrible shock,' he remembered. 'It broke my heart.'[9] Cy told police that he had gone in search of Vera the night before when she failed to return home, but had to give up because their children were alone in the flat.

Dr Reuben Woodcock began the post-mortem at 12.30 p.m., with Gee and Domaille observing. Vera had died approximately twelve hours earlier, following three hammer blows to the head; a piece of bone was lodged inside her fractured skull. The first blow had been struck from behind while she was standing, the other two after she had collapsed. One wound to her body had been penetrated three times, the blade only slightly retracted on each withdrawal, passing between her ribs and damaging her remaining lung, liver and stomach. The larger injury to her stomach was eight inches long. A series of cutting movements had left the wound with jagged edges, causing her intestines to bulge. All the injuries to her body had been inflicted when Vera was close to death.

The *Manchester Evening News* broke the story of a second Ripper killing in the region, reporting that Detective Chief Superintendent John Domaille was in liaison with Greater Manchester Police. But otherwise, both regional and national press paid relatively little attention to Vera's murder. The Byford Report stated that coverage 'again reflected the fact that the victim was a prostitute'.

DCI Fletcher recalled that further examination of the crime scene yielded several clues: 'From the position of tyre tracks, footprints, blood and the spot where the body was found it was assumed that the murderer had driven through the opening in the wire mesh at the southern end of the compound and had veered sharply to the right; he had then reversed his vehicle until the bonnet was pointing towards the exit, ready for a quick getaway.'[10] The tyre treads matched those from the scene of Irene Richardson's murder and the attack on Marylyn Moore; further examination narrowed the range of relevant vehicles down to eleven and then two, one of which was a Ford Corsair. The Farina previously included was eliminated, although West Yorkshire Police continued with the Farina enquiry until the Ripper's eventual arrest.

On 18 May, police launched 'a massive operation' in Manchester's red-light areas, consulting prostitutes in Moss Side, Chorlton and Whalley Range to piece together Vera's working life.[11] Five hundred posters bearing her photograph and description were distributed throughout the city. The man who had heard Vera's screams at the hospital that night came forward, as did her regular Tuesday client. Both were eliminated from enquiries. With nothing further to go on, Ridgway made a grim assertion: 'When you have eliminated the obvious motives of robbery and sex, there's very little left except murder for its own sake.'[12]

Cy Birkett returned to Jamaica with his son and daughter, but Vera's death left her five children with Yusef Sultan orphaned; their father had passed away in 1975. She was laid to rest in the Roman Catholic section of Southern Cemetery, close to Jean Jordan. Both graves are unmarked.

In June 1978, the results of the review conducted by Domaille's homicide investigation team were sent to all British police forces in the form of a confidential report. 'Murders and Assaults upon Women in the North of England' formally attributed more crimes to the Ripper: ten murders instead of eight and four attacks instead of one. The news caused shockwaves when it was made public after the annual September meeting of the Association of Chief Constables in Preston. 'Ripper's Death Toll Rises to Ten' read the *Daily Express* headline, informing readers that the killer was now deemed responsible for the murders of Yvonne Pearson and Joan Harrison.

Investigating officers in Yorkshire and Lancashire had already explored a possible link between Joan's 1975 death in Preston and the Ripper killings. The 1981 Byford Report acknowledged that it was a mistake to include it, since Joan's murder was later confirmed as not being part of the series, but the initial decision to regard it as such proved 'very significant' in the investigation overall, 'especially in regard to senior police management decisions'. Byford described Joan as 'a known prostitute and alcoholic', but her friends remembered her as the 'bubbly and vibrant' daughter of a Chorley baker.[13] Following marriage and motherhood, an illness left Joan addicted to cough medicine. Her husband's death soon after their separation resulted in the loss of the family home. A second marriage floundered as Joan became increasingly dependent on alcohol. Moving from one bedsit to another, she turned in desperation to sex work.

Three weeks after Wilma McCann's murder, Joan's naked body was found in a disused garage on Preston's Berwick Road. She had been raped vaginally and anally before being kicked to death. She was twenty-six years old. A deep bite to her left breast revealed that the killer had a gap between his upper front teeth, while semen analysis showed that he was a blood group B secretor, placing him within only 6 per cent of the UK's male population. Similarities between Joan's death and Irene's murder fifteen months later – including the boots laid across the legs of both women – convinced Hobson to re-examine the earlier killing.

Also now officially included in the series were the attempted murders of Anna Rogulskyj, Olive Smelt, Maureen Long and Marylyn Moore, but attacks on Tracy Browne and Marcella Claxton remained absent. Olive's response was unequivocal when detectives called her before the news was made public: 'He is a coward. Something must have happened in his life to put him off women, but things happen to a lot of men and they never do anything like this. He has ruined my life.'[14]

The attack had a profound effect on Olive's family. Rumours that Harry Smelt had carried out the attack on his wife abounded, leaving their daughter Julie filled with anger and Linda finding it almost impossible to bear. Stephen Smelt developed a compulsion for checking the locks whenever his mother was home to ensure her safety. One reporter asked Harry how he felt about his wife working as a prostitute. Olive struggled to cope with this and many other untruths almost as much as the physical consequences of the attack: 'Everywhere I went, I felt I was being stared at. It got to the stage when I wondered how I was ever going to walk down the street again and that's when I began to wonder if I would have been better off dead.'[15]

Harry strove to support his wife as she became withdrawn and depressed; on one occasion she struck him. 'The mental scars are still there and always will be,' he reflected. 'I remember my wife as full of energy and enjoying a night out with her friends. Now she rarely goes out.'[16] Olive agreed that she had 'lost interest in everything. One of the first things to happen was that I couldn't stand a man near me. I just rejected my husband completely. If he made any sort of advance, well, I just shuddered in horror … I could not bear to be near a man or even look at one without feeling funny. I just could not stand men and I know it sounds horrible but sometimes I would look at my own husband sitting there. My mind used to play all sorts of tricks.'[17] She refused psychiatric help and medication, overcoming her fears by taking a cleaning job at a men's hostel 'so that I would be forced to see men, to talk to them, help them and mix with them. I am glad that I did. I am still not back to normal. I don't think I ever will be, but at least it's a major step.'[18]

Journalist Christa Ackroyd witnessed Olive's battles first-hand over a thirty-year friendship. 'I was eighteen years old,' Christa recalls. 'And had just begun working for the *Halifax Evening Courier*. It was obvious very quickly that as a female reporter my job would be to report on fluffy dogs and ruby weddings. All the serious stuff – the attacks – were the domain of the crime reporter, who was of course a man.'[19] Christa fought to cover the bigger stories and succeeded, meeting Olive in the process: 'When she first saw me, she said, "Oh! A woman – that makes a change." She was very bright, very sharp in that way that northern women are. The first thing she did was to grab my hand and put it onto the back of her head, saying, "Feel that – that's what he did to me." It was a sort of challenge in a way, a test from her.'[20] Christa's fingertips touched the appalling physical legacy of the attack. 'Her skull was caved in at the back. She had lots of hair though, and every single week without fail she would go to her local salon to have it backcombed so that nobody could see the damage. Every week.'[21]

While Olive's children felt deeply protective towards her, the psychological fallout for those sons and daughters whose mothers did not survive took a different form. Three years after Wilma MacCann's murder, her eight-year-old son Richard believed it was up to him to avenge her death: 'I wanted to kill random males and fantasized about attacking them from behind with a hammer. In my mind, they represented society as a whole and ultimately everything around me that had caused my mother's untimely and violent departure.'[22] He fantasized about committing the murders in a pattern, so that when police began plotting them on a map, they would form the letter 'R' for 'Richard' and 'Ripper'. At the same time, the idea that his mother's killer might return forced him into an abject state of terror: 'I was petrified this man was going to kill me. I was walking around with that for years. I was convinced that "he knows where we're living now", and I can remember being petrified at going into the kitchen on an evening – I imagined him appearing at the window, out in the garden.'[23]

In practical terms, the inclusion of other crimes in the series meant adding the relevant paperwork to the Millgarth Incident Room, where the floor had to be reinforced to bear the weight of so much documentation. More than two hundred officers of the West Yorkshire Police continued to be permanently engaged on the inquiry, and another fifty in Manchester. The official cost of the inquiry was around £2 million; in November 1978, West Yorkshire Police themselves increased the reward to £20,000 for information leading to the killer's arrest. Chief Constable Gregory declared: 'We will be pressing on and on and we will get this man in the end. You don't think in terms of how much money it is costing, or as some people might put it, the fact that all but one of these women were prostitutes. They were members of society. I can honestly say there is a burning keenness to solve this mystery – and we will.'[24]

JOSEPHINE

The covert monitoring of red-light districts in West Yorkshire was extended to Manchester, Sheffield and Hull in summer 1978. Denise Cavanagh, then a WPC based in Manchester, recalls that the volume of traffic overwhelmed resources: 'Two of us would go out together in our little cars to observe vehicles. At first, we had to record the results on paper – one of you would call out the number and the other would write it down. But there were too many cars passing through and we didn't have time to get them all jotted down. So then we were given hand-held tape recorders, but that wasn't much better. There were loads of punters and it was really hard to keep track.'[1] Results were checked against the Police National Computer database, and if a vehicle was identified in two separate red-light districts, the driver would receive a visit from detectives.

Senior police officers admitted being exasperated that women were still soliciting on the streets where attacks had taken place. Most sex workers felt they had no choice but to continue, either because the men who ran them demanded it, or to support their families, or to feed an addiction – the reasons were many. Nineteen-year-old Sasha worked the same patch as the Rytka twins in Huddersfield and was fatalistic about the killer: 'If I get him, I get him and that's all there is to it. No one would miss me, only my young son, Justin, who is the only one I work and care for. I'm afraid of him, but I'm more afraid of going into prison. I couldn't stand it.'[2] She relied on alcohol to get her through every encounter at the flat she shared with another sex worker, charging £10 for ten minutes. Most of her clients were married: 'A lot of men think only about their own satisfaction. They are like animals.'[3]

Bradford police made some attempt to promote safer working practices among prostitutes, which included the advice 'not to work when drunk, to work in pairs, to note down the registration numbers of each other's clients'.[4] The city introduced the first approved 'tolerance zone', permitting women to solicit without fear of arrest. Officers wearing plain clothes and in unmarked cars monitored sex workers while recording client registration numbers. Some viewed it as a cynical ploy on the part of the police, who seemed less concerned with protecting the women and more interested in using them as 'live bait'.[5] The designated approved area was small, forcing women to stand in clusters and thereby leading to a drop in business. Sex workers outside the region turned up after hearing about the scheme, which added to the problem of overcrowding.

According to one media report, a number of women working in prostitution relocated to Europe. In 'Good Time Girls Flee Shadow of the Ripper', a girl named Patricia described how she had left Chapeltown to earn more money dancing in a Zurich night club, returning home once a month to visit her two toddlers: 'I used to get £18 a week from the Social Security. Take £10 from that [for bills, etc.] and you don't have much left to look after yourself and two kids. You just have to get money and hustling is the easiest, quickest way of doing it.'[6] Women who stayed working the streets sought new ways to protect themselves. 'Dotty' had been a sex worker since she was fifteen years old; then in her thirties, she had never felt the need for a weapon until the attacks, but had recently begun carrying scissors in her handbag. She was part of a group of women who had asked police whether they could carry mace, and were refused because it was classed as an offensive weapon. 'I think they thought we might blast the odd client and roll him if we had tear gas,' Dotty said wryly. 'One copper said why didn't we carry sticks? Sticks! I ask you. I mean, who's going to pick a girl up if she's carrying a fucking big stick?'[7]

The rigorous monitoring of sex workers and their clients clearly had an effect on the killer himself who realized red-light areas were now too dangerous for him. With the exception of the woman with him at the time of his arrest, none of the killer's acknowledged victims or survivors from 1979 onwards worked as prostitutes or were passing through known red-light districts. Some sex workers suspected that this led to increased reluctance among authorities for the creation of safe areas in the future.

The first attack following the implementation of the scheme took place in Halifax. Josephine Anne Whitaker was born there in December 1959, one month before her parents ended their marriage. For the next four years, she and her mother Avril lived in a terraced house on Huddersfield Road with Avril's parents, Tom and Mary Priestly. Avril eventually married local builder Haydn Hiley. The couple, together with Avril's children, Josephine and younger brothers Michael and David, moved into 10 Ivy Street, a smart terrace in the Bell Hall area, close to the popular recreation spot of Savile Park.

From early childhood, Josephine loved the outdoors. As a teenager at Highlands School she was a rare 'all-rounder', proficient academically and at sports; weekends were spent riding at Norland Moor stables. Josephine's only serious boyfriend remembered her as a 'confident and fearless' sixteen-year-old, tall, slim and brunette, with a ready smile.[8] Craig Midgeley was one year older, and got chatting to her on a local bus. For a while, they were inseparable and Craig frequently accompanied Josephine to her grandparents' home. 'They were very, very special to Josephine,' he recalls. 'She loved them deeply. During the two years I went out with her, we went there to tea every Sunday. You could see there was a very special bond between them. She loved all her family and they all made me feel very welcome.'[9]

Josephine's 'great love of life' was what he remembered most about her: 'She really enjoyed meeting people and was very popular with a lot of friends. There was nothing she liked more than a night out in Halifax among people. She was an outgoing girl who liked all the things a normal girl of nineteen likes – dancing, clothes and having fun.'[10] They were engaged for a few months, but Craig was less keen than Josephine to marry young and have children. In May 1978, they split up. She focused on work and was rewarded with a rise in wages and promotion as a clerk at the Halifax Building Society's head office in town. A part-time job as a barmaid at the Tower House Hotel in Master Lane brought in a little extra money too.

Wednesday 4 April 1979 started well. As a treat to herself, Josephine had ordered a silver cocktail watch from a catalogue. It was delivered to her workplace, where she slipped it happily onto her wrist, but her mother was unimpressed when she showed it off at home; £65 seemed an unnecessary extravagance. Avril remarked on the value of money, adding that the filter in Josephine's fish tank cost more than she realized to run. 'I'll get rid of it then!' Josephine retorted before heading for her room, where she fumed for the better part of an hour before deciding to visit her grandparents, who could always be relied on to support her regardless of the situation. She changed out of her work clothes, slipping a leather hacking jacket over a pink top and multi-coloured skirt with a lace hem, then set out for Huddersfield Road.

Twenty minutes later, her grandfather, Tom, greeted her warmly, glad to have company while Mary was at a party across the road in St Andrew's Methodist Church. They sat down together to watch the news, where the lead story concerned the execution of the deposed Prime Minister of Pakistan. Josephine remarked that no one deserved such a fate.

'What about the Yorkshire Ripper?' Tom asked.

'He doesn't deserve to be killed either,' she replied firmly.[11]

Mary arrived home at 11 p.m. She admired her granddaughter's watch, told her not to worry about the silly row with her mother, and asked if she wanted to stay the night in her old room, given the late hour. But Josephine explained that she was wearing contact lenses and had left the little storage barrel for them at home. Tom offered to accompany her on the walk back, but Josephine wouldn't hear of it, especially since he suffered with emphysema.

It was 11.40 p.m. when she left, crossing the road to Dryclough Lane, then Skircoat Moor Road before cutting across the park. Wainhouse Tower, a nineteenth-century folly, loomed in the distance through a light rain. The area was fairly well-lit and populated with dog walkers and late night visitors to the Refreshment House.

Around midnight, a man passing through the park heard a sharp and eerie sound. It was, he said afterwards, 'the type of noise that makes your hair stand on end'.[12] He squinted in the direction of the cry and thought he saw a figure but could not be certain. He listened for a while, but there was only the light patter of rain in the trees. After a moment, he walked on.

Ronald Marwood's shift the following morning saw him drive the first bus of the day along Savile Park Road at 5.30 a.m. As the vehicle trundled past the Refreshment House in the mist he caught a glimpse of something – a bundle – on the grass. Back at the depot, he told his employers about it, expecting them to contact the police but they took no action.

An hour later, Jean Markham, a worker at Rowntree Mackintosh, also spotted something while she waited for her bus on Savile Park Road: 'I thought it was just a bundle of rags until I saw a shoe nearby. I went across the road and was just about to pick up the shoe when I realized someone was lying there.'[13] She rushed home to telephone the police, who arrived soon afterwards. At 7.20 a.m., an officer called the bus depot to request a temporary move for the Savile Park Road stop and learned that Ronald Marwood had tried to inform them earlier.

The hands on Josephine's new watch stopped at precisely that moment, 7.20 a.m. The first policeman on the scene noticed drag marks in the soil and grass from her body to the brown shoe standing upright on the field, twenty yards from Free School Lane. Bloodstains in the same area made him question whether Josephine had been involved in a hit-and-run, crawling to the spot. But the arrival of Detective Superintendent Dick Holland, Assistant Chief Constable George Oldfield and Detective Chief Superintendent Jack Ridgway put an end to speculation: they realized that the young woman concealed behind a hastily produced privacy screen had been murdered by the Ripper.

Thirteen-year-old David Whitaker saw the police gathered by the screen when he cycled by on his paper round. Peddling closer, he squeezed the brakes hard: the single shoe standing upright like a sentinel on the grass belonged to his sister. He rode at speed through the busy streets, throwing down his bike before bursting into the house with a breathless explanation. Josephine's family had assumed that she was in bed, but when Haydn opened the door to his stepdaughter's room, it was empty.

Police turned a young team of lacrosse players away from the Savile Park pitch. While dog handlers patrolled the area, Professor Gee crouched near a path of purple crocuses, next to Josephine's body. Her blood-streaked face and feet were visible, but she had been covered with a blanket, which he drew back carefully. All the signs of a Ripper murder were present: the displaced, blood-soaked clothing, the terrible head injuries and stab wounds – this time to the young woman's breasts, stomach, vagina and thighs. When Detective Chief Superintendent Trevor Lapish spoke to the press later that morning he was cautious nonetheless: 'We will not know the cause of death until after examination later today. It could have been a road accident. There are scuff marks indicating that she might have been dragged and with her being found so close to the road, she might have been dragged from a car across the grass.'[14]

Josephine's body was driven to the mortuary of Halifax Royal Infirmary on Free School Lane. The post-mortem took six hours but yielded new forensic evidence. Minuscule flecks of engineering oil were found in some of Josephine's wounds, along with tiny metal particles from the sharpened point of a weapon which Professor Gee could not identify. There were nine wounds to the front of Josephine's body and twelve to the back, some of which had been penetrated twice. A tiny puncture above her left nipple appeared to be the result of a bite from the killer. Her skull had been fractured by two hammer blows to the back of her head.

When Gee pronounced himself satisfied that the murder was part of the Ripper series, senior detectives made no attempt to hide their dismay. Still exercising caution, Oldfield announced on 5 April: 'If this is connected with the previous Ripper killings, then he has made a terrible mistake. As with Jayne MacDonald, the dead girl is perfectly respectable.'[15]

The following day Oldfield confirmed that the 'mentally deranged' Ripper was responsible and that Josephine's murder marked a dangerous change in pattern because

this girl was perfectly respectable, in an open space and legitimately going about her business. We always felt he would strike again, but we are now faced with a new situation. We cannot stress how careful every woman must be. Unless we catch him, and the public must help us, he will go on and on. This was another particularly brutal and savage attack on an innocent young woman who was most respectable. There are many similarities with other murders of women which we have been actively investigating for the past three and a half years. I have good reason to believe that one man is responsible for all those horrific crimes. Clearly, we have a homicidal maniac at large and I believe he lives in West Yorkshire. I have repeatedly said in the past that this man will continue to kill until he is caught. I am still of that opinion and I am more determined than ever to catch him.[16]

His attitude was shared by senior officers even after the investigation ended; in 1981, Lawrence Byford described Josephine's murder as different because 'the victim was a young woman of good character, murdered in a respectable residential area of the town, and who could not possibly have been looked upon as a prostitute by the murderer'. Police and press had likewise regarded Jayne MacDonald's murder as a 'mistake' on similar terms, but Byford seems to have taken a different view simply because Jayne was killed in Chapeltown and had lived on the nearby Scott Hall estate.

Oldfield urged all women never to walk home alone or accept lifts from strangers. The national press carried similar warnings to those in the following day's *Yorkshire Post*, namely: 'Every woman in the north of England was last night in danger from a maniac police now fear could be on the verge of more shocking attacks. In 42 months, the Yorkshire Ripper has compiled the worst catalogue of horror – eleven murders, four attempted murders, in Yorkshire and Lancashire – that this country has known.'[17] The *Daily Express* announced that previous victims were 'nearly all prostitutes. But not Josephine. She was a respectable working girl. And this change in pattern could prove a mistake by the Ripper and produce vital new clues.'[18] The paper later queried whether Josephine had died 'after the Ripper failed to find the fun girl he had marked down as his next victim' because 'a known prostitute lived near her in Ivy Street'.[19]

Oldfield was aware that the general public reacted more proactively when a victim was regarded as a model of female propriety. The murder of building society clerk Josephine, in a town without a red-light district, bore this out: where previous attacks, with the exception of Jayne MacDonald, had resulted in only a trickle of useful information, now there was a deluge. Within a matter of days, the incident room had taken a thousand calls, as the tangible shock at Josephine's killing continued to reverberate with people who felt they could relate to her. One female reporter recalled: 'We could all see her lying there on the playing field, her face peeping from under the screen the police had covered her with, and I kept thinking, "My God, this could be me or my sister or my mother. This is an ordinary working girl and this is not a red light area."'[20]

A photograph of Josephine lying on the dewy grass as forensic experts bent over her was published in the *Halifax Courier*, which acknowledged the furore in an editorial:

> The picture was used in the knowledge that it would shock. It was used in the hope that the message would be driven home that it is unsafe for women to be out late at night unaccompanied, that it may help in speeding justice. Use of the picture was not for "sensationalism" in the sense that has come to be accepted in newspaper terms, as a titillating stimulant for sales, although it was anticipated that something of a sensation may be created. It was an awful picture of yet another awful crime and was seen by the editor, who acknowledges responsibility for its use, as part of the newspaper's duty to impart information. It is a duty which is often distasteful. One that sometimes offends.[21]

Despite the newspaper's defence of its decision, publication and reproduction of the image undermined the previously cordial relationship between police and press, which deteriorated from then onwards.

Easter leave was cancelled for all two hundred and fifty officers engaged in the hunt for the Ripper after Josephine's

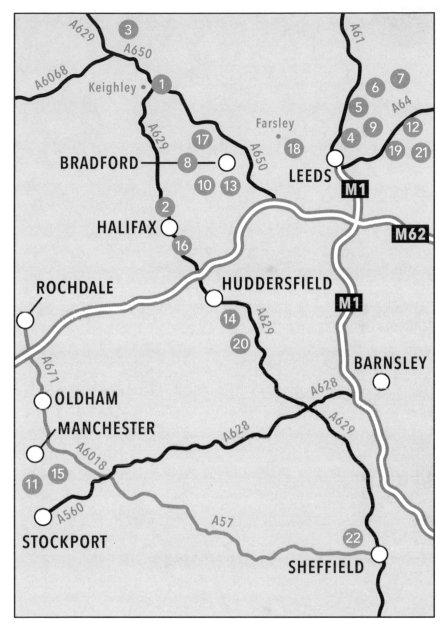

A map of the area where the attacks took place.

1. Anna Rogulskyj
2. Olive Smelt
3. Tracy Browne
4. Wilma McCann
5. Emily Jackson
6. Marcella Claxton
7. Irene Richardson
8. Patricia Atkinson
9. Jayne MacDonald
10. Maureen Long
11. Jean Jordan
12. Marylyn Moore
13. Yvonne Pearson
14. Helen Rytka
15. Vera Millward
16. Josephine Whitaker
17. Barbara Leach
18. Marguerite Walls
19. Upadhya Bandara
20. Theresa Sykes
21. Jacqueline Hill
22. Olivia Reivers

THE RIPPER'S VICTIMS

The victims are habitually presented as a montage of faces. From left to right: Wilma McCann, Joan Harrison (not actually a victim of Sutcliffe), Emily Jackson, Irene Richardson, Patricia Atkinson, Jayne MacDonald, Jean Jordan, Yvonne Pearson, Helen Rytka, Vera Millward, Josephine Whitaker and Barbara Leach. Jacqueline Hill, the last young woman to die at Sutcliffe's hands, is not shown.

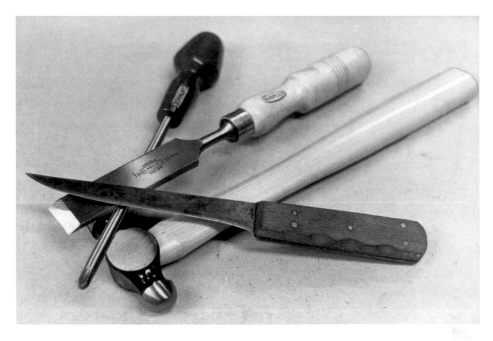

Brutal reality – the tools used by Sutcliffe to mutilate and kill women.

CLOCKWISE: The first three women to survive attacks by the Yorkshire Ripper, all in the summer of 1975: Anna Rogulskyj at the Old Bailey, Olive Smelt at the scene of her attack, and Tracy Browne, who recovered from her encounter aged just fourteen.

ABOVE: Wilma's son and daughters (Richard, Sonia, Angela and Donna), photographed in the children's home a few days after her murder in 1975.

BELOW: Barbara Leach with her beloved dog at home in Kettering.

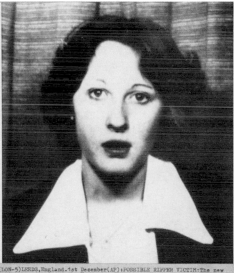

CLOCKWISE FROM THE TOP LEFT: Survivors Marcella Claxton,
Marylyn Moore, Theresa Sykes and Upadhya Bandara.

Josephine Whitaker crime scene in Halifax. Josephine's body is visible in the background to the far right of the photo. Her shoe is in the foreground.

Barbara Leach crime scene, Bradford 1979.

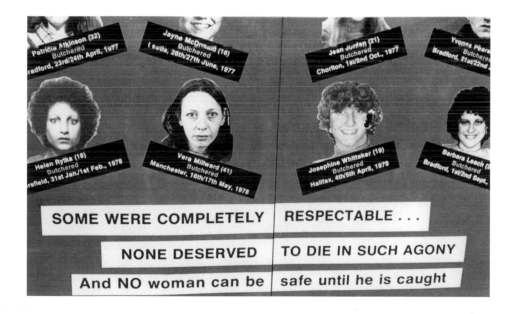

ABOVE: 'Flush Out The Ripper' campaign boards were displayed in shopping centres and other public places from late 1979.

LEFT: Survivor Maureen Long listens to the broadcast of the 'Wearside Jack' tape in 1979.

RIGHT: Olivia Reivers narrowly escaped murder; she was with Sutcliffe when two police officers questioned him about the false number plates on his car. She testified against the killer at the Old Bailey in May 1981, helping to put him behind bars.

To put that person in the agony and the pain that I was in.

ABOVE: Survivor Mo Lea contemplates the artwork that formed part of her long recovery process. Shown here in the film *Facing Evil*, directed and produced by Roberto Duque, Mo still waits for the authorities to officially recognize that the man who attempted to kill her was Peter Sutcliffe.

death. The temporary relocation to Halifax of the Millgarth inquiry team stemmed the processing of all outstanding actions while officers conducted house-to-house enquiries and evaluated evidence from the crime scene. Footprints in the mud near Josephine's body had been made by a size-seven industrial boot, similar to that found at the crime scenes of Emily Jackson and Patricia Atkinson. It was subsequently established that a person taking a size eight-and-a-half shoe could also comfortably wear the boots, but there was a clear pattern of wear to the right print, suggesting a manual worker. The evidence regarding the substances found in Josephine's wounds supported the possibility that the killer operated machinery as part of his job. Gee spent several months trying to track down the sort of instrument that had been used to inflict the wounds. An engineer's scraper, used to clear bores on piston engines, was the closest match.

The man who had broken off his walk after hearing a chilling cry near the Refreshment House on the night of Josephine's murder came forward. He described the sound as 'a laugh or a wail' and was sure he had seen a figure or two at the spot where Josephine's body was found the following morning. The couple who ran the Refreshment House informed Oldfield that they had heard a woman's footsteps running into the toilet at the back of the lodge between 12.10 a.m. and 12.15 a.m. on the night of Josephine's murder. A dog walker recalled seeing a woman who resembled Josephine strolling with a bearded man in Manor Heath Road around 11.40 p.m. Police also interviewed a hundred and fifty members of the Bradford Pennine Insurance Sports and Social Club, who had attended a party at Standeven House off Broomfield Avenue that same evening. One of the guests had seen a man running at speed across nearby Savile Park around 1.15 a.m. that night, but he was never traced.

Detectives sought to track down the drivers of three cars in the area at the relevant time: a dark, dirty Ford Escort saloon parked on the grass between the Refreshment House and Skircoat Moor Road; a dark-coloured Datsun, possibly an estate, parked in Free School Lane at the junction with Moorfield Street; and a new style orange or tan-coloured Rover, parked on Savile Park Road outside the café just after midnight. The Ford Escort had been linked to an incident in the town centre around 9 p.m., when a woman walking towards a bus stop was propositioned by a man driving the same make of car. Her reaction caused the man to accelerate away, but she provided sufficient detail for a photofit, which featured in the *Yorkshire Evening Post* on 9 April and afterwards in the national press. The driver was described as a scruffy white male, about thirty years old, averagely built, with blond curly hair, a square jaw and 'Jason King'-style moustache. This last detail rang a bell with the Ripper inquiry team: Marylyn Moore had also described her attacker as having a 'Jason King' moustache. Despite the lighter coloured hair, the Halifax photofit bore a strong resemblance to that produced by Marylyn, who insisted after seeing it: 'That's the man who attacked me. I still dream about that swine. I still live in fear of that man. I must have come back from the dead after he attacked me. He has the same eyes, eyebrows, nose – the face is the same. It's the same guy.'[22]

Josephine's mother and stepfather were too distressed to speak to the press initially, but eventually Haydn Hiley told reporters that Josephine must have ignored their warnings never to cross the park at night, although 'she was a tall girl and capable of looking after herself. I'm sure she would have put up a struggle against this monster, if it had been at all possible ... I don't hate anyone, but I think I should. I would just like everyone to try and help catch this man.'[23] Josephine's grandparents wept openly when reporters turned up on their doorstep and her ex-fiancé took time off work, describing himself and his colleagues as 'absolutely shattered by her death'.[24]

Josephine was remembered at the Palm Sunday service in St Jude's Church, where she had attended Sunday School. Her brother Michael had been a choir boy there, and attended the service with their younger brother David. Reverend Michael Walker asked the congregation to hold everyone affected by her death in their prayers – even her killer, who 'needs help. He is someone's child, husband or father. Most probably he will be a quiet, ordinary, well-loved person who is somehow triggered off. In one accepted term, he is in need of help. Pray not only for Josephine and her family but for the Ripper and his family.'[25] Josephine's stepfather thanked everyone for their 'kind thoughts' but had no comment to make about Reverend Walker's plea on behalf of her killer.[26]

Following a private burial, more than five hundred people joined a memorial service for Josephine, where the lesson was read by the chairman of the Halifax Building Society. Jayne MacDonald's mother Irene had wept when she read of Josephine's death and extended sympathy towards her family: 'I pray for them and I pray this killer will be caught. I just keep hoping and praying that if there is a God this monster will be caught and will be stopped from doing these terrible things. But I cannot take the same attitude as Josephine's [step]father, who has said he has no hate for the killer. I hate the Ripper, whoever he is, for what he did to Jayne and to our family. I would find some way of killing him myself if he was caught.'[27] Wilf MacDonald's health had declined following their daughter's murder; he suffered with severe nervous asthma and would never be able to work again. 'No one can ever know what it's like when your child is murdered,' Irene mused. 'For those they left behind there will never be any peace again. A murder doesn't just end with the victim. It spreads hideous ripples throughout a family. In its way, it kills them all.'[28]

17

BARBARA

Sergeant Megan Winterburn popped on the headphones. Sitting at a desk in Millgarth Police Station, she pressed 'play' on the tape recorder. Revolving spools hissed and the man's slow, deliberate voice intoned: 'I'm Jack. I see you are still having no luck catching me ...'

Two years earlier, Sergeant Winterburn had accompanied Maureen Long around Bradford in an attempt to find her attacker; now she sat transcribing a tape purporting to contain his voice. The more she listened, the more sinister it became. 'It made hairs stand up on the back of my neck,' she recalls. 'It was horrible, a real low point for me.'[1]

The recording had landed on Assistant Chief Constable George Oldfield's desk that morning. He had asked Sergeant Winterburn to produce a transcript, rather than entrusting it to one of the civilian typists. She took shorthand notes first to make sure she missed nothing, then typed it all up. 'I felt sick to the pit of my stomach,' she reflects. 'Just the thought that it might actually be this man's voice, instead of being elated, made my stomach churn.'[2]

The tape recording was the fourth communication from the same sender in Sunderland since March 1978. A letter addressed to 'Chief Constable George Oldfield, Central Police Station, Leeds, West Yorkshire' was the first. Written in a spiky, forward-slanting hand on lined notepaper it read:

Dear Sir,

I am sorry I cannot give you my name for obvious reasons i am the ripper. Ive been dubbed a maniac by the press but not by you You call me clever and I am. You and your mates havent a clue That photo in the paper gave me fits and that lot about killing myself no chance. Ive got thing to do, My purpose to rid the streets of them sluts. mu one regret his that young lassie Macdonald did not know cause changed routine that nite, Up to number 8 now you say 7 but remember Preston 75, Get about you know, you were right I travel a bit You probably look for me in Sunderland don't bother I am not daft, just posted letter there on one of my trips. Not a bad place compared with Chapeltown and Manningham and other places

Warn whores to keep of streets cause I feel it coming on again. Sorry about young lassie.

Yours respectfully
Jack the Ripper

Might write again later I am not sure last one really deserved it. Whores getting younger each time. Old slut next time I hope, Huddersfield never again too small close call last one.

A second letter, using similar phrasing, arrived at the *Daily Mirror* offices in Manchester later that month. Both were postmarked 'Sunderland' and neither bore any fingerprints from the criminal database.

Several people had made obviously fraudulent claims about being the Ripper, but there was something about the Sunderland writer's tone that struck Oldfield as plausible. He was further persuaded by the reference to Joan Harrison, mistakenly believing there had never been any public mention at that stage of a possible link between the Preston murder and the Ripper attacks. In reality, the *Yorkshire Post* had made the connection only one day after the discovery of Irene Richardson's body in February 1977: 'Mr Hobson also plans to examine the file on the murder of a prostitute found battered to death in Preston in November 1975 … because of striking similarities.'[3] Hobson had indeed liaised with Lancashire CID about the matter, but Oldfield was unaware of it.

Nor did he grasp that the letter writer had failed to include the murder of Yvonne Pearson while gloating over the number of victims. Although Yvonne's body was not found until a fortnight after the letter arrived, she had been missing since January, weeks before. The only reason for him not to mention her murder was if he had no knowledge of it. But neither Oldfield nor Holland – who was similarly persuaded – took those issues on board. As a result, writer Joan Smith points out, 'the inquiry began to head inexorably for disaster'.[4]

Both men mistook tradition for authenticity: the anonymous correspondent not only signed his letters 'Jack the Ripper', he mimicked the original in taunting the police about their inability to catch him, in contacting the press, in warning of future murders, in the tone of his writing, and in claiming to loathe prostitutes.

Oldfield sent copies of both letters to detectives in Northumberland, asking if they could shed any light on the sender. They were unable to assist, and with insufficient evidence to pursue 'Wearside Jack', the letters were filed away until the *Daily Mirror* exclusively revealed their existence on 25 February 1979. Oldfield gave credence to the letters by telling the press that the handwriting has been analysed by a graphologist who 'confirmed many of the impressions we have about the man we are looking for'.[5] His words inspired the hoaxer, who wrote again on 23 March 1979:

Dear Officer,
Sorry I havn't written, about a year to be exact but I havn't been up North for quite a while. I was'nt kidding

last time I wrote saying the whore would be older this time and maybe I'd strike in Manchester for a change. You should have took heed. That bit about her being in hospital, funny the lady mentioned something about being in the same hospital before I stopped her whoring ways. The lady wont worry about hospitals now will she I bet you are wondering how come I hav'nt been to work for ages, well I would have been if it hadnt been for your curserred coppers I had the lady just where I wanted her and was about to strike when one of your cursen police cars stopped right outside the land, he must have been a dumn copper cause he didn't say anything, he didnt know how close he was to catching me. Tell you the truth I thought I was collared, the lady said dont worry about coppers, little did she know that bloody copper saved her neck. That was last month, so I don't know when I will get back on the job but I know it wont be Chapeltown too bloody hot there maybe Bradfords Manningham. Might write again if up north.

Jack the Ripper

PS Did you get letter I sent to *Daily Mirror* in Manchester.

Oldfield was more convinced than ever that this was the man they were hunting. In the previous letter, the writer mentioned hoping to kill an 'old slut next time', and although Vera Millward was far from elderly at forty-one, she was twice the age of the two women whose deaths had preceded hers: Yvonne Pearson and Helen Rytka. A second reference to Vera having received treatment in the hospital where her body was found further swayed Oldfield; again, he and Holland believed the killer could only have known about Vera's operations from her, but both Detective Chief Superintendent Jack Ridgway and Vera's partner had told local reporters about her hospital visits. The *Daily Mail* had also mentioned it in their coverage of the murder.

There was more significance as far as Oldfield and Holland were concerned. Following receipt of the third letter, analysis of saliva on the envelope seal showed it belonged to someone from the 'B' secretor blood group – and Joan Harrison's killer had been identified as a 'B' secretor. Scientists found oil on one of the envelopes, similar to the milling oil detected in Josephine Whitaker's wounds. Taking all that into account, Oldfield threw himself into the investigation afresh, despite his ailing health.

The tape recording arrived in June 1979, two months after Josephine's death. 'Jack the Ripper' was scrawled on the underside seal of the envelope and again the saliva present belonged to a 'B' secretor. Oldfield sent for a tape recorder and listened as the flat, unmistakably north-eastern voice rolled out:

I'm Jack. I see you are still having no luck catching me. I have the greatest respect for you, George, but Lord, you are no nearer catching me now than four years ago when I started. I reckon your boys are letting you down, George. You can't be much good, can you? The only time they came near catching me was a few months back in Chapeltown, when I was disturbed. Even then it was a uniformed copper, not a detective.

I warned you in March that I'd strike again. Sorry it wasn't Bradford. I did promise you that, but I couldn't get there. I'm not quite sure when I'll strike again, but it will definitely be sometime this year, maybe September or October, even sooner if I get the chance. I'm not sure where, maybe Manchester; I like it there, there's plenty of them knocking about. They never learn, do they, George? I bet you've warned them, but they never listen.

At the rate I'm going, I should be in the book of records. I think it's eleven up to now, isn't it? Well, I'll keep on going for quite a while yet. I can't see myself being nicked just yet. Even if you do get near, I'll probably top myself first.

Well, it's been nice chatting to you, George.

Yours, Jack the Ripper.

No good looking for fingerprints, you should know by now it's as clean as a whistle. See you soon. Bye. Hope you like the catchy tune at the end. Ha-ha.

A short segment of Andrew Gold's minor UK chart hit, 'Thank You for Being a Friend' followed.

Oldfield consulted other senior officers about releasing the tape publicly and called a press conference in Wakefield on 26 June 1979 to play the recording. There was an awkward interlude when he couldn't operate the tape recorder and Holland had to step in, but then the lugubrious voice rang out in a hushed room: 'I'm Jack. I see you are still having no luck catching me ...' Afterwards, Oldfield maintained that they were now closing in on the killer and had identified the specific region associated with his accent. Reporters pointed out that the Black Panther had duped detectives into believing he had a West Midlands accent when in fact he hailed from Bradford. But Oldfield was obstinate in his refusal to concede that the letters and tape might be an elaborate hoax.

The tape was broadcast on national television and radio that evening. West Yorkshire Police also set up a free telephone hotline that allowed callers to listen to the tape; almost a million people rang the number during the time it was available. The hotline was part of a colossal publicity campaign in the North and North-East aimed at drawing attention to the letters and tape. Together with a Leeds-based advertising agency, West Yorkshire Police established 'Project R Designers', for which distributors and photographers worked free of charge. The collaboration produced six thousand posters displayed in six hundred locations with the grab line: 'The Ripper would like you to ignore this. The man next to you may have killed twelve women.' Newsagents gave away two million copies of a four-page leaflet featuring excerpts from the letters and a transcript of the tape recording, which was played everywhere from bingo halls to shopping centres and on radio and television several times a day.

Listening to the recording was an unsettling experience for anyone, but it was deeply disturbing for those women who had survived the attacks and for victims' relatives. The latter believed they were hearing their loved one's murderer glorying in his autonomy to kill while the former realized how far the police had travelled down the wrong path. Tracy Browne recalls: 'My mum got a phone call from George Oldfield, wanting to come and see me, to listen to a tape of a Geordie man. I listened to the tape and he said, "Does this sound like the guy that attacked you?" I said, "No, because he wasn't a Geordie. He was definitely Yorkshire." He kept saying, "Are you sure he wasn't Geordie?" And I said, "Yes, I'm sure." I said, "I know who I spoke to for those thirty minutes. His voice is imprinted in my mind." There was no comparison. There was no doubt in my mind that the police had got this one wrong. It was frustrating.'[6] Marylyn agreed: 'I had to listen to this tape over and over again. But I knew he wasn't the Ripper. Because he didn't sound like that, he had a Yorkshire accent.'[7]

Wilma McCann's children were enjoying bottles of pop and bags of crisps at a Liberal Club with their uncle Isaac one Sunday afternoon when they heard the tape recording for the first time. It was one of the most powerful events of Richard's childhood: 'I thought, "My God, that's the man that killed my mum. That's the man that I think is going to kill me." That chilling recording has remained with me ever since.'[8] His sister Sonia recalled: 'We listened for that voice. Every man that spoke. We listened for that voice.'[9]

The *Yorkshire Post* ran a perceptive feature just one day after the tape was first broadcast to the nation, reflecting on the obvious care taken by the sender to imitate the Victorian killer by referring to the original 'Dear Boss' letter of September 1888. In Sunderland, Detective Inspector David Zackrisson had noticed the similarities. He juxtaposed the modern letters with the nineteenth-century missives and studied contemporary newspaper reports to find out which details of each case had been published. West Yorkshire Chief Constable Ronald Gregory acknowledged Zackrisson's research in his memoirs: 'He studied every newspaper article written about our inquiry and proved that everything in the letters could have been gleaned from them. He also compared the phraseology and vocabulary used by the 1888 Ripper and again found striking similarities.'[10] Among the immediate parallels was the modern-day line, 'That photo in the paper gave me fits ...' and the Victorian killer's remark: 'That joke about Leather Apron gave me real fits ...' Zackrisson concluded that the letter writer was nothing more than a malicious hoaxer who had immersed himself in the Ripper myth and craved publicity.

'This is the terrible mistake, the appalling blunder, that lies at the heart of the case,' writer Joan Smith observed. Oldfield remained blindly certain that the letter writer was genuine, a conviction that stemmed as much from the hoaxer having appealed to the assistant chief constable's vanity as from the content of his communications. Oldfield believed the most wanted man in the country had a personal interest in him, thus acting out that staple of crime fiction: a war of wits between detective and villain. 'I would like to talk to this man,' Oldfield declared at a press conference after the tape recording aired. 'And I feel he wants to talk to me. This has become something of a feud. He obviously wants to outwit me, but I won't pack it in until he's caught.'[11] He and his fellow detectives were as entrenched in the Jack the Ripper myth as the Sunderland letter writer, leading them to believe that they 'knew' the killer and would recognize him instinctively. In 1978, a senior Manchester police officer remarked that the killer could not have been interviewed yet because 'I am positive we will realize and nail him'.[12] Two years later, Oldfield confirmed: 'If we had twenty or thirty suspects in one room we would know very quickly which one was the Ripper.'[13]

The horrifying extent of their assumptions would only fully emerge after the investigation. For the time being, the inquiry continued to be derailed, shunted off track by a hoax whose authenticity lay merely in tradition: master criminal versus master detective, elevating both parties at unfathomable cost to women everywhere.

Barbara Janine Leach was born in the Northamptonshire town of Kettering on 5 January 1959. Her brother Graham, always known as 'Crow' to Barbara, was two years older.

The Leaches lived on Hazel Road in a comfortable semi-detached house close to Henry Gotch Primary School and Southfield Girls' School; Barbara was a pupil at both. Her mother Beryl worked at Henry Gotch, while David Leach was employed at Barclays in town. They were a close family, and Barbara missed her brother when he left for Cambridge University in 1974. Arriving home at the end of his first term, he told them about the fear on campus generated by the 'Cambridge Rapist'. Barbara had read about the attacks and demands for the perpetrator to hang. 'She was absolutely against it,' Graham recalled. 'So are all the family.'[14]

Graham's post-graduate career took him to Hampshire on a permanent basis, but he remained in frequent contact with his parents and sister, now a slim brunette in her teens. Barbara was passionate about animal welfare, lavishing attention on her own cat and dog, and loved horse-riding, funded by a Saturday job at Boots. She achieved high grades in A level English and Religious Knowledge, giving her a choice of universities. Graham recalled that her decision to read Social Psychology at Bradford was influenced by her 'totally cosmopolitan type of feminism' and desire to mix with 'real' people after growing up in middle England.[15] Barbara loved the city and her studies, returning to work in Kettering between terms – first at the local Prime Cut processing plant and then at a handbag manufacturer's in nearby Desborough. She saved enough money to travel abroad with a friend in summer 1979, flying out to Greece and Italy and planning to visit Crete the following year.

The final year of Barbara's degree course started on 1 October 1979. She returned to her student digs that summer to study for her finals. Her parents had always worried about the attacks on women in the north of England, especially given Barbara's predilection for late night walks in the rain. 'We had all talked about the Ripper,' her father said. 'But we felt safe in the knowledge that when she went out at night, Barbara would always walk with a friend. We all thought it would never happen to us. Barbara was pretty strong and could give a good account of herself. Once, when she had an argument with her elder brother, she playfully hit him – and practically floored him.'[16] Beryl prayed that her daughter would be safe: 'She was at that stage where she was becoming independent. We were at the stage of entering a new phase of our relationship. It was because of her I had my ears pierced and things like that.'[17] She knew that Barbara 'didn't feel unsafe or worried about it. She thought she was in a comparatively safe area.'[18] But for Beryl and her husband David, 'the terrible murders in Yorkshire were always at the backs of our minds'.[19]

Barbara rented an attic room on Grove Terrace, in the heart of student Bradford and a short walk from the campus across Great Horton Road. She shared a property with four boys and two girls who knew her as Babs, 'a fun-loving girl'.[20] Lecturer Tony Oxley spoke on behalf of Barbara's tutors when he described her as 'a cheerful girl with a pleasant personality whom it was a pleasure to teach'.[21] A keen student who loved socializing, she had also joined a riding club affiliated to the student union. Once a week she caught a bus to the village of Tong, four miles south-east of the city, where Raikes Hall Riding School was situated. Janet Hanson, who ran the stable with her mother, remembered Barbara was 'an experienced rider. She talked a great deal about horses and riding but not much about her home life. She was quiet but friendly and I liked her.'[22] A gentle, eight-year-old grey mare was Barbara's first choice: 'She was always good to Dina, rubbing her down after every ride. Dina became her favourite horse. She had ridden others but for some reason she liked Dina most of all.'[23]

In August, Barbara's parents visited and she introduced them to the stray kitten she and her housemate Lynne had found in a nearby street. Barbara adopted him as her own, giving him the moniker 'J.C.' in honour of the Lancastrian punk poet John Cooper Clarke. It was the last time Beryl and David ever saw their daughter. 'I can remember waving goodbye to her,' Beryl said years later, struggling to speak through the memory. 'She was standing just against the low wall in front of the house. And that was it ...'[24]

Barbara's father, David, celebrated his birthday on Saturday 1 September. Barbara was mortified when she realized she had forgotten to post a card and ran to the nearest phone box to call home. She promised to deliver the card herself on Monday, when she expected to arrive home for a week's holiday. She said goodbye after asking her mother, Beryl, to make her an appointment at the hairdressers, then headed for the shops to buy a birthday present before returning to Grove Terrace.

It was a beautiful late summer's day; Barbara's attic room was stuffy that afternoon. Most of the sash windows along the terrace had been pushed open, letting in the smells of cooking and joss sticks. A party was planned for that evening in a ground-floor flat on Ash Grove. It was only a few streets away, but she had already made plans to visit her local pub with friends.

The heat became cloying after dark. Barbara got ready to go out, slipping into a beige cheesecloth blouse, blue jeans, and knee-length red leather boots. She did her hair and make-up, throwing an army surplus haversack over her shoulder, then went downstairs.

Six students headed out together: Barbara, her twenty-one-year-old flatmate Paul Smith, and four others, including a lad named Stephen Greenough, who lived in the house on Ash Grove where the party was being held. They walked to the Manville Arms on the junction of Great Horton Road where Barbara put her name down for a game of darts and enjoyed a steak and kidney pie with two pints of cider. The jukebox belted out chart hits: The Police, Tubeway Army, Thin Lizzy and the current number one from the Boomtown Rats: 'I Don't Like Mondays'. 'We had a good night there,' Paul remembered.[25] Their group stayed behind to help the landlord clean up and were rewarded with free drinks. It was quarter to one when they emerged into the street, where a steady rain had begun to fall.

There was some discussion about whether to visit a favourite Indian restaurant that stayed open until 2 a.m., but home won out. As they neared Grove Terrace, Barbara decided that she fancied a walk and asked Paul to wait up; she had lost her house keys two days before, and her best friend had the spare set. Paul tried to change her mind but she assured him she'd be no time at all and with a wave, turned away.

The party on Ash Grove was in full swing as Paul waited, listening to faint laughter and thumping music. When Barbara failed to appear, he assumed she had gone to the party and went up to bed, leaving the door on the latch.

Barbara did not return that night. The following morning, Paul got in touch with her best friend, twenty-two-year-old social science student Gabrielle Rhodes. She hadn't seen Barbara since Friday and wasn't expecting to see her again until Monday, when they had arranged to meet for lunch before Barbara went home to Kettering. The news that Barbara was missing spread rapidly, and when the Manville Arms opened its doors again at midday, Paul and Stephen contacted the police.

The response was immediate; officers spoke to Barbara's friends and told Gabrielle to keep her appointment the following day because she might turn up, but the possibility faded as the hours wore on.

At 8 p.m., the telephone rang in the Leaches' home. David got up from his chair in front of the television, turning down the sound on *The Onedin Line*. 'A voice asked if Barbara was here,' he recalled. 'I said, "No, she comes home on Monday." I was just going to say I would take a message for her when the policeman told me she had gone for a late night walk and had not returned.'[26] In the silence that followed David replacing the receiver, Beryl's mind began to race; she pictured her daughter 'being held somewhere. And I thought "Oh, she won't have her glasses with her." She wouldn't be able to see where she was or – just all sorts of things. That she wouldn't be able to escape. That she wanted me and I couldn't get to her.'[27] After a sleepless night, David drove to work. Beryl was not due at school until Tuesday and stayed next to the telephone with her brother, Les Larkman, joining her in the afternoon.

At 12.30 p.m., Gabrielle arrived at Bradford Interchange and waited thirty minutes. Pinning her hopes on Barbara getting confused about their arrangements, she then walked to the Shoulder of Mutton pub where they had met the previous Friday. Gabrielle waited another half an hour, but

> once it was past 1.30 I knew she wasn't going to come. I knew something was gravely wrong. At the back of my mind was the thought of the Ripper. I couldn't get Barbara out of my mind all afternoon and couldn't concentrate. I went back to Barbara's flat and let myself in – Barbara had given me a key. There was no one in the house but J.C. – Barbara's kitten. I went home and tried to take my mind off what might have happened to

Barbara. My boyfriend told me to go out for a drink to stop me worrying. About 9 p.m. on Monday evening I telephoned my mother and she told me that a body had been found. I knew that it just had to be Barbara.[28]

The police search had begun around Great Horton Road, working outwards from Grove Terrace. At 3.55 p.m., PC Simon Greaves headed down the overgrown cobbled alleyway that ran behind the backyards of Ash Grove. Saturday night's party had been held at no. 16; directly opposite was no. 13, where a dustbin stood in the gap between two properties. Thinking its placement odd, he moved forward to the recess where bins were normally stored.

In the alcove lay a length of old carpet weighed down by large stones. A red boot protruded from one corner. Greaves lifted the edge of the carpet: Barbara was slumped against the corner of the recess, her head towards her right shoulder, left arm resting on the ground. Her legs were bent at the knees and twisted to the right, with her feet against the wall. Her bloodstained blouse and bra had been pushed up to expose her body; the belt and zip on her jeans had been undone and partly pulled down. Next to her lay the brown haversack she had favoured over a handbag.

Greaves radioed in his discovery. A forensic scientist arriving before Professor Gee noticed blood on the wall near Barbara's head and more on the ground a short distance away. There were stab wounds to her body, and he thought it likely she had fallen on her side after the injuries were inflicted. The killer had then wedged her into the debris-strewn alcove and covered her with carpet. A quick inspection of the area convinced him that she had been hit from behind as she passed the alleyway on the main road, then dragged down the cobbles, into the yard and murdered in the recess. The killer had only needed to take a couple of steps to the side to see into the open window where the party was underway. Barbara's friend

Stephen Greenough was visibly shaken when told later, responding: 'I was more than likely at the house when it happened. But I didn't hear anything at all.'[29]

Within an hour, a hundred-strong task force had descended on the area, cordoning off Ash Grove and Back Ash Grove alley. Officers conducted a fingertip search of the cobbles, cutting down weeds as they progressed. They found a screwdriver head, a wallet, two knives and a spanner, but none related to the murder.

In the yard of no. 13, Professor Gee manoeuvred Barbara's body out of the recess and onto a black polythene sheet on the ground. Rigor mortis had set in and she was cold to touch. Her hair and exposed skin were soiled with blood. At the back of her head was an oval-shaped laceration and a depressed fracture to the skull below, probably the result of a single hammer blow. Eight deep stab wounds had penetrated her vital organs; these were inflicted by a weapon very similar to the one employed in Josephine Whitaker's murder. When Gee performed a post-mortem later that evening in the city mortuary, he noticed a black, greasy substance in some of the wounds.

Detective Chief Superintendent Peter Gilrain took charge of the investigation from an incident room in Bradford. Dick Holland abandoned a family holiday in Scotland to supervise from Millgarth and Detective Chief Superintendent Jim Hobson joined him from his wife's hospital bedside; she had suffered a fall the previous week. Manchester-based Detective Chief Superintendent Jack Ridgway travelled to Bradford, but Oldfield remained absent until the following January on doctor's orders, following a period of ill health.

A sergeant and WPC arrived in Kettering at 9.15 p.m. to escort Barbara's parents to Bradford. David identified his daughter in the mortuary. Beryl could not face it: 'I was terrified. Because they called him the Yorkshire Ripper. I couldn't ask for weeks how she'd been killed. My imagination – you can imagine – it was running riot. I couldn't ask my husband and I couldn't speak of it to anyone. Eventually, I got my friend. I said, "Would you ask David if she was badly hurt." And no – she'd got scratches on her face, but [the injuries were] mainly on her body.'[30]

On Tuesday morning, the Leaches visited Barbara's digs on Grove Terrace. The house was overrun by forensic experts and after a few minutes in Barbara's room the couple were driven home by PC Greaves, who had found their daughter's body.

Barbara's brother Graham boarded a train from Havant for the journey to Kettering. He sat in a corner of the restaurant car as the Hampshire countryside raced by, weeping as he remembered family holidays in Cornwall and Snowdon. He got up and walked to the corridor to clear his head; on the floor next to the guard's van was a stack of *Daily Mirrors* bearing his sister's smiling face.

All newspapers carried the story of Barbara's murder. The *Yorkshire Post* tied it in with the Sunderland recording: 'Police believed early today that the Yorkshire Ripper had murdered his twelfth victim following the discovery of the mutilated body of a woman in the backyard of a Bradford house. They feared he had carried out a bizarre promise in a taped message delivered to police to kill again in September.'[31] Hobson confirmed later that day: 'We are now satisfied this murder is linked with other unsolved murders in Yorkshire and Manchester.'[32] Two sightings were explored without success: a white man in his thirties with short dark hair and a moustache, who had been seen putting a bundle into a green Hillman Avenger estate parked near the murder scene, and a blue Datsun saloon that was also of interest.

The media stressed Barbara's background, with the *Yorkshire Evening Post* quoting a detective – 'She was a perfectly respectable young woman with a good home' – while its sister paper, the *Yorkshire Post,* announced that the Ripper had 'got it wrong. His victim was not a prostitute but a much-loved daughter and undergraduate who made the mistake of taking an early morning stroll ... Miss Leach, like his last victim, Miss Josephine Whitaker, a building society clerk at Halifax, was a perfectly respectable young woman. Detectives involved in the case feel the Ripper will not be able to resist the temptation to explain why his plan went wrong and special checks of all police post will be made each morning. His hatred of prostitutes has evolved into a duel with the police, with every woman in the north of England now a potential victim.'[33] Detective Chief Superintendent Gilrain declared: 'No woman in this part of the world should go out alone at that time. These are extremely brutal attacks and he is now picking them at random, not just concentrating on prostitutes.'[34]

Barbara's uncle Les denied press insinuations that her decision to walk alone was the result of excessive drinking: 'She had been at her flat working on her studies until about one in the morning. She was working hard towards her finals next year and she wanted a walk to clear her head and settle her down before she went to bed. It was something she often did, but never alone.'[35] He added: 'What can you say? You bring a child up and see her embark on a worthwhile career and then something like this happens. Why her? She enjoyed university life and had all the usual interests of a girl of that age. But she often came home on visits, even if it was only for a couple of days. They are a very close-knit family.'[36] Graham spoke briefly to reporters, telling them his sister was 'not the sort of girl who would have stopped to talk to [the killer]. If he gave her any trouble, she would have been more likely to knee him where it hurts. She had some sense.'[37]

Relatives of previous victims expressed anger that the killer remained at liberty. 'That man is a monster,' Wilf MacDonald stated. 'How many more innocent girls have to suffer before he is caught? It is hard to describe the hatred a parent of a victim feels for this animal. I may be a sick man, but I'd just like a few minutes with him. A prison sentence would be too good for him. He should be hanged. Our house is strangely quiet. It has brought back all the heartache.'[38]

Barbara's university friends spoke of the girl they had felt privileged to know. Her housemate Paul reflected: 'She did not have any special hopes or dreams. She lived for today. She really was a great girl. She loved to play mother to the lads and make us meals. She was very close to her mother and father and even when she saw them at weekends she wrote to them. She was a prolific letter writer. She did not have a special friend really – everyone was special to Barbara.'[39] John McGoldrick was among those students who had attended the party in the house close to where Barbara's body was found:

> There was plenty of noise right into the early hours of Sunday and the window downstairs was wide open. In fact, one bloke was lying under the window as I sat talking and drinking with him. We were in full view of the street but saw nothing unusual. It seems incredible that Barbara should have been murdered just a few yards away, while we were drinking so nearby. There is nothing particularly unusual for a girl student to wander around on her own at night in this area; we're a tight-knit community and there is usually someone around.[40]

Barbara's best friend Gabrielle was distraught when she spoke to reporters before her father arrived to take her home to York. 'Don't forget Barbara,' she urged the public. 'And don't forget what happened to her. Do everything you can to help bring her killer to justice.'[41]

A stark warning was issued to Bradford's female students: never walk anywhere in the city alone, never stay at home alone, and always use the transport laid on after university functions. The *Yorkshire Post* flagged up the advice in a special editorial that implied not all victims were equal, adding:

Nobody would wish women to go around in perpetual fear. It would be foolish, unnecessary and unhealthy for them to do so. But even if the Yorkshire Ripper were not still on the loose after his twelfth gruesome and sadistic murder, and even if he had never existed, there would still be certain places and routes, especially at night, which girls and women should strive to avoid if unaccompanied. Every week seems to bring tragic stories from various parts of the country of lone women victims brutally injured or done to death. Almost always they are totally innocent victims who had believed they had nothing to fear, often treading familiar paths and sometimes being attacked within a few hundred yards of their home or destination. One can only appeal for public vigilance and the utmost co-operation with the police.[42]

Twenty-four-year-old WPC Barbara Terry re-enacted Barbara's last walk. She found it an unsettling experience even though Holland and Gilrain were present: 'I was scared. It was very weird. When I was asked to do the reconstruction I accepted without thinking. When it came to wearing the clothes and actually doing the walk I began to feel a little nervous. I had a funny feeling that the Ripper may be lurking in the background, watching me. I know the way women are reacting to these murders. There is a real fear hanging over almost everyone.'[43]

The inquest into Barbara's death was opened and adjourned on 20 September. Afterwards, Bradford coroner James Turnbull handed a letter to her parents, expressing sympathy on behalf of the people of Bradford. When reporter Christa Ackroyd interviewed David Leach some time later, he told her that he had questioned the expense of the outfit chosen by his wife for Barbara's funeral. 'I'll never forget what he said to me because it underlined the extent of all the relatives' loss and grief,' Christa recalls. 'When he commented on the cost of the outfit,

Beryl turned to him and said quietly, "It's not just for Barbara's funeral. It's for her graduation, her wedding and the christening of her babies. That's what's been taken from us."[44]

The following month, Barbara's parents travelled to Bradford to collect her belongings and to attend a memorial service recognizing her contribution to university life. An Acer Goldsworth Purple sapling was planted with an accompanying plaque: 'This tree was planted on 20th October 1980 by the Students Union and the University of Bradford in memory of Barbara Janine Leach, a student in the School of Social Sciences who died in September 1979.' The tree remains there still, tall and strong, its leaves turning a rich, purple-hued gold each autumn, around the anniversary of her death.

After the service, Barbara's parents returned to the house on Grove Terrace. In the corner of the attic were her new riding boots and on the desk was a half-completed form for student financial aid. It lay next to the mug she had bought for her father's birthday with the cheery inscription: 'Life is Too Short Not to Live It Up a Little!' Beryl walked across to her daughter's cassette player and pressed the button to find out what she had been listening to last. Singer Melanie's voice filled the room: 'I will not weep, nor make a scene, I just say: "Thank you, Life, for having been", and the hardest thing under the sun above, is to say goodbye to the ones you love ...'

Detective Chief Superintendent Gilrain spoke of his disappointment in the response to Barbara's death: 'We have had a lot of help from the public, but not as much as we have had on previous occasions.'[45]

In desperation, David Leach asked a journalist if he knew of anyone who might be able to help and was put in touch with Jim Lyness, an Ulster-born private detective in his forties who ran a security company based in Oldham. 'I haven't got much money, but I want you to find out whoever killed my daughter,'

David Leach told him during their first conversation.[46] Working free of charge, Lyness spent almost a year investigating the murder without access to police records. His meetings with Anna Rogulskyj and Olive Smelt convinced him that the Sunderland letter-writer was a fraud.

Detectives had expected the killer to contact them again, but failed to realize when he actually did, in a muddled poem sent from Manchester three days after the discovery of Barbara's body. Sent to the editor of the *Sheffield Star*, it was written in capitals on lined notepaper, and suggested with good reason that the police had allowed themselves to be deceived:

'CLUELESS
POOR OLD OLDFIELD
WORKED IN A COALFIELD

HOBSON HAD NO CHOICE
MISLED BY A VOICE

RELEASED OF DRURY
AROUSED FURY

BRADFORD WAS NOT ME
BUT JUST WAIT AND SEE

SHEFFIELD WILL NOT BE MISSED
NEXT ON THE LIST.

THE STREETCLEANER (T.S.).'[47]

18

MARGUERITE

On 13 September 1979, West Yorkshire Police issued an updated version of the Domaille report from the previous year to all police forces in the UK. In addition to detailing the murders and attacks attributed to the Ripper, it also included data from the tyre-tracking enquiry, and left no doubt about the credibility given to the Sunderland letters and tape. Officers were instructed to eliminate any suspect not born between 1924 and 1959, or 'an obvious coloured person', if he took a shoe size nine or larger, was not of blood group B, and if his dialect was 'dissimilar to a North Eastern (Geordie) accent'.[1]

The dossier is extraordinarily revealing of the police attitude to victims and survivors, explicitly stating that 'most of the earlier victims are prostitutes or women of loose moral character'.[2] Only Josephine (the most recent victim at the time of the report) was held completely blameless; on the morning of her death, the notice sent out to regional forces had declared: 'She was not a prostitute, nor was her moral character questionable.' The dossier indicates that class and geography were additional factors in this regard: the fact that Jayne MacDonald lived on the borders of Chapeltown and had walked through the district alone at night to reach home appears to have counted against her.

In her penetrating analysis of the dossier, Joan Smith observes that the division was made on two grounds: 'First, that this is a case in which the early victims are morally flawed;

and second, that any woman who doesn't come from a middle-class family and who presumes to venture out alone at night is little better than a prostitute – a type of woman for whom, it is clear, the police themselves feel a barely concealed disgust.'[3] Smith rightfully makes an example of the dossier's treatment of Anna Rogulskyj, of whom it is written:

> She is a very heavy drinker and has cohabited with a number of men. She has a history of mental instability. In July 1975 she was associating with a local man who had moved into her home. She was apparently unhappy with her sexual relationship and left her home on the night of Friday, 4th July 1975 saying she was going to Bradford to see her Jamaican boyfriend. She visited Bradford that night and had some drink. About midnight she left Bibby's Club and got a lift in a car with two Jamaicans who took her back to Keighley and dropped her off at home.[4]

No evidence was produced to support their claims about Anna's 'moral character', which in any case played no part in her attacker's decision to target her. A similar character assassination was extended to Olive Smelt, of whom the dossier baldly declares: 'She is of loose morals' simply because she was a married woman whose 'usual custom several nights a week [was] to visit public houses in Halifax on her own'.[5]

Tracy Browne's attack is glaringly absent, presumably because no amount of manipulation of the facts could mould her into the perceived victim profile. In his memoir, Chief Constable Ronald Gregory gave a nonsensical explanation for the omission: 'Tracy was not a prostitute; we thought at the time she was hit with a piece of wood; and all the other attacks were in city areas.'[6] Although the police discounted Tracy's attack, they continued to visit her whenever another woman was murdered to ask if she had remembered anything further.

'I felt so frustrated because I'd told them all I could at the time,' Tracy recalls. 'My family got so angry but we didn't know what else we could have done.'[7]

Working from the same criteria, Joan Harrison's murder was included in the dossier because her profile *did* fit the victim profile as imagined by the police. There were certain similarities from an evidential viewpoint for adding her murder to the list, but it was ultimately the perception of Joan herself that convinced detectives, given that they regarded her simply as 'a chronic alcoholic' who had 'close associations with other alcoholics, drug addicts and prostitutes in the Preston area. She had previous convictions for theft and, although not convicted of prostitution, it is known that she resorted to this in order to provide money for her drinking habits.'[8] West Yorkshire Police were so certain that Joan matched their victim criteria, they threw out the fact that she had not been subjected to a hammer attack or the stabbings consistent with the Ripper, and even dismissed the post-mortem report. Ignoring the pathologist's observation that Joan's injuries were due to her having been kicked to death, instead they declared the wounds were 'consistent with being struck by a hammer-type instrument'.[9]

Joan Smith concludes:

> How on earth, given their own attitudes to women and female sexuality, did the police expect to be able to recognize the killer if they came face to face with him? If, as they believed, the man was disgusted by prostitutes – well, so were they. If he expressed disapproval of married women going to pubs without their husbands, or said he couldn't stand women who drank too much, or remarked that women who went out alone late at night were no better than whores, would they really think something was wrong about this one and arrest him? Or would they dismiss him as an average bloke, the

kind who can be found leaning on the bar in the local pub – not to mention the police club – any night of the week?[10]

Detective Chief Superintendent James Hobson's remarks about the killer at a press conference in October 1979 bore out Smith's assertions: 'He has made it clear that he hates prostitutes. Many people do. We, as a police force, will continue to arrest prostitutes. But the Ripper is now killing innocent girls. That indicates your mental state and that you are in urgent need of medical attention. You have made your point. Give yourself up before another innocent woman dies.'[11] It was an extraordinary statement. According to Hobson, it was only when the killer apparently became indifferent to the occupation of his victims that he showed madness; killing prostitutes, on the other hand, was somewhat reasonable.

Anger among sex workers was palpable. In a statement to the Metropolitan Police Commissioner, the English Collective of Prostitutes demanded: 'To the Ripper and to the police, prostitutes are not decent, we are not "innocent victims." What are we guilty of to deserve such a death? Seventy percent of prostitute women in this country are mothers fighting to make ends meet and feed our children. But because we refuse poverty for ourselves and our children, we are treated as criminals. In the eyes of the police we deserve what we get, even death.'

Following the dossier's release, the homes of Anna Rogulskyj and Olive Smelt were 'besieged by reporters', who referred to them as 'good-time girls', that catch-all phrase covering everything from a woman drinking with friends in a pub to prostitution.[12] Anna consulted a solicitor, threatening legal action against the Chief Constable and the *Yorkshire Post*.

Newspapers reminded female readers yet again that if they wished to avoid attracting the Ripper's attention, they should be mindful of their clothing and conduct. The *Sunday Mirror* issued a handy 'Checklist for Survival' in which women were invited to consider questions that might apparently save lives, including, 'Do you think you are safe because you are not a good-time girl?'; 'Do you go out alone at night, even to walk just a few yards?' and 'Do you make any secret of the fact that when talking to a man you don't mind having sex?'[13]

The police repeatedly advised women to think carefully about whether they could trust their male relatives and friends, while telling them to rely on the same menfolk for protection. In Leeds, where the university had stopped their night bus service and the city's late night buses no longer ran, outraged women vandalized notices reminding them not to walk alone after dark. Taxi companies introduced a price hike and surcharges, admitting that 'business has never been better'.[14] At the city's Royal Park pub, staff noticed that on the rare occasion when a woman entered the bar alone, male drinkers would berate her for being so thoughtless. One female student described the climate of fear that existed in the north, explaining: 'I went to Brighton last week and I was delighted to walk the streets alone, late, and the thing is, I would have been worried about that normally but you just think, "There's no Ripper here", and feel safe.'[15]

Equally insidious was the underlying sense that some men admired the 'anonymous loner who was eluding the largest manhunt in British criminal history', manifesting itself on the football terraces, where crowds sang 'There's only one Yorkshire Ripper' to the tune of 'Guantanamera'.[16] The Wearside Jack tape was drowned out when it was played over the loudspeakers at Elland Road as Leeds United fans chanted, 'You'll never catch the Ripper, 12–nil, 12–nil!'

The media bore some responsibility for the elevation of an unknown misogynistic killer to the status of modern folk hero. Newspapers consistently invoked the spectre of Jack the Ripper to enhance the Yorkshire Ripper's notoriety, transforming the north of England 'pockmarked with soot-stained mills and ramshackle factories' into a contemporary version of the gaslit

East End.[17] *Evening News Magazine* informed its readers: 'Bradford on Saturday night is pure Victorian Gothic ... dank, slate roofs gleaming, the blackened brick ... even the quarter moon obliges, fitfully disappearing behind windswept clouds.'[18] The *Sunday Mirror* described the city as a region of 'ill-lit streets with derelict houses and waste grounds; some near the huge arterial roads from where you could hear the thunder of freight lorries and smell their cancerous exhausts. There lurked the women of the night, gaunt creatures asking if they wanted to do "business."'[19] Other newspapers discussed Chapeltown's 'vice spots', complete with maps of its 'mean streets' while *Esquire* intoned: 'A good deal of the British Empire was made in this part of Yorkshire, but these dark, steep, cobbled towns have been used up.'[20] Background pieces suggested that the murders could not have happened elsewhere; they were 'the product of a particular environment: tough, northern, working-class, patriarchal, sordid and commercial'.[21]

This ongoing mythologizing was a global phenomenon in which fact and fiction, past and present did not simply meet – they merged into one. *US* magazine ran an article in October 1979 titled, 'A New Jack the Ripper is Terrorizing England', featuring a black and white shot of a caped copper with the caption: 'West Yorkshire Police Constable Alan Firth patrols a lonely stretch of his beat in the heart of Ripper Country'. On the opposite page was a feature on a new film, *Time After Time*, in which Jack the Ripper travelled to modern day San Francisco. *Time* magazine referred to the murders as 'The Ripper's Return', using both the Josephine Whitaker crime scene and an illustration of the 'Whitechapel terror' in an 1888 edition of *Punch*.

Renewed interest in the crimes of Jack the Ripper as a direct result of the Yorkshire murders was a key factor in the April 1980 opening of Madame Tussauds' 'Ripper Street'. The waxwork Chamber of Horrors had lacked a recreation of the Victorian killer because no face could be put to him, but a 'consuming desire to re-enact and resolve the mystery' while the current murderer remained at large led to the creation of the Chamber's most popular section.[22]

There were some dissenting voices in the media. The *Guardian* addressed the issue of dividing victims into good and bad girls a month after the publication of the dossier: 'Barbara Leach was said to be the Ripper's "second innocent victim", a "deadly error." The official police poster in the area described Barbara Leach as a "respectable girl" from a "good family." Can you imagine them saying of a man who had been robbed that he'd never been in debt? And why did the *Sun* assure us that she was not drunk? Presumably because if she had been, she would have been a bad girl getting her just deserts. The Ripper clearly hates all women – prostitutes are just an easy target.'[23] The article took issue with the demonstrations in Bradford that followed Barbara's murder, asking why feminists had apparently remained silent when Yvonne Pearson and Patricia Atkinson were killed.

Spare Rib magazine responded by insisting that the march had been organized on behalf of 'all victims of the Ripper and all women victims of murder, rape, assault and battering by men ... Barbara Leach lost her life partly because of the police's insistence that only prostitutes were prey. This is not the case, we are *all* prey.'[24]

Marguerite Walls had been sensible to wear her mackintosh on Wednesday 20 August 1980. Light showers during the day kept the temperature cooler than average and when she walked home after leaving work late that evening, it was fairly chilly. Although she would be attending a colleague's funeral on Friday in Newcastle, she had ten days' holiday ahead, intending to clear the city air from her lungs with plenty of bracing walks in the Lake District.

Born on 17 December 1932 in Lincoln, Marguerite was a lifelong 'rambler'. An intensely private person, she had never married and caused some curiosity among her colleagues, who liked her but found her slightly aloof. If she had any close friends, she never mentioned them, but nor did she discuss her family, to whom she was extremely close. 'Margot was very special to us all,' her mother Kathleen Walls confirmed, speaking on behalf of Marguerite's father and her younger brother and sister.

The family had moved to Northern Ireland when Marguerite was in her early teens. She completed her education in Londonderry and had a few casual jobs before joining the Women's Royal Army Corps in 1963. Five years later, having reached the rank of sergeant, she joined the civil service in London. After a couple of years, she changed jobs but decided to return to the civil service in Basingstoke. She then joined Customs and Excise in Leicester, working at the VAT office until 1978.

Marguerite's colleague Tony Nash and his wife were her closest friends and she was their trusted and much loved babysitter. When Marguerite's long-standing relationship with a local man ended, she applied for a position with the Department of Education and Science in Pudsey, Leeds. In March 1978 she began working as the company's Executive Officer, having dipped into her savings to buy a modern, detached house at 7 New Park Croft in Farsley, midway between Leeds and Bradford. Unless the weather was exceptionally poor, she walked one and a half miles every day to and from work, determined to keep as fit as she had been in the army. She also joined the Leeds and Bradford Fell Walking Club and took a second job as an adult-literacy tutor in Pudsey. A small, slim brunette with a strong jaw and an intelligent, direct gaze, she liked her own company and was perfectly settled in her life.

Marguerite remained at work until 10.30 p.m. on 20 August 1980, eating a Chinese takeaway at her desk and making sure everything was in order before she left, reached for her canvas shopping bag and coat. The Department of Education and Science was in a three-storey modern block on Richardshaw Lane. After locking up with her own key, she walked towards Westroyd Park and got as far as Claremont House on New Street. It was a large property divided into three separate homes, one of which was occupied by Peter Hainsworth, chairman of Pudsey and Otley Magistrates; his son Richard was a reporter who had covered the Ripper killings for the *Yorkshire Evening Post*. The house stood behind stone pillars in extensive and partly overgrown grounds. A pupil at Westroyd Primary School across the road explained: 'It's murky and mysterious. We're not supposed to go in there but sometimes we do and it's creepy if you're there by yourself. We all call it the "Secret Garden" after we saw the story on television, because nobody knows what happens in there.'[25]

Farsley PC Kenneth Stevens and his wife Lynn lived next to the property in the old police house. Lynn was responsible for the upkeep of the Claremont's garden but she and her husband were away, leaving her parents to keep an eye on things. At 9 a.m. on 21 August 1980, the Harrisons headed out into the garden to see what needed doing.

A pair of shoes lay on the path and near the rockery was a violet wrap-around skirt, its lining ripped. They spotted a cheque book on the grass and then a large shopping bag. Deciding to look no further, they telephoned the police.

Dog handlers discovered Marguerite's body under a pile of lawn cuttings near the stone garage. She was naked but for her tights and the mackintosh tossed across her torso. Under another heap of grass were her purple cardigan and blouse.

Detective Chief Superintendent Peter Gilrain arrived a short while later with Professor Alan Usher of Sheffield University's Department of Forensic Pathology. The road nearby was sealed off and house-to-house enquiries launched. Coincidentally, survivor Maureen Long had lived on Donald Street, scarcely a minute's walk from Claremont House, but she had moved away.

Upon examination of Marguerite's body, Usher found two lacerations to the back and side of her head and a deep ligature line around her neck. Bloodstains and drag marks on the ground indicated that she had been struck by the stone pillars. Her killer had then pulled a ligature around her throat before hauling her twenty yards out of sight, across the rockery, into a wooded area. Defensive marks on her body and bruising on her knuckles showed that she had put up a considerable fight, punching her attacker several times. Three of her ribs were fractured, and Professor Usher believed the killer had knelt on Margeurite's chest to strangle her fully. The post-mortem revealed three fingernail scratches on her vagina, leaving him in no doubt that the murder was sexually motivated.

Detective Chief Superintendent Hobson headed the inquiry into Marguerite's death, setting up an incident room at Pudsey Police Station. Reporters were swift to speculate, but Hobson was keen to play down links with the Ripper, following consultation with forensic experts. They advised that Marguerite's murder was unlikely to be part of the series in view of the element of strangulation and lack of stab wounds, although she had the requisite head injuries. 'My feelings are that it is a local man who did this murder,' Hobson informed a press conference. 'I have a team of detectives at Miss Walls' house looking for addresses of male and female friends. She had boyfriends in the past but that was about twenty-odd years ago.'[26] Local men convicted of sexual attacks would be interviewed first for elimination from the inquiry.

Robert Walls travelled alone from his home in Lye, Stourbridge, to identify his sister's body. His parents and younger sister were unable to face the journey. Although Marguerite's death was ruled out of the series, Hobson felt compelled to reiterate that she was 'a perfectly respectable woman going about her legitimate business', who spent her leisure time walking and gardening.[27]

'This is a savage killing,' he declared.

A great deal of strength and violence was used to kill this woman. The person we are looking for is somebody that was able either to drag or carry this woman a fair way into the grounds. I think the struggle probably took place at the gates and inside. The woman's garments were torn. There are certain injuries to the body which could have been inflicted by a blunt instrument … It might be that her attacker had followed her from work or he may have lain in wait for her behind the walls of the garden of Claremont where he could be hidden in the shadows.[28]

A nearby resident had heard a woman screaming at about 10 p.m. that night, but Marguerite was still at her desk in Pudsey then. A bus driver also contacted detectives to say that he had seen a woman matching Marguerite's description walking down the Leeds–Bradford Road at 9.45 p.m., leaving the probable time of her death under review.

Mrs Kathryn Vater lived next door to Marguerite, whom she described as 'a very lonely person and very difficult to talk to. I used to help her with the garden but she didn't really get friendly with anybody in the area.'[29] At Richardshaw Lane, Divisional Inspector Gordon Hamflett learned that Marguerite had left her workspace tidy and up to date: 'It was not unusual for her to remain at the office after hours. She was the sort of woman who liked to work on her own and she liked to finish her business in the peace and quiet after other people had gone away. It was consistent with her conscientiousness that she should want to clear her desk.'[30] Hobson was puzzled by the lack of friendships in Marguerite's life, given that she was a personable woman: 'We have not traced anyone who will say they went out with her on a night. She seemed to come home about 6 or 7 p.m. and then stay in the house for the rest of the evening. Even the people who worked with her eight hours a day knew very little about her personal life.'[31] Her diligence led to a thinly veiled remark in the *Daily Mirror* on 23 August about the dangers of female ambition: 'A career woman's devotion to work led to her murder in a savage sex attack ...'[32]

Two days after the murder, police officers armed with scythes hacked their way through overgrown areas in the garden of Claremont House while detectives searched Marguerite's home in Farsley. They found several diaries and letters which they hoped would help them build a picture of her life. Unfortunately, the news of the discovery led to headlines that would have appalled the very reserved woman who had been murdered; the *Yorkshire Evening Post* queried on 25 August: 'Did Margo Have Secret Lover? Home-loving spinster Margo Walls – savagely slain by a sex killer – may have had a secret lover. Detectives hunting the killer are investigating the possibility ...'[33]

Two days later, after detectives had travelled to Worcester to speak to her relatives, it emerged that several years earlier Marguerite had stopped a man from indecently assaulting her by reprimanding him. Further enquiries focused on establishing exactly when she had left Richardshaw Lane. A reconstruction led to residents of West Street confirming that the light in Marguerite's office, which overlooked their homes, might have been shining as late as 10.30 p.m., but definitely not after 11.10 p.m.

The police remained unwilling to link Marguerite's murder with the previous attacks and killings, but the *Keighley News* warned:

> We've said it before and we say it again: local women must not think that just because they live outside a city they are safe from the beast. The sad fact is that the Ripper can strike anywhere. Police are convinced he started his macabre trail of death right here in Keighley ... Yet despite all the warnings and despite the horror of last week's Ripper savagery in Leeds, it is still menacingly

common to see women walking alone at night through the streets of Keighley and neighbouring villages. The cost of ignoring the police warnings to stay at home or only go out when accompanied could be a hideous assault ending in death.[34]

The inquest into Marguerite's death was opened and adjourned in Leeds on 24 November 1980. Professor Alan Usher confirmed that strangulation was the cause of death. Four months after Marguerite's murder, her father Thomas Walls passed away. His widow and surviving children were certain that he had died of a broken heart.

19

UPADHYA

Like Marguerite Walls before her, Dr Upadhya Anandavathy Bandara was also looking forward to leaving Leeds for a holiday. Work had brought her to the city from Singapore, where she was the youngest in a family of eight sisters and three brothers. After graduating from the University of Singapore in 1967, she was given a position with the Ministry of Health in the city centre. Aged thirty-three, she won a World Health Organization scholarship for a postgraduate course in health service studies. In August 1979, Upadhya arrived in Leeds. One year later, after completing her course at the Nuffield Medical Centre, she was preparing to return to Singapore, breaking her journey home with a ten-city break in Europe.

Upadhya spent the evening of Wednesday 24 September 1980 with friends in Cottage Road, about a mile from her digs in another part of the leafy, student-dominated district of Headingley. She left her friends shortly after 11 p.m. It was a dry, warm night and most of the way was well-lit. As she headed down Otley Road, past the squat brown bulk of the Arndale Centre on her left, she noticed a man watching her from inside the KFC takeaway. She averted her eyes and carried on, past the quirky shops and other late night eateries, until she reached the Skyrack pub on the corner of Otley Road. Crossing over, she passed the war memorial and turned left down St Michael's Lane, then left again into Chapel Lane.

The long cobbled alleyway was a short cut to her digs on Cardigan Road. To her right were the small back gardens and yards of St Michael's Crescent. As Upadhya reached the curve in the lane, she heard quick footsteps and stood aside to let the person pass. Turning slightly, she caught a glimpse of a dark-haired man with a closely cropped beard. She had no time to react: he struck her savagely, then pulled something rough and knotted around her neck, causing her to slip unconscious to the ground.

Mrs Valerie Nicholas lived closest to where the attack occurred; hearing noises, she rushed through the back door, shouting for her husband. They entered the lane to find Upadhya, 'lying face down with blood all around', her beige cardigan pulled around her head.[1] No one was nearby. After calling the emergency services, the couple waited with Upadhya, who was still unconscious. Valerie noticed bloodstains on the young woman's brown trousers and red shirt, and bloodied drag marks on the cobbles where she had crawled from the site of her attack.

A police car skidded round St Michael's Lane, its headlights on full beam. Upadhya had regained consciousness and groaned as she tried lifting her head. 'She was concussed,' Valerie recalled. 'When she came round in the ambulance she did not know who she was or what had happened.'[2]

Upadhya spoke to pathologist Dr Michael Green after surgery at Leeds Infirmary, telling him that her attacker had dark hair and a trimmed beard. Green examined the injuries to her face and the back of her head, noting that the laceration was curved and reminiscent of those inflicted by the Ripper. About her neck was a red welt, left by a length of plaited material, perhaps a dressing-gown cord, which had been tightened from behind like a garotte; she had clearly tried to prise it loose before being dragged along the cobbles. Injuries behind her left ear were consistent with having been kicked.

No one had yet been held accountable for the murder three years earlier of a woman strangled with a ligature in Shipley, nor for the recent killing of Marguerite Walls, whose death had been very similar. Dr Green considered the two murders, in which neither woman had been stabbed. Nor had Upadhya suffered any knife wounds, which suggested to him that her assailant – and perhaps the killer of the two earlier victims – was someone other than the Ripper.

Detective Superintendent Tom Newton took charge of the investigation from the same Pudsey Police Station incident room used for the inquiry into Marguerite's murder. He too decided that the attempt on Upadhya's life was not the responsibility of the Ripper, therefore acknowledging the presence of two serial killers operating within the city and its environs.

The *Yorkshire Evening Post* broke the story on 25 September, informing readers that an as yet unnamed woman had been 'attacked and left in a pool of blood' but was 'said to be comfortable at Leeds Infirmary with head wounds'.[3] The police had informed the press that the attack might be linked with a second incident ('not an assault') in the same area two hours later, which involved a dark-haired, bearded man.[4]

Within a couple of days, the inquiry into Upadhya's attack had moved to Woodhouse Moor, where a fairground visited every year as the central attraction of Woodhouse Feast. Thirty police officers and dog handlers arrived early on Wednesday morning to interview fairground workers about the attack and search the premises. Newton, the senior investigating officer, afterwards declared the information gleaned from the visit as 'useful' but did not elaborate further.[5]

In Singapore, Upadhya's employers at the Ministry of Health had been informed about the attack. She implored them not to say anything to her family, not wishing to worry them 'unduly'.[6] When Upadhya's mother eventually learned the truth, she remarked of her daughter: 'That's just like her, always trying to keep worries away from the family.'[7]

Discharged from hospital within the week, Upadhya cancelled her European trip and agreed to take part in a reconstruction aimed at jogging people's memories. Dressed in the same outfit she had worn that night, Upadhya retraced her entire route from Cottage Road to Chapel Lane. 'She was nervous, but composed,' Newton told reporters. 'It was an ordeal for her to go through – but nevertheless she went through it to help us. The operation has resulted in lots of useful information being brought to light.'[8]

Upadhya flew back to Singapore in early October. Her mother recalled: 'When she first came home from England, we noticed a slight scar near her forehead and naturally we were anxious and inquired about it. She refused to say anything except that she had had an accident while in Leeds.'[9] It was only after the news broke worldwide of the Ripper's arrest that Upadhya finally revealed the truth. Even then, she tried to play down the seriousness of the attack. 'After we had learnt what happened in the newspapers, we asked her again,' her mother remembered. 'But all she told us was that everything was alright and we should not worry.'[10]

Upadhya refused all interview requests from the media. She continued her work at a government outpatient dispensary and never spoke publicly about the attack that so nearly ended her life thousands of miles from home.

Dr Upadhya Bandara died in 2006, at the age of sixty.

Eighteen thousand calls were received during the first six weeks of Project R, necessitating interviews of seventeen thousand suspects. The response was so overwhelming that the project had to be jettisoned. West Yorkshire Police's failure to control the publicity campaign led to a restriction on the flow of information to the press. The Byford Report observes that as a result 'the whole mood of media coverage changed and articles and broadcasts became critical, rather than supportive of police action'. The *Daily Express* began a dogged campaign to 'bring in the Yard'.

Two months after the attempted murder of Dr Bandara, victims' relatives and survivors of the Ripper attacks participated in a powerful edition of BBC's *Newsnight*. Looking directly at the camera, each speaker addressed the Ripper with their thoughts. In every clip, anger was the overriding emotion.

'Doesn't it bother you that you are hated?' survivor Maureen Long asked. 'Don't think you are a sort of god. I rate you so low. You are not a man, for you can only prove you are a man by killing women. Someone wants to get hold of you and do the same things to you as well. Which they might do, if they come face to face with you. You'd be better off killing yourself before someone else does it.'[11]

Jayne MacDonald's mother Irene declared: 'I just see you as a beast with no feelings. And you're a coward. Why do you come up and stalk young girls? Innocent girls, as well. You come up from behind them, they don't have a chance. You're not a man, you're a beast and I hate you. And I believe that all the population in Leeds and everywhere hate you. I wonder who you think you are. Do you damn well think you're God or something? I think you are the devil himself.'[12] Beryl Leach, whose daughter Barbara had been murdered the previous year, echoed: 'If I were you, I'd look over your shoulder. Somebody's looking for you. Many people are looking for you, and they all hate you.'[13] Avril Hiley, Josephine Whitaker's mother, was scathing: 'I think you're probably a very inadequate person. Certainly physically and probably mentally too. You're not significant at all. I don't think you can make a relationship with a woman, certainly not a live one. Possibly the only relationship you can make is with a dead one, as you've proved.'[14]

Irene's husband Haydn Hiley was one of the few men to address the Ripper:

> You are the lowest of the low. You did mention, I believe it was in your tape to the police, that you wanted to be mentioned in the *Guinness Book of Records*. I'll go

along with that. You should be classed as the biggest coward the world has ever known. Put that in the *Guinness Book of Records*. I think the person who is harbouring the Ripper is as bad as he is. I cannot understand the mentality of anyone who could cohabitate with such a loathsome creature. People are frightened of the deeds you do, but you are probably a very insignificant little man.[15]

Survivor Olive Smelt's husband Harry also took part in the programme, declaring frankly, 'Of all the women you've killed, if you were to take a census of them all, I think given the opportunity to do as you wish with them, I think they would rate you pretty low, sexually. I think that's what it's all about – you're "proving" you're a man by killing them. Most men don't have to kill women to prove that they're a man.'[16] He then spoke to the person harbouring the Ripper: 'My advice is this: if you're a young woman, there's lots of life for you, lots left. If you don't give him up you'll be despised by every woman in the country. You'll probably hate yourself too. If you do give him up you'll be admired by every woman, indeed everybody, in the country.'[17] Olive herself addressed the person shielding the killer, warning: 'Maybe he's going to hurt you in the end, anyway. Aren't you frightened of that? Why don't you go straight and give him up. Go to the CID and give him up because I'm sure you won't have to fear anything. And I think you'd be a much happier woman once you knew he'd been put away. Just like a lot more women will feel, when he's been caught.'[18]

After the programme aired, Irene told the press that the person she despised most of all was the one who protected the Ripper: 'This man is a coward but the biggest coward of them all is the person shielding him. If it is his mother, wife, sister or indeed a male, they should put themselves in the position of we women who have lost someone we loved. It makes my stomach churn to think that someone is saving his neck.'[19]

Marylyn Moore did not participate in the recording, explaining to the press from her home in Leeds that she was unable to work due to poor health and depression. Her children were in care. Every night she took her childhood teddy bear to bed for comfort: 'I still live in fear of that man. I must have come back from the dead after he attacked me. I moved around the country because I was terrified. I am frightened he will come for me because I can identify him.'[20]

Olive had a similar experience to the one haunting Marylyn. Around the time of the *Newsnight* special, her home telephone rang. When Olive answered, a male voice said: 'I'm coming to finish you off, Olive. I didn't do a good enough job last time.'[21] Reeling with shock and fear, Olive immediately telephoned the police, who told her it was almost certainly a hoax. But Olive had no doubts: 'I know it was the man who attacked me.'[22] She remained convinced until the end of her life.

Among the records in the charts that autumn was one by Irish rock band Thin Lizzy. 'Killer on the Loose' reached number ten with contentious lyrics that placed the singer in the role of Jack the Ripper, referring to himself within the song's boundaries as a mad sexual rapist and warning that there was a ladykiller on the loose. The B-side to the track, 'Don't Play Around', was a revenge fantasy against an unfaithful lover, with lyrics that described a woman being knifed in the gut.

When the video for 'Killer on the Loose' aired on *Top of the Pops*, showing scantily clad women falling to the ground on a foggy street, it provoked an immediate response. The Brighton Women's Centre were among many to express their abhorrence, writing to the BBC: 'We are horrified that this record clearly encourages and revels in sexual violence against women. Not only is this song an attempt to make money out of the horrific murders perpetrated by the man known as the Yorkshire Ripper, but it also encourages a sick admiration of his activities, and a desire to emulate him.'[23] Thin Lizzy were not the only male rock singers putting themselves in the Ripper's shoes; Trevor Rabin, musician with the band Yes and then a film composer, included a song called 'The Ripper' on his album *Face to Face*. Mimicking the Sunderland hoaxer, he intimated that the killer was indeed a 'streetcleaner' of vice who was set on ridding the world of its 'shame', referring, like the letter writer, to George Oldfield by name.

There were signs that discussions arising from the case were having an unexpectedly positive effect, as the Ripper became 'a catalyst for social change'.[24] Certainly the women's movement had emerged from an entirely political base and university background to become more accessible. One social commentator notes: 'When feminists raised a clamour against male callousness and the incompetence of the police, they reached a wider and more receptive audience than all the debates about gender-specific language and patriarchal structures ever had.'[25] Feminism, in short, was going mainstream, and rather than accepting the advice to stay at home until men had eliminated the threat on their behalf, women began mobilizing. 'Self-defence classes are packed out,' reported the *Yorkshire Evening Post*, as workplaces, colleges and schools brought in experts to teach women and girls how to fight an attacker. Disgusted at being told to depend on men to escort them about after dark, women turned to each other, organizing support networks of car shares, telephone links and walking groups.

In November 1980, the first Sexual Violence Against Women conference in Leeds saw an eight-hundred-strong march through the city centre, accompanied by shouts to 'Slap a Curfew on Men!' Thirty women broke into *Dressed to Kill* at the Odeon, throwing rotten eggs and paint bombs at the screen before escaping through the fire exit. Other cinemas showing 'sexploitation' films, such as *Violation of the Bitch* in Bradford, were similarly targeted. Sex shops had their windows smashed and locks glued, angry slogans about women's rights were spray-painted on walls throughout the country, and at

BBC Radio Leeds, crowds of women gathered to chant: 'Men Off The Streets!' and 'Women Are Angry, Not Frightened!'

To some extent, the press treated the protests as the latest chapter in a long tradition of women behaving in a 'disorderly' fashion, and as mildly amusing sidelines. 'Girls in Ripper Riot Fury' thundered the *Daily Mirror* front page, relating how 'the frenzied mob attacked several men and stormed cinemas' and a male reporter was 'left bruised and bleeding'.[26] At the same time, the political right and campaigners against 'smut' bandwaggoned the protests. Mary Whitehouse, leader of a campaign to clean up the media, declared: 'It has taken the Ripper murders and the attacks by women on the sex cinemas in Leeds to bring into the headlines again what is surely one of the political and social scandals of our day.'[27] But feminists made it clear that their campaign was not going to be hijacked for anyone else's political or social ambitions. While debates raged on every side, the Ripper made his presence felt again.

20

THERESA

Bonfire Night 1980 was wet and windy in Huddersfield, but the firework displays across town went ahead as planned. Sixteen-year-old Theresa Sykes was happy to be staying in; she and her boyfriend Jim Furey, a millworker and fitness fanatic nine years her senior, had recently become parents to a boy they named Anthony. 'Life was really good,' Theresa recalled. 'We had just got a new house. My boyfriend was working. We were just a normal couple.'[1]

Born in Huddersfield, Theresa had attended Deighton Secondary School while her parents, Raymond and Margaret Sykes, ran the Minstrel pub in town. Theresa was delighted to be a young mum and enjoyed decorating the council house she and Jim had been allocated on Willwood Avenue in Oakes, two miles west of Huddersfield's centre. Although the Ripper had already killed one teenage girl in the area, Theresa had never given him much thought, reflecting years later: 'You don't think anybody's going to go out and hurt you. And at the time he was just going for prostitutes. I was sixteen years old. You don't think, at sixteen years old.'[2]

Anthony's bedtime was between six and half-past. As Theresa settled him down for the night, the television played in the background: *Crossroads* was followed by *This Is Your Life*. By the time Eamonn Andrews had closed the big red book, Anthony was sleeping peacefully, oblivious to the high whistle of rockets going off and bonfires crackling around the estate.

Theresa and Jim were smokers, and as she settled down to watch *Coronation Street*, they realized neither of them had any cigarettes. Theresa tried to persuade Jim to go for some, but he preferred to wait until morning rather than battle through wind and rain. Annoyed with him and the situation, Theresa grabbed her coat and set out towards the park.

There were a few kids around, waving sparklers in the air as she walked down to the main road and then Acre Street, where a board outside the newsagents announced that Ronald Reagan had defeated Jimmy Carter to become the new American President. Theresa paid for her cigarettes and headed outside again. She noticed a man standing inside a nearby telephone box but was too concerned with getting home to pay him much attention.

It was a ten-minute walk to Willwood Avenue. Along the path at the edge of the park, Theresa realized someone was following her. She turned fearlessly and glared at the man, recognizing him from the phone box. He looked at her, then turned down one of the streets on the estate. Theresa quickened her step, hoping he had gone for good. She had counted two lampposts when she saw a shadow in the pool of light at her feet. 'I knew something was going to happen,' she recalls. 'I was saying to myself, "Run" and I couldn't. I literally froze.'[3]

Theresa stumbled forward, reaching blindly for the nearest garden gate. She felt the first blow: 'It will live with me, night and day, for the rest of my life. Apparently, he hit me three times over the head with a hammer … the second time he hit me, that brought me round and I started screaming.'[4] Fireworks exploded in a burst of colour, but Theresa's scream was loud enough to sound above them, alerting her neighbour, Stephen Humphreys, who recalled: 'We heard this firework go off and then there was this screaming. The wife put the milk bottles out and there was somebody shouting for help.'[5]

Jim had seen the attack from where he stood at the sitting-room window only thirty yards away, looking out across the front garden at fireworks. At first he assumed it was a couple of lads fighting and padded barefoot to the door, ready to break them up if necessary. Then he heard Theresa scream and yelled out himself, causing her attacker to sprint away. Jim raced straight past Theresa, who had collapsed on the ground with her head in her hands. He saw the figure swerve into Millfield Close towards Reinwood Road.

'I'll fucking kill you!' Jim shouted as the assailant vanished. Jim reached the end of the close and looked about frantically but the road was empty. 'He was like lightning,' he remembered. 'I didn't get very close to him.'[6] He ran back to his girlfriend, who was half-sitting, half-lying on the floor with one leg bent beneath her and the other splayed forwards. Three neighbours tried to help her up as she cried, 'He's hit me, he's hit me.'[7] Mrs Rita Wilkinson helped Theresa into the house, followed by Jim and Stephen Humphreys, who rang for an ambulance. Barely conscious, Theresa felt her way into a chair. When she realized that the sticky substance on her head and chair was blood she began screaming.

It was one of the busiest nights of the year for the emergency services, but the ambulance arrived quickly, taking Theresa to Huddersfield Royal Infirmary on Acre Street, where only an hour ago she had bought a packet of cigarettes. After a consultation, she was transferred to the specialist neurosurgical unit at Chapel Allerton Hospital for emergency brain surgery: she had suffered several blows to the head with a hammer and sustained compound fractures to her skull. She remained in hospital for five weeks.

The local police station stood only two hundred yards from the scene of the attack. Detective Superintendent Dick Holland inspected the area with several officers and a dog handler. The dog picked up a scent but the attacker had long since fled. They conducted house-to-house enquiries, but without success. Possibly as a result of the orange street lights, the description of the attacker they were given by witnesses identified him as having a ginger beard and moustache. When Theresa was able to be interviewed she corrected the description, remembering black hair and a beard.

Theresa's attack scarcely featured in the media; even the regional press coverage was slight, with only a brief reference to the possibility that it might be part of the Ripper series. West Yorkshire Police refused to be drawn on the issue. Senior investigating officer Detective Superintendent Hickley spoke testily to reporters: 'I said at the time that this was a local incident and that I was convinced a local man was involved. Nothing has happened to change my mind. All this talk that Theresa may have been attacked by the Ripper is making it more difficult to catch her assailant.'[8] Other senior detectives disagreed, causing friction as the attack remained categorized as an isolated incident. One detective told Theresa's parents that their daughter had been attacked by the Ripper but he advised them strongly not to mention it publicly.

Theresa underwent further surgery on 1 December for a hole the size of a fifty pence piece in the centre of her skull. On the same date, the *Daily Express* referred to the Ripper, claiming that police were 'now investigating the possibility that a girl in hospital with serious injuries was one of his victims'.[9] An interview with Raymond Sykes, naming the Ripper as his daughter's attacker, featured in the following day's paper. He was convinced that the killer had targeted Theresa after seeing her in their pub: 'I have always believed it was him, even when the police told us it was a local man. When I took over the pub two years ago, a few prostitutes were using it. We have cleaned it up since, but I think the Ripper must have seen Theresa and marked her as one of them. I think he followed her out of the pub to find out where she lived. The terrible thing is that I probably chatted to him and served him with a drink.'[10] He added, 'She is a very sensible and intelligent girl but now she won't let anybody stand behind her. She is forever looking over her shoulder and has great trouble sleeping at night.'[11]

In a swift piece of damage limitation, West Yorkshire Police told the press they were now completely satisfied that Theresa's attack was not the work of the Ripper. Their announcement was reported the following day in regional newspapers.

Raymond Sykes talked at more length about the emotional effect on his daughter: 'Her whole personality has changed; she was always quick with a smile but now she seems to flare up at the slightest thing. She only seems happy in the company of the baby, Anthony. She argues about every little thing. In fact I am sad to say that she has become a bit of a tyrant. It will never be the same for any of us again. Even now we tell each other when we go out and where we are going. We are all very nervous, particularly with Theresa.'[12]

She agreed with her father's assessment, reflecting: 'I used to go up to my bedroom of a night and put the wardrobe behind the door, put the dressing table behind the door. I had to sleep with a knife under the pillow, which my mum used to go barmy about, but that was the only thing that made me feel that bit safer. He took away my freedom, he took away a lot of my life the night that he attacked me and that I'll never get back, never, ever get it back.'[13] She learned to walk again with the aid of a frame and worked hard to correct the speech anomolies that had been caused by the injuries to her brain.

The house that had represented their future as a family became somewhere Theresa could not bear to be. She broke off her engagement and moved back in with her parents. 'I have a great mistrust of men at the moment,' she explained.

Jimmy and I had planned to get married in the near future, and when I came out of hospital we got back together for a while but it just didn't work out. I am on edge all the time and frightened at being alone with him. All that mattered was that he was a fellow, and I didn't feel safe. I preferred being with my mother and sisters. I am obsessed with having my back to the wall all the time, even when I am surrounded by friends. I have tried to stop myself but I simply can't stand anyone to my back.[14]

A year later, the Byford Report observed that the refusal to accept Theresa's attack as part of the series was 'less easy to explain' than the exclusions of Marguerite Walls and Upadhya Bandara. The denial issued to the press was 'little more than an attempt to reduce the public, media and Parliamentary pressure to which the force was being increasingly exposed'. Part of the difficulty in catching the Ripper lay not with lack of effort but simple disorganization: everything was recorded on paper. The government offered West Yorkshire Police use of the computer at the Atomic Research Establishment in Harwell, for a fee of £25,000 plus an annual rent of £156,000; it was rejected as too expensive.

The Millgarth incident room should have been the nerve centre of the police operation. Instead, it sagged under the backlog of unprocessed information, resulting in various strands of vital information remaining isolated instead of being cross-referenced. The killer continually slipped through the net as evidence against him was split and divided on the card index system. There was no centralized file of forensic reports or post-mortem findings, and few officers knew precisely what sort of weapons the killer favoured. Witness descriptions of the assailant and photofits created from survivor testimony languished apart; some, such as Marcella Claxton's excellent photofit, were shelved almost as soon as they were compiled.

It was an archetypal pressure cooker environment that reached boiling point when, only eleven days after Theresa's attack, the Ripper killed again.

21

JACQUELINE

Born on 22 May 1960, Jacqueline Hill grew up in a large detached home on Lealholm Crescent in Ormesby, three miles from Middlesbrough. She was the eldest child of Jack and Doreen Hill, but still close in age to her siblings Adrian and Vivienne.

At Eston Grammar School, Jacqueline was regarded as 'a model student who worked hard and got on with her studies'.[1] *Radio Times* columnist Alison Graham was at school with her; they stayed close friends at South Park Sixth Form College. Alison recalled:

> Jackie was the lovely, kind girl with the endearingly silly sense of humour. We sat together for two years of O level French lessons at our northern comprehensive school. She was much better at French than I was. We became pals, we giggled at Jackie's daft jokes, we had the kind of friendship that fourteen-year-old girls are so good at. I remember she bought me bath cubes for Christmas one year. I can't remember what I bought her. Later, at sixth form college, we'd chat in the common room and share our delight in one of our A level set-texts, Evelyn Waugh's *A Handful of Dust*.[2]

Jacqueline became a Sunday School teacher at the small parish church of St Cuthbert's in Ormesby where she had been baptized. She created a beautiful visual aid for the children: a painted wood shield depicting St Francis of Assisi surrounded by animals and birds. After lessons, if the weather was good, she took the children for nature rambles on the North Yorkshire Moors. During college holidays she worked at a camp in Ipswich for deprived children, earning a bronze Duke of Edinburgh Award. 'She was hard-working, generous, intelligent and reliable,' her friend Patti Hewstone recalled. 'It's impossible to find a bad word to say about her. She was everything people want their daughters to be.'[3]

Towards the end of her A level studies, Jacqueline decided to pursue a career in the probation service, gaining practical experience through volunteer work. She hoped to combine it with marriage and motherhood; her boyfriend Ian Tanfield was two years older and a junior technician in the RAF at Kinloss in Scotland. They planned to get engaged on her twenty-first birthday. Before then, with eight O levels and three A levels to her credit, she enrolled at Leeds University.

Originally, Jacqueline rented a room on the city outskirts. Her parents were so worried about her travelling to and from lectures during the Ripper attacks that she switched to women-only lodgings in Lupton Court, a large, modern complex of student residences on Alma Road in Headingley. More than six hundred students lived in the flats, just past a tract of empty ground behind the Arndale Centre and facing a row of handsome Bauhaus semi-detached properties dating back to the 1930s. Jacqueline shared a first-floor apartment with four girls and never failed to call her parents around 9 p.m. every Friday. She rarely went out to parties, preferring to concentrate on her studies, but was sociable nonetheless and enjoyed communal living.

By November 1980, Jacqueline was in her last year at university and had completed her training with the probation service. On Friday 14 November she sounded 'excited and carefree' when she rang her mother from the noisy Student Union bar.[4] She had two things to tell her parents: she had paid the deposit on a fortnight's holiday in Majorca with Ian the following summer, and she had an interview for a probation officer's job. She chatted about the outfit she had bought for the interview: a beautiful soft-grey suit.

The following Monday, 17 November, was a miserable day in Leeds – constant icy drizzle and dark, dank clouds. In the evening, Jacqueline attended a probation officers' seminar on Cookridge Street in the city centre. When it finished at 9 p.m. she caught the Beeston–Holt Park bus home to Otley Road, disembarking twenty minutes later at the stop opposite the Arndale. It was still raining; the car headlamps were a yellow blur as she crossed the road and hitched her raffia handbag further up her shoulder.

Alma Road was in darkness. The few streetlamps were obscured by dripping, overhanging trees, gathered at the entrance to 'Oakfield', a large, derelict old house. Jacqueline drew parallel with the wasteground behind the shops, where tall, unkempt shrubs grew about the concrete walkway from the car park. She made it no further.

Half an hour later on the same street, thirty-one-year-old Amin Hussain, a postgraduate student from Iran, spotted a red-striped raffia bag lying crumpled on the ground. He took it home to ask his flatmates what he should do with it. Thomas Curtis offered to take it to the university site office in the morning, leaving it in their hands. Amin agreed, but when he returned to the kitchen shortly before midnight, he noticed spots of blood on the bag. Two other students joined him, one of whom was mature student Tony Gosden, a former Chief Inspector with the Hong Kong police. He examined the bag and found a Barclaycard in the name of Miss Jacqueline Hill. Given the bloodspots, he thought the police should be informed immediately.

Student Paul Sampson made the call, which was logged by the Eastern Area control room in Leeds at 12.03 a.m. A message was passed to Ireland Wood Police Station on Spen

Lane, two miles from Alma Road. The police officers who arrived at Lupton flats gave the bag a cursory look, then asked Amin to fill in a lost property form. Paul Sampson was taken aback by their lack of urgency: 'I kept saying, "What about the blood?" And I kept thinking that somewhere there might be a young girl bleeding but breathing.'[5] He demanded that the two officers should at least visit the spot where the bag had been found, rather than sit drinking tea. Amin led them back to the road where the rain had begun pelting down. Torches in hand, the officers made a perfunctory search of the wasteground's perimeter, then turned and shone the lights across Oakfield's empty facade. They returned to their car at 12.30 a.m. to investigate a possible burglary.

The following morning, passersby on Alma Road found a pair of Fair Isle mittens and spectacles at the edge of the wasteground. At 10 a.m., shop manager Donald Court was on his way to the bank with a bag of silver and heading along the concrete walkway when a dark shape twenty feet below caught his eye through the sleet. He peered over the wall, drew in a sharp breath, and ran to raise the alarm.

Jacqueline's body lay two yards from the wall, near a single ash tree. She had been partially covered with her grey checked duffle coat. Officers screened her from view with a sheet of black tarpaulin held down by stones. Pathologist Dr David Gee made his way from Alma Road across hastily laid duckboards to examine Jacqueline's body. Accompanying him were Detective Chief Superintendent Peter Gilrain and Detective Superintendent Alf Finlay, deputy head of Leeds CID.

Gee realized immediately that Jacqueline had been struck from behind on the roadside and dragged some fourteen yards into the undergrowth. She lay on her back, clothes in disarray: her dark-blue jeans were about her ankles with a collection of keys attached to the waistband; her blue woollen knee-length socks were in place but her bra had been pulled up. A necklace holding a small, heart-shaped silver locket was tangled in her hair, which was matted with blood. There was a stab wound to her chest which, together with the head wounds and the state of her clothing, immediately suggested a Ripper attack with one appalling difference: the killer had stabbed Jacqueline through the right eye with a tool, penetrating her brain by one and a half inches.

Gee studied the injuries in more detail during the post-mortem, finding five lacerations to her head and fractures to her skull caused by a ball-pein hammer. He thought it unlikely that she had died immediately; had the two police officers searched only a short distance further into the wasteland, Jacqueline's life might have been saved.

The Hills were informed later that day. Jacqueline's father was only forty-eight years old but had taken early retirement after being diagnosed with cancer. Her mother was two years younger, still teaching arts and crafts. Jacqueline's brother had just finished school and her fifteen-year-old sister was in her final year of studies. While they travelled north to identify Jacqueline's body, 'prostrate with grief', a solicitor spoke to the press on their behalf, describing a situation from which there was no escape: 'If the Ripper is caught, a blaze of publicity will keep this nightmare alive. If he commits further murders, the family are still going to suffer.'[6]

Jacqueline's mother eventually spoke to journalists herself, telling them: 'The irony is that she was killed by the very type of person that she wanted to help. We have lost our strength and our faith. Even now, we still half-expect Jackie to walk in and shout, "I'm home!" and dump her pile of washing in the hall. We were worried about her being in Leeds. I told her not to go out alone, especially at night. But it was only a short walk from the bus stop to the flat – even I would not have thought twice about walking along there. I will never go to Leeds again.'[7]

Jacqueline's boyfriend, Ian Tanfield, was given compassionate leave from his RAF course in Lincolnshire. He felt 'shattered, angry and sick. I cannot believe what has happened. It makes me want to hit someone.'[8] Jacqueline's schoolfriend, Alison Graham, was training as a journalist in the South West and was numb with horror: 'I read about her murder in the "stop press" of my own newspaper. Later, I sat in my tiny flat, staring at nothing.'[9] Jacqueline's housemates at Lupton Court were deeply shocked and scared. Deborah Haworth spoke on behalf of them all: 'We are going to have to think very seriously about going out at all on our own – even about going as far as the supermarket after dark.'[10]

Again the police were cautious about confirming Jacqueline's death as part of the series. Senior Investigating Officer Detective Superintendent Alf Finlay told a press conference: 'There is no evidence at the moment to link this death with the so-called Yorkshire Ripper. We have not ruled him out yet but we have nothing to suggest it is him.'[11] Three days after the discovery of Jacqueline's body, police efforts were focused on tracing a car that had been spotted heading the wrong way down Alma Road at about 9.30 p.m. that night. There were sightings of several men in the Otley Road area, one of whom was described as having a Mexican-style moustache and a dark donkey jacket, resembling Marylyn Moore's first recollection of her attacker. The photofit she had compiled was reissued, but without result.

The media reacted angrily to the news of the latest murder, especially when Chief Constable Ronald Gregory told a press conference: 'It is easy to say with hindsight that officers should have found the body. There were three bloodspots on the handbag. At this stage the girl had not been reported missing. So here was a report of a handbag with one or two spots of blood on it. This was not significant.'[12] As jeers rebounded about the room, Detective Superintendent Finlay came close to erupting himself, snapping that he would no longer engage with the press unless he had something specific to tell them.

The *Guardian* observed: 'A definite change has occurred in police attitudes towards the media. Police were particularly reluctant yesterday to talk about the discovery of Jacqueline's handbag twelve hours before her body was found ... Over the past few months the police have discouraged any publicity about the murders and have said privately that a virtual campaign of silence may tempt the killer to either contact the police or to attack again. It is clear that they intended to pursue this approach.'[13] The irony was that Jacqueline's murder generated more newspaper coverage than any of the other attacks or killings. The Byford Report states: 'The murder of this respectable university student, coupled with apparently clear evidence of inefficiency and suspected lack of concern on the part of the police, promoted media pressure thereafter which was to undermine the confidence of the West Yorkshire Metropolitan Police to a very serious extent.'

The lack of urgency regarding Jacqueline's bloodstained handbag resulted in several calls being put through to the police to test the speed of their response; items of property were also reported to have been found, with cameramen primed to record the police reaction. A permanent press liaison officer was brought in to restore harmony between the two factions, but the damage had gone too deeply to be repaired.

George Oldfield, back on duty after a prolonged rest period, announced that the Ripper was responsible for Jacqueline's death:

No woman is safe while he is at large. To catch him we need all the help we can possibly get. Miss Hill was a most respectable, intelligent and educated young woman. Regretfully, our inquiries to date leave no doubt in our minds she is another victim of the so-called Ripper. I have always held the view that this man will continue to kill until he is caught. I ask anyone who believes they may have seen Miss Hill either on a bus travelling from the city centre, or who may have seen her near the Arndale Centre or in Alma Road, to get in touch with us. We believe that she met her death soon after she alighted from that bus.[14]

With the Union Jack flying at half-mast over Leeds University as a mark of respect for Jacqueline, fear rippled through the campus. A number of female students departed for home, most at their parents' beseeching. The Women's Action Group at the university chaired an emergency meeting to discuss how women could most effectively protect themselves. A spokeswoman declared: 'We are terrified. It's a disgrace that it takes something as horrifying as this to make people sit up and notice. Women are virtually under curfew in West Yorkshire now and that is a sad reflection on our society. We cannot go out alone after dark with any degree of safety.'[15]

Posters across the campus warned women: 'After Dark, Take No Risks', 'Do Not Go Out Alone' and 'Keep Your Doors and Windows Locked'. Greater restrictions were placed on women's activities, with some workplaces ordering shift changes to avoid female staff having to leave after dark. One woman recalls: 'It was always there, in the background, you couldn't get away from it. It was either affecting how you logistically got round places or it was in your face in that you were getting tapes played ... The normality of somewhere like Headingley, that it could happen, just seemed unbelievable.'[16] Another former student reflects: 'We became a bit obsessed by it. We were very frightened and I suppose we were a lot more careful about what we did. Making sure that you locked up and kept your windows closed ... That has an effect as well. Normally you might want to have your windows open at night, but we didn't do that. It felt like we were under siege.'[17]

The *Yorkshire Post* demanded to know, 'Why Can They Not Catch The Ripper?' pointing out that police efforts focused on the Ripper to the detriment of all else, including twelve attacks by 'the hooded rapist of Bradford', who had begun his assaults in June 1979. The report predicted with some accuracy:

'It is almost impossible to establish whether, relatively, West Yorkshire is worse than any other area for unsolved crimes of violence. Yet there is little doubt that even if the Ripper were caught today and given 13 life sentences at Leeds Crown Court six months hence, his name will be writ large on the minds of police officers for a very long time.'[18]

Three days after Jacqueline's body was discovered, Leeds University's Students Union Executive issued special notices to all four thousand female members, warning them again of the dangers of going out after dark. Twenty-year-old Sian Stephens lived close to Jacqueline's former digs and was deeply distressed by the restrictions:

> Girl students are virtually prisoners in their homes at night. Personally I hate Leeds now – I am so scared and all my friends feel the same. One girl I talked to today was in tears, she was so frightened. We can't go anywhere at night, even down to the library unless we have someone to walk home with. At the moment I don't think I can cope with my work because I am so frightened. My mum phoned me and asked me to go home. She comes from Devon where nothing like this ever happens and she is petrified for my safety. But I don't want to give in and go home. I have to stick it out. I told my mum I would never be out by myself.[19]

Melanie Barrett lived in Jacqueline's block and told a reporter who asked about morale among women: 'The atmosphere is terrible now. Everyone is terrified and depressed. All my friends want to get away from Leeds. It is suffocating everyone.'[20]

Student Union Officer Martin Blakely insisted that it was up to young women to 'act sensibly' and be 'personally vigilant. They must not, I repeat must not, go anywhere in Leeds themselves after dark.'[21] His statement, and others like it, provoked a surge of anger; demonstrations and marches were held in Leeds throughout the entire month. One indignant male *Yorkshire Post* journalist reported:

> Police lost their helmets as they struggled with a score of obscenity-shouting women who tried to get into the science and technology compound. The attempt failed and the marchers made for the refectory where they tried to interrupt a pop concert by the Iron Maiden band. A window was smashed as they struggled at the doors but concert stewards managed to bar the entrance. The women continued through the campus into Clarendon Road, where about 50 halted near the Grammar School and stood briefly on a pedestrian crossing, preventing traffic crossing the junction ... In Clarendon Road, I was assaulted as I walked behind the marchers, five women pinning me against a wall and kicking at my legs. I was rescued by three policemen.[22]

In Downing Street, the woman charged with running the country appeared equally furious. On 25 November, Margaret Thatcher summoned three government ministers to her office, telling them that police had so far 'failed totally' in their investigation into murders which constituted 'the most appalling kind of violence against women' and it was now 'a matter of public confidence'.[23] Thatcher's biographer recalls: 'So vexed was the Prime Minister by yet another murder, [she] announced her intention of going to Leeds that weekend to take personal charge of the investigation. Nobody but her, she thought, really cared about the fate of these wretched women. Certainly no man could care enough.'[24]

But steps had already been taken to shake things up. The following day, Regional Inspector Lawrence Byford informed the Home Office that George Oldfield had been removed from the case and replaced with a 'team from outside'.[25] To save him from embarrassment, it would be publicly announced that

Chief Constable Ronald Gregory had instigated the move. With the existing team exhausted beyond reason, Byford placed Detective Chief Superintendent Hobson in charge of the 'Ripper Squad' advisory team and made him temporary Assistant Chief Constable. The five-strong team, which included Stuart Kind, director of the Home Office Centre Research Establishment at Aldermaston, were tasked with reviewing the case and reporting their findings to Gregory.

Only three days after the Prime Minister's intervention, the Ripper Squad declared the letters and tape from Sunderland to be 'an elaborate hoax' and recommended immediately calling off the hunt for a suspect with a Wearside accent.[26] Shortly afterwards, Stuart Kind advised West Yorkshire Police that the killer was in all likelihood a man 'living in or near Bradford'.[27]

On 25 November, Doreen Hill's plea for help in tracking down her daughter's killer was reproduced in several newspapers: 'I want to ask everyone not just in Leeds or around Leeds but all over the country, to help us find the person who killed my daughter. Please think. Perhaps he lives in your house. He could live in a mansion, a block of flats, down the street. He lives somewhere, he works for someone – please think … If anyone has any money to spare will they please plaster Leeds and all the big towns with posters, large and small, in huge capital letters with just the simple words, "The Ripper is a Coward."'[28] A psychiatrist advised against this course of action, on the grounds that it might inflame the killer all the more. However, a number of newspaper offices in the area agreed to add £30,000 to the present reward on offer, bringing the total to £50,000.

Jacqueline was laid to rest in Ormesby on 19 December – the day she had expected to return home for Christmas with her family. Two hundred people attended her funeral service at St Cuthbert's, where she had planned to marry her boyfriend, who dropped the shining silver florin she had given him as a lucky talisman into her grave. It was a poignant tribute to the 'silver girl' of Jacqueline's favourite song, 'Bridge Over Troubled Water', which played at the burial. Reverend Michael Wright told the congregation: 'All who knew her speak with admiration of Jacqueline Hill. And we are glad that we knew her. We feel a deep sense of shock, grief and anger because her death was not an accident and we hope and pray there may be no more funerals like this one.'[29]

Finally, after five long years, those prayers were answered.

22

OLIVIA

In the early 1960s, while growing up in Jamaica, Olivia St Elmo Reivers had dreamt of becoming a nurse or a singer. When she was thirteen years old her family moved to Birmingham, where her father found employment in a factory. She left school two years later, working in shops until she gave birth to a daughter at nineteen and moved to Sheffield. In 1977, with little financial support from her partner, Olivia turned to prostitution. 'When the baby came along, that squashed it all,' she reflects. 'It wasn't meant to be like that. It's just the way things turned out.'[1]

Four years later, Olivia had a conviction for soliciting and was on a suspended sentence. She lived with her five-year-old daughter and three-year-old son in a narrow, red-brick terraced house on Wade Street in Grimesthorpe, a north-eastern suburb of Sheffield.

On the bitterly cold evening of Friday 2 January 1981, Olivia left her children with a babysitter and set out in the fur coat she kept for work. She met her friend Denise Hall at 9 p.m., and together they headed for the red-light streets of Broomhall. The two girls walked on opposite sides of Wharncliffe Road, a short residential street popular with kerb-crawlers. When a brown Rover with a black vinyl roof pulled up alongside Denise, she leaned in. The driver was in his thirties, smart and bearded with thick black hair. He asked if she was 'doing business', but something about him unnerved her and she drew back, mumbling an apology.

'I don't know why Denise was suspicious, but she turned him down,' Olivia recalls. 'Obviously, something must have warned her off. You might think you can judge people's characters by looking at them, but *I* can't look at a person and decide what sort they are. Of course, we were all worried about the Ripper, but no one knew what he looked like, so we wouldn't have known him if we saw him. Anyway, you can't afford to turn down the chance of £10 in this game.'[2]

The Rover pulled away, but Olivia spotted it again an hour later as she was strolling down Broomhall Street. 'The driver asked me if I was doing business and I said I was. I told him it was £10 in the car with a rubber. He said that it was okay.'[3]

They drove to nearby Melbourne Avenue, where the driver turned his car into the courtyard of Light Trades House. He parked near the building and switched off his lights. 'I said to him, "Would you like to pay first, please?"' Olivia recalled. 'He gave me a £10 note and I took a rubber out and had it in my hand, putting the money into the packet. He asked, "Do you mind if I talk to you a bit?" I said, "No." He said that he had had an argument with his wife. He did not say what about or what the result of the argument had been. He asked me my name and I said, "Sharron." He said his name was Dave.'[4]

The man took off his overcoat and suggested moving into the back of the car. Olivia told him she preferred to stay in front and pushed her seat back. They spent ten minutes trying to have intercourse, but 'Dave' was unable to get an erection. Olivia thought he seemed edgy. She had just asked him about it when twin beams of light swung towards them from the end of the driveway.

The police car parked directly in front of the Rover, dipping its headlights. Two uniformed police officers climbed out. Olivia's client said quickly, 'Leave it to me. You're my girlfriend.'[5]

Police Sergeant Robert Ring and Police Constable Robert Hydes had noticed the Rover as they passed the driveway at 10.50 p.m. Hydes asked the man sitting nervously in the driver's seat if he owned the car. He nodded, giving his name as 'John Williams' and an address in Canklow. Ring asked him about his passenger. 'John' replied that she was his girlfriend, but had trouble remembering her name. Olivia told the officers her real name, seeing no point in a denial.

The two men returned to their vehicle. They radioed divisional headquarters, requesting a check on the registration number. The control room told them that Olivia was on a suspended sentence for soliciting, and that the number belonged to a Skoda – not a Rover. The officers walked back to the car and escorted Olivia to their vehicle. The driver disappeared momentarily, returning with apologies for having needed to urinate. At the police station, he did exactly the same before sitting down to be questioned.

In an interview room at Hammerton Road, the dark-haired bearded man admitted that he was Peter Sutcliffe of 6 Garden Lane, Heaton in Bradford, and he had stolen the Skoda plates from a scrapyard near Brighouse.

In accordance with procedure, Ring informed the incident room at Millgarth of the situation, asking if Sutcliffe had ever been questioned with regard to the Ripper attacks. He was told that he had been interviewed in connection with the £5 enquiry arising from Jean Jordan's murder, and was logged as a cross area-sighting in the red-light district observations. There was also a reference to his handwriting, shoe size, the gap in his teeth, and his occupation as a long-distance lorry driver. He denied visiting prostitutes. His wife and close family had always provided him with alibis. On that basis, Ring was instructed to keep him in custody.

At 3 a.m., Olivia arrived home, trembling with the realization that a few hours earlier she had been alone with a man now strongly suspected of being the Yorkshire Ripper. She sat up until dawn, smoking one cigarette after another and letting cups of tea go cold as she replayed her last sighting of him at Hammerton Road, 'looking like a little boy lost with the bobbies giving him a right grilling. He looked so pitiful – someone you could cuddle, someone you could twist round your little finger. You wouldn't think in a million years that he could be the Yorkshire Ripper.'[6]

From Sheffield, Sutcliffe was transferred to Dewsbury Police Station. While he was being questioned the following evening, Sergeant Ring returned to Light Trades House. Remembering Sutcliffe's brief disappearance, he checked the ground near an oil tank and lifted out two objects: a ball-pein hammer and knife.

Four days later, Ring also thought to check the toilet at Hammerton Road, which Sutcliffe had asked to use upon arrival. Feeling along the water cistern, he discovered a wooden-handled knife.

By then, Peter Sutcliffe had confessed to being the Yorkshire Ripper.

His details had been on record in Wakefield and at New Scotland Yard since committing various motoring offences in the mid-1960s. He claimed his attacks on women began at the end of the decade in revenge for being short-changed by a prostitute who laughed about it in front of other people.

The first attack he admitted to was in September 1969, within a month of the alleged incident. He had gone out in Bradford that evening with his friend Trevor Birdsall, intending to find the woman who short-changed him. Birdsall parked his mini-van on St Paul's Road near Manningham Park, where Sutcliffe got out and disappeared. Ten minutes later, he returned breathlessly and told Birdsall to drive away. As they raced home, Sutcliffe described how he had followed an 'old cow' to a house and struck her on the head with a stone in a sock.[7] He then removed the sock from his pocket and threw the broken stone out of the moving vehicle.

The woman was more observant than Sutcliffe realized; she had made a mental note of the van's registration number and called the police. Two officers turned up on Birdsall's doorstep and he directed them to Sutcliffe, who admitted to hitting the woman, but with his hand, rather than the stone in the sock. The police issued a verbal warning and said he was fortunate the woman didn't want to press charges; her partner was in prison and had no idea she was soliciting.

Details of the attack were never committed to paper. At his trial, Sutcliffe declared: 'I was out of my mind with the obsession of finding this prostitute. I just gave vent to my anger on the first one I saw ... I got out of the car, went across the road, and hit her. The force of the impact tore the toe off the sock and whatever was in it came out. I went back to the car.'

He confessed to a second incident that took place later that same month, September 1969. A police officer had noticed him sitting in his Morris Minor in Manningham late at night with the engine running and lights off. Realizing he had been spotted, Sutcliffe sped off with the officer in pursuit. Sutcliffe managed to get away, but the officer was tenacious and found the car abandoned a short distance away. He soon discovered Sutcliffe crouched in a garden, clutching a hammer. His explanation was that one of his hubcaps had worked loose and he needed the hammer to thump it back into place.

He admitted after his arrest in 1981 that on this occasion, he had also had a knife in his possession which the police failed to find. He told detectives that he had gone out that night in 1969 in search of a sex worker to attack, believing that God had instructed him to do so in a mission against prostitution. He had been charged with being equipped for theft and was fined £25. The Central Criminal Record Office made reference at the time to him being 'in possession of a housebreaking implement by night, namely, a hammer'. The Bradford Criminal Record Office carried three photographs of Sutcliffe on file from that period. All three clearly showed him as being dark-haired, dark-eyed and with a beard and moustache.

Sutcliffe had been interviewed by police twelve times between attacking Anna Rogulskyj and being charged with the murders and assaults. Nine of those interviews were conducted specifically in relation to the Ripper inquiry. In addition to the points outlined when Ring telephoned Millgarth for further information about him, Sutcliffe was one of only three hundred men who could have received the £5 found in Jean Jordan's handbag in his wage packet. He also closely resembled some of the photofits.

Detective Constable Andrew Laptew had been unaware of these details when he and another officer interviewed Sutcliffe in Heaton after his Sunbeam Rapier was seen thirty-six times in Manningham's red-light district. Nonetheless, he was unsettled enough to submit a report recommending that Sutcliffe should be examined more closely. He took his report personally to Holland, who only wanted to know whether the suspect had a Geordie accent. Laptew replied, 'No, he's local, he's from Bradford. He's a dead ringer for the photofit—' but Holland cut him off, roaring, 'If anybody mentions photofits to me again, they'll be doing traffic for the rest of their service.'[8] Laptew's report was filed away.

Sutcliffe had his own views on the photofits. After seeing the one based on Tracy Browne's recollections, he remarked to his mother-in-law that it was such a good likeness it could have been him.

Trevor Birdsall described having had suspicions about his friend ever since the attack on Olive Smelt. He later claimed that he was convinced Sutcliffe was guilty after watching Olive on *Newsnight,* coupled with the discovery that a car matching his friend's Rover was sought by the police, and seeing the latest photofit. On 25 November 1980, Birdsall wrote an anonymous letter to the police, naming Peter Sutcliffe as the killer.

The following day, Birdsall's girlfriend urged him to visit the police in person. They arrived together at Bradford police headquarters, where Birdsall ran through his suspicions with the young constable on duty. An action note was sent to Millgarth Police Station requesting that Sutcliffe be interviewed again; it remained in the filing tray into the new year. Two weeks after visiting the police, Birdsall telephoned them for an update but no one seemed able to tell him anything. He assumed his friend had been cleared.

An unprecedented media storm erupted at the news that the Yorkshire Ripper had been captured. Olivia, who was so nearly his last victim, and would almost certainly be called to give evidence at trial, was taken by police to a secluded hotel in an effort to keep the press at bay. Soon afterwards, however, she told a reporter: 'I go cold all over when I think how I touched this man, felt his skin on mine. My flesh still creeps.'[9] She feared returning to sex work: 'I think I've used up all my luck and there would always be the feeling that some crank would want to harm me if they found out I'd been with the Ripper and had escaped. They might fancy doing the job properly. There are mad men about like that.'[10]

She added: 'I can't tell you all that happened, but it was the worst moment of my life. I am so very tired. I have still not got over the shock of it all. I have no idea if I will stay on the game. I need time to think things out … The police have done a good job and I have to thank them for coming up when they did.'[11]

23

'AN INNER COMPULSION TO KILL'

Following his arrest, Peter Sutcliffe confessed to several attacks and murders, often recalling the details with remarkable clarity. The excerpts reproduced here are taken from his original statements to police and at trial.

Anna Rogulskyj

Sutcliffe claimed that he drove alone into Keighley on the night of 4 July 1975 after being told by colleagues that there was 'a plague of prostitutes in Keighley'. He admitted to having seen Anna Rogulskyj twice in the area before that evening, and when questioned about her attack in January 1981, nodded: 'Yes, that was me. She had a funny name and I asked her if she fancied it. She said "not on your life" and went to try and get into a house. When she came back, I tapped her up again and she elbowed me. I followed her and hit her with the hammer and she fell down. I intended to kill her but I was disturbed ... I was certain she was a prostitute – scum. I was being given instructions on what was the best moment to attack. I waited till she turned to walk back home. Then I hit her on the back of her head with a hammer. I knew that was safest. I knew she wouldn't see me. It was all over in less than ten seconds. I didn't mean her to suffer. I meant her to die.'

Olive Smelt

Together with Trevor Birdsall, Sutcliffe headed into Halifax on the evening of 15 August 1975. He noticed Olive at the bar of the Royal Oak: 'She annoyed me, probably in some minor way. I took her to be a prostitute.' On the journey back to Bradford with Birdsall, he spotted Olive again as she walked home along Woodside Road. 'I said to Trevor, that is a prostitute we saw in the public house,' Sutcliffe recalled. 'She fell down. I was going to kill her. I had the knife with me at that time. I was going to kill her, but I did not get the chance …' He confirmed he had 'hit her on the head and scratched her buttocks with a piece of hacksaw blade or maybe a knife. My intention was to kill her but I was disturbed by a car coming down the road.'

In court, Birdsall stated: 'The next evening I read in the *Telegraph & Argus* a report about a brutal attack on a woman in Boothtown. It crossed my mind that Peter might be connected with it.'[1]

Wilma McCann

Sutcliffe recalled driving into Leeds on 30 October 1975: 'That was the incident that started it all off, I was driving through Leeds late at night, I'd been to somewhere having a couple of pints, you'll know the date better than me. It was Wilma McCann. I was in a Ford Capri, K registered, a lime green one with a black roof with a sun grill in the back window. I saw this woman thumbing a lift where the Wetherby Road branches to the right, but you can carry straight on. She was wearing some white trousers and a jacket. I stopped and asked her how far she was going. She said, "Not far, thanks for stopping," and she jumped in.

'I was in quite a good mood and we were talking on the way. She said something about, just before we stopped, did I want business. To me I didn't know what she meant by this. I asked her to explain and straight away a scornful tone came into her voice, which took me by surprise because she had been so pleasant. She said, "Bloody hell, do I have to spell it out?" She said it as though it was a challenge. My reaction was to agree to go with her.

'She told me where to park the car. It was just off this road, we turned left, we came to this field which sloped up. I parked near the field. We sat there for a minute talking then all of a sudden her tone changed and she said, "Well, what are we waiting for, let's get on with it." Before we stopped she had said that it would cost a fiver. I was a bit surprised, I was expecting it to be a bit romantic. I think she had been drinking because she was being irrational. I couldn't have intercourse in a split second, I had to be aroused. At this point she opened the car door and got out. She slammed the door and shouted, "I'm going, it's going to take you all fucking day!" She shouted something like, "You're fucking useless."

'I suddenly felt myself seething with rage. I got out of the car wanting to hit her to pay her back for the insult. I went to her and said, "Hang on a minute, don't go off like that." She was only three or four strides away, she turned and came back to me. She said something like, "Oh, you can fucking manage it now, can you." She sounded as though she was taunting me. I said, "There's not much room in the car, can we do it on the grass?" This was with my idea of hitting her. She said, "I'm not going to do it here bloody well next to the car." With that, she stormed up the hill into the field.

'I had a tool box on the back seat of the car and I took a hammer out of the tool box. I followed her into the field. I took my car coat off and carried it over my arm, I had the hammer in my right hand. I put my coat on the grass. She sat down on the coat. She unfastened her trousers. She said, "Come on then, get it over with." I said, "Don't worry, I will." I then hit her with the hammer on her head. I was stood up at that time behind her. I think I hit her on the top of the head, I hit her once or twice on the head. She fell down flat on her back and started making a horrible noise like a moaning gurgling noise. I thought, "God what have I done?"

'I knew I had gone too far. I ran to the car intending to drive off. I sat in the car for a while, I could see her arm moving. I was in a numb panic, I still had the hammer in my hand. I put it back in my tool box. I half expected her to get up, and realised I would be in serious trouble. I thought the best way out of the mess was to make sure she couldn't tell anybody. I took a knife out of the tool box, it had a wood handle with one sharp side. The blade was about 7" long, about 1/2–3/4" wide. I went to her. She was still lying on her back. I thought that to make certain she was dead I would stab her in places like the lungs and the throat. I stabbed her at least four times, once in the throat. Before I stabbed her in the body, I pulled her blouse or whatever it was and her bra, so I could see where I was stabbing her. I was in a blind panic when I was stabbing her, just to make sure she wouldn't tell anyone. What a damn stupid thing to do just to keep somebody quiet. If I was thinking logical [sic] at the time, I would have stopped and told someone I'd hit her with the hammer. That was the turning point. I realise I overreacted at the time, nothing I have done since then affected me like this.

'After I'd stabbed her I went back to the car, I remember that I'd taken my coat off the ground after I'd hit her with the hammer, and I'd taken my coat back to the car. I started the car and shot off backwards along the narrow road leading to the road, swung the car round, and drove away towards Leeds. I drove home as soon as possible. I was then living at my mother-in-law's house at 44 Tanton Crescent, Clayton, Bradford. I was very frightened and don't even remember driving there. I thought I was bound to get caught. I parked my car outside the house. I'm trying to remember if it was my mother-in-law's house I was living at then. I've thought it out now, it must have been her house. I looked over my clothing before I went in the house. I went straight to the bathroom and washed my hands and went to bed. I don't have any of the clothes I was wearing that night, they are worn out. I cannot honestly remember what I did with the hammer and the knife, I don't remember chucking them away that night. I haven't got the knife now, I may have kept the hammer in the tool box, but I'm not sure of that even.'

He added in his statements to the police that 'I'd gone there [Leeds] for the purpose of picking up a prostitute with the intention to kill her. I realised shortly after she had got into the car that she was a prostitute because she asked me if I wanted business and the evil chain of events went on from there.' He was keen to impress upon detectives that it was never his intention to have sex with her; their alleged conversation about it was 'just a preamble leading up to the true purpose of my killing her. It was my idea to get her to go up a distance up the field. To accomplish this I had to put up with all kinds of language and abuse because she couldn't see the point. I had the tackle (a hammer and a kitchen knife) with me in my pocket and, in fact, I didn't go back to the car and return to it. I hit her with the hammer, she still made loud noises and I hit her with it again, and the noises still didn't stop. I then took the knife out of my pocket and stabbed her about four times, as I've previously described.'

The following day he saw the murder discussed on the local news: 'I felt sick and I still half expected a knock on the door by the police. I carried on trying to act as normal, living with my wife and in-laws. At that time I worked at Common Road Tyre Services at Oakenshaw. After that first time, I developed and built up a hatred for prostitutes in order to justify within myself the reason why I had attacked and killed Wilma McCann.'

Emily Jackson

'This time I drove to Leeds looking for a prostitute because I felt I could not justify what I had done previously and I felt an inner compulsion to kill a prostitute,' Sutcliffe told police. He had driven to Leeds in his Capri at about 8 or 9 p.m. on 20 January 1976. Near Wetherby Road he saw a woman dressed in a heavy coat and headed towards her: 'I stopped and wound the window down. I said, "How much?" She said, "Five pounds." She got in the car. I remember when she got in there was an overpowering smell of cheap perfume and sweat, this served all the more for me to hate this woman even though I didn't even know her. Looking back, I can see how the first murder had unhinged me completely.

'She had an overcoat on and she was heavily built and had brown hair. She said she knew where we could go. I knew from the outset I didn't want intercourse with her. I just wanted to get rid of her. At that time, I think I was dressed in my working clothes, at that time I used to wear wellington boots at work. At her direction, I turned the car round and drove back the way I'd come. We had just gone about 400 yards and she told me to turn left. I turned in and then turned left again and drove behind some old buildings, it was a cul-de-sac. I couldn't bear even to go through the motions of having sex with this woman. On the journey she told me that she could drive. I wanted to do what I'd got in mind as soon as possible. I remember turning on the ignition again so that the red warning light came on, and pretended that the car would not start. I said I would have to lift up the bonnet to sort it out. I asked her if she would give me a hand. We both got out of the car.

'I lifted up the bonnet of the car. I had picked up a hammer which I had put near my seat for that purpose. I told her I could not see properly without a torch. She offered to use her cigarette lighter to shine under the bonnet. She was holding her lighter like this [he demonstrated], I took a couple of steps back and I hit her

241

over the head with the hammer. I think I hit her twice. She fell down onto the road. I took hold of her hands or wrists and pulled her into a yard which had rubbish in. I then made sure she was dead by taking a screwdriver and stabbing her repeatedly. I pulled her dress up and her bra before I stabbed her to make it easier. To be truthful, I pulled her clothes up in order to satisfy some sort of sexual revenge on her as on reflection I had done on McCann.

'I stabbed her frenziedly without thought with a Phillips screwdriver all over her body. I had taken the screwdriver with the hammer in the well of the driving seat. I was seething with hate for her. I remember picking up a piece of wood from the yard, about 2–3ft long and 3" x 1" [wide], and pushing up against her vagina with it as she lay on her back. I cannot recall taking her knickers down. I threw the wood away in the yard. I left her lying on her back, I never took anything from her.

'Just as I was about to get into my car, a car came round with its lights on and stopped a few yards from where my car was. I don't know what make of car it was, but it scared me. I put the hammer and screwdriver on the car floor and drove away. I went straight home to my mother-in-law's house. At that time I had a feeling of satisfaction and justification for what I'd done. I found that I didn't have any blood on my clothes which I could see, so I had no need to dispose of them. I am still unable to recall if it was the same hammer I used on Jackson as I did on McCann, but I do recall buying a new hammer from a hardware shop near the roundabout in Clayton. It had a flat head on one side and a nail extractor on the other, which I later used on women. The hammer I used on the first two had a flat head on one end and a ball on the other.'

Marcella Claxton

Sutcliffe was cruising Chapeltown in his white Ford Corsair in the early hours of 9 May 1976. He claimed that Marcella responded to his advances as if she were soliciting, telling detectives: 'I picked her up in the Chapeltown area, she asked me if I was the police, I said, "No, do I really look like a policeman?" She decided to get into the car, and suggested where we go. We ended up in what I knew later as Soldiers Field. We got out of the car at my suggestion, and she took off her trousers whilst leaning against a tree, and she sat down on the grass and suggested we started the ball rolling. Straight after she said this I hit her with the hammer. Again, I don't know what it was this time, but I just couldn't go through with it, I could not bring myself to hit her again for some reason or another and I just let her walk away, possibly to tell the nearest policeman or passer-by what had happened.

'I went back to the car in a stupefied state of mind, I just had a feeling of morbid depression, I didn't care whether she told anybody or not, and I drove back home. I only recall hitting her once, as she got up and walked away, but owing to my state of mind I'm not sure whether I hit her more than once.'

Irene Richardson

After the pubs closed on the evening of 5 February 1977, Sutcliffe drove out to Leeds in his white Ford Corsair; he also owned a red version of the same car. He spotted Irene not far from the Gaiety and later claimed that she had offered him sex: 'It was my intention to find a prostitute to make it one more less. I saw this girl walking in some cross streets in the middle of the vice estate near a big club. I stopped my car and she got in without me saying a word. I told her I might not have wanted her, she said, "I'll show you a good time. You are not going to send me away, are you?"

'She told me to drive to the park. At this time you knew where I was picking them up. She told me where to drive and we came to this big field which was on my left. I drove off the road onto the field and stopped near some toilets [close to the scene of his previous attack on Marcella]. She wanted to use the toilets, so she got out and went over to them. She came back and said they were locked. Before she went to the toilet she took off her coat and placed it on the ground. When she came back she said she would have a wee on the ground. She took her boots off and placed them on the ground, then she crouched down to have a pee.

'By this time I was out of the car and I had my hammer in my hand. As she was crouching down, I hit her on the head from behind, at least twice, maybe three times. She fell down. I then lifted up her clothes and slashed her in the lower abdomen and also slashed her throat. I left her lying face down and I covered her up with her coat. I put her knee boots on top of her before I covered her up. I then got into my car and drove off the field. I cannot remember whether I drove off or backed off. When I got to the road, I saw a couple sitting on a bench near the toilets. I did not see a car.

'I was living with my wife at 6 Garden Lane, Heaton. I drove straight home. I looked at my clothes before I went in, I did not see any blood stains. I was wearing jeans and I believe I had some boots on. I don't remember throwing any of my clothes away. I kept the Stanley knife, but I haven't seen it for a long time, I think I may have lent it to someone.'

He added: 'By this time, after the Richardson killing, prostitutes became an obsession with me and I couldn't stop myself, it was like some sort of a drug.' Asked why more than a year had passed since his last murder, he paused before replying: 'I was having a battle in my mind. My mind was in a turmoil whether I should kill people.'

Patricia Atkinson

Sutcliffe recalled travelling through Bradford on the evening of 23 April 1977: 'I drove off Lumb Lane into Church Street, I knew this was a prostitute area. I was in my Corsair, either the white one or the red one. I saw this woman in St Paul's Road at a junction with another road, she appeared drunk and was banging on the roof of a white Mini and was shouting and bawling, "Fuck off!" and such things to the driver, who then drove off at speed. I pulled up to her and stopped and without me asking she jumped in the car. She said, "I fucking told him where to get off!" She said, "I've got a flat, we can go there." She told me where to go.

'We turned right at the junction with Manningham Lane, turned left down Queens Road, left into Oak Avenue, and turned second left and stopped at her flat. She told me she lived alone. I parked up outside her flat and she got out and went in. I picked up a hammer as I got out of the car. I remember this was a claw hammer that I had bought at the Clayton hardware shop. I followed her into the flat, she closed the curtains, and I hung my coat on the hook on the back of the door. She took her coat off and sat on the bed, her back was slightly towards me. I went up to her and hit her on the back of the head with the hammer. She fell off the bed onto the floor. I picked her up and put her back on the bed.

'That was the first time I had noticed the red blood, before it had always been dark, but this time in the light I saw lots of blood on the bed and on the floor. When she was on the floor I hit her another twice, or three times, before I put her on the bed. I pulled the bedclothes back before I put her on the bed. She had already pulled her jeans down before I hit her. I pulled her clothes up and I hit her several times on her stomach and back with the claw part of the hammer and I saw that I was making marks on her body doing this. I then covered her up with the bedclothes. I think she was lying face down or on her side when I left her.

'When I first hit her she was making a horrible gurgling sound, and she carried on making this noise even though I'd hit her a few times. She was still making a gurgling noise when I left, but I knew she would not be in a state to tell anybody.

I drove home and put my car in the garage. I looked at my clothes in the garage. I saw that I had some blood on the bottom of my jeans. I went in the house, my wife was in bed. I took my jeans off and rinsed them under the cold tap and hung them up. I also saw some blood on one of my shoes or they may have been boots, I rinsed this under the tap and wiped it with a sponge. I believe I was wearing a pair of brown Doc Martins [sic] boots at that time. I'm trying to think what I did with the claw hammer, I think I used it again on a woman. I have thrown it away over a wall near Sharps Printers at Cottingley, I can't remember when it was exactly. At that time I carried on as though nothing had happened.'

Jayne MacDonald

Sutcliffe spent the evening of 25 June 1977 drinking with male friends before heading alone to Leeds at closing time: 'The next one I did I still feel terrible about, it was the young girl Jayne MacDonald. I read recently about her father dying of a broken heart and it brought it all back to me. I realised what sort of a monster I had become. I believed at the time I did it that she was a prostitute. This was on a Saturday night. I drove to Leeds in my Corsair, I think it was the red one, but I'm not one hundred percent sure. At this time the urge to kill prostitutes was very strong and I had gone out of my mind.

'I saw this lass walking along quite slowly towards the crossing near the Hayfield pub in Chapeltown Road. She stopped on the corner before crossing over Chapeltown Road. I anticipated that she was going to walk up one of the streets up past the Hayfield. I drove my car into the Hayfield pub car park and got out. I took my hammer out of the car. I think it was the claw hammer. I also had a knife with me that time, it was a kitchen type knife with a black ebonite handle and a thin blade. I walked towards the narrow street behind the Hayfield to see where she was, and just as I got there, she was walking up.

'I walked behind her, I was very near to her, I followed her for short distance [sic], she never looked round. I took the hammer and I hit her on the back of the head and she fell down. I then pulled her by the arms face down into a yard behind a fence. I recall that her shoes were making a horrible scraping sound on the ground. I pulled her into the corner of this yard. I hit her another once at least, maybe twice, on the head. I pulled her clothes up exposing her breasts, and I stabbed her several times with the knife in the chest. Before this I stabbed her in the back. I left her lying in the corner. I cannot remember whether she was lying face up or face down. She was wearing a jacket and a skirt. I walked back down the same street to where I had parked my car. As I got to the car park, I saw a group of people walking up the narrow street (Reginald Street) from Chapeltown Road. I got into my car and drove away into Reginald Terrace, into Chapeltown Road, and drove straight home.

'I think my wife may have been working that night. I have remembered that my wife started working some Friday and Saturday nights at Sherrington Private Nursing home in Bradford. That is why I have done a lot of my attacks on a Saturday night. I don't think I had any blood on me following this one. I cannot recall what I was wearing then. I cannot remember what I did with the knife, I must have taken it home with me and washed it. I feel I may have left it in the Corsair when I scrapped it. The hammer may have been the one I threw over the wall at Sharps Printers.'

He added that he was troubled when he read in the newspapers that Jayne was only sixteen years old and not a sex worker: 'I felt like someone inhuman and I realised that it was a devil driving me against my will and that I was a beast. When the Ripper came up in conversation at work or in a pub I was able to detach my mind from the fact that it was me they were talking about, and I was able to discuss it normally. This amazed me at times that I was able to do this.'

Maureen Long

Sutcliffe spotted Maureen shortly after she left the Mecca Ballroom in Bradford on 10 July 1977: 'She was just past the hamburger stand when I saw her. I stopped my car and said, "Are you going far?" She said, "Are you give [sic] me a lift?" I said, "If you want one." She got in. She told me she had been to the Mecca. She told me where she lived, and that she lived with a man who was an ex-boxer and that he was a spoilsport and would not take her to the Mecca.

'She directed me where to drive to her house, which was somewhere off Leeds Road to the left. She pointed out a house in a row of terraced houses where she said she was going. She told me not to stop outside but to drive past. I drove about 20 yards past and stopped. She got out of the car. She had told me that if there was no one in the house we could go in. She had asked me if I fancied her and I told her that I did, just to please her. She went and knocked at the door of the house and she was banging away for a minute or two. Then she came back and got into the car and told me she knew a place where we could go.

'She told me where to drive, and I drove eventually into Bowling Back Lane and turned right down a cobbled street. I stopped the car some way down the street. There was some spare unlevelled land on the left and a big high wall on the right. She got out of the car and said she was going for a piss first and she went to the spare land and crouched down and had a piss. I had my hammer ready as she got out of the car and I also had a knife. I think it was the same knife I had at MacDonald. I got out of the car whilst she was having a piss and as she was crouching down I hit her on the head with the hammer. She slumped down. I pulled her by the hands further onto the spare ground. She was not making any sound. I pulled up her clothes and I stabbed her three or four times with the knife in her chest and back. I did see a caravan with a light on over the spare land, but it didn't put me off what I was doing. I thought that I had stabbed her enough when I left her.

'I went back to the car, got in, and drove off. I was under the impression that the street I was in may be a cul-de-sac, so I reversed my car by turning it round in the street I was in. No, I didn't, I remember that I backed out of the street into Bowling Back Lane facing towards the City. I drove along Bowling Back Lane towards the general direction of the City centre, and drove home to Garden Lane. I believe my wife may have been working that night, or else she was in bed. I don't think I found any blood on myself on that occasion.'

Again, Sutcliffe read about his actions in the press the following day but 'got a nasty shock' when he discovered that Maureen had survived. He thought it was 'the end of the line there and then. I thought she would be able to identify me. I think it was about that time that I threw the hammer over Sharps' wall.' He was relieved to read a few days later that Maureen was suffering from amnesia, which made him 'less worried about being caught. My desire to kill prostitutes was getting stronger than ever and it took me over completely. I was in a dilemma, I wanted to tell someone what I was doing, but I thought about how it would affect my wife and family. I wasn't too much bothered for myself.'

Almost as an afterthought, he remarked to detectives: 'I saw Maureen just a couple of weeks ago. I was in the Arndale Shopping Centre with my wife when I came face to face with her. I recognised her immediately, she seemed to look at me, but she obviously didn't recognise me.'

Jean Jordan

On 26 September 1977, Sutcliffe and his wife Sonia moved into their own home in the Bradford suburb of Heaton. He arrived in Manchester alone just after 9 p.m. on 1 October, having resolved to avoid the places now associated with him: 'I realised things were hotting up a bit in Leeds and Bradford. People had dubbed me the Ripper. I decided to go to Manchester to kill a prostitute. I had read in a paper somewhere, or a magazine, of a priest chastising what went on in his parish at Manchester where there obviously were prostitutes.

'One Saturday night in October 1977, I drove over to Manchester. I believe it was in my red Corsair. I had a look at my map in Road Atlas to see where Moss Side was and I drove there. I went through Manchester town centre, Princess Street I think it was, followed it all the way down past the University, which eventually came out near the Moss Side area. It was a run-down area and almost immediately on arriving there I saw several girls plying for trade. I pulled up at the kerb side and asked a girl if she wanted business. She was very slim with light coloured hair, not bad looking. She told me if I waited further along the road she would meet me there. I drove on two hundred yards and made a right turn, then a three-point turn to face the main road once again. After a couple of minutes the girl drew level. She saw my car just as she was going to get into another car which had stopped for her. I think this was an 1100, a light coloured one, either grey or fawn. She didn't get in but came over to me, which I suppose was the biggest mistake she ever made.

'She came up and got into my car. She told me she was going to go with the man in the other car until she saw me. She told me she wanted a fiver for business, and she told me she knew a place. I drove at her direction until we came to an allotment. She told me to drive in the entrance to the allotment, which I did. I said to her, "Fancy coming here, you see that greenhouse?" I pointed to a greenhouse that was about 30 yards away. "That belongs to my uncle." I said this to her thinking she would get out the car to use the greenhouse for business. I told her there was plenty of room and some heating in there. I was wanting to see her off. She then asked for the money, she said, "You're not forgetting about the money, are you?" I said, "Of course not," and I promptly gave her a five pound note. She got out of the car and headed for the greenhouse.

'I followed her, and seeing there was no entrance into the greenhouse from where we were, I told her we would have to climb over a low fence. While she was starting to climb over the fence I hit her over the head with the hammer. She fell down and was moaning quite loudly. I hit her again and again on the head until the moaning stopped. At this time I saw some car headlights suddenly come on. These were from a car parked further into the allotments than I was. I had turned sharp right when I drove in and I was parked up close to the hedge. This car was parked about 60 yards further into the allotment. The car started up and I knew it would be moving within seconds, so I pulled the girl under the bushes, the perimeter bushes, and threw her belongings, handbag, etc., out of the way. On reflection I think there was just her handbag. I stood with my back to the hedge and threw the bag diagonally to my right.

'I stayed where I was, I saw the car out into the road. No sooner had the car gone, when another car driving along the road, which was a dual carriageway, slowed right down. I saw through the bushes it was indicating left to come into the allotments. Thinking this was a very dangerous position to be in, I hid behind my car. I saw this car drive into the allotments, the car drove up the road, turned round, and stopped in the same place the other car had just left from. I didn't wait around any longer, I jumped into my car and drove off towards the centre of Manchester, and drove home.

'The hammer I used that night was the one I had found lying in my garage after I had taken over my house. I took the hammer back with me. Having driven half way back, I realised suddenly that this didn't put me in the clear, because I had given her from my wage packet a brand new five pound note. I was working at Clarks then. I was in a dilemma once again. I kept on driving towards home, I didn't realise whether she would be found or not. I decided I could not risk going back to retrieve my £5 note, and I carried on home. My wife was either working, or in bed, when I got home. I was puzzled when no mention of this was made in the newspapers or television over the next few days. I decided before a week was out that she was lying there undiscovered and that I would go back to retrieve the £5 note.

'One night, about a week later, the opportunity arose for me to go back as we were having a house warming party with family and gathering the coming weekend. My mother and father, brothers, and sisters came from Bingley to my house, and at the end of the party I ran them home. Then I made my return trip to Manchester. This was about 11pm on either the Saturday or Sunday. I drove to the allotments in my red Corsair and arrived there within 45 minutes. I turned left off the dual carriageway into the allotments. To get to there I had to drive to a roundabout and double back to that side. I turned right when I got into the allotments, as I had done before, and parked up about the same place.

'I found the body still hidden in the place I left it. I pulled it out from the bushes and pulled off her clothes and boots. I went through them desperately trying to find the £5 note. I just threw the clothes about as I took them off. I realised that she hadn't got the £5 note in her clothes, and that it must have been in her handbag. I roamed about all over the allotments frantically searching for the bag, but I couldn't find it. I was cursing the girl and my luck all the time.

'Having not found the £5 note, I gave vent to my frustrations by picking up a piece of broken pane of glass and slashing it across her stomach. When I did this there was a nauseating smell which made me reel back and immediately vomit, it was horrendous. I forgot to say that before I did this it was my intention to create a mystery about the body, I felt sure this was the end for me anyway. I had taken a hacksaw out of my car intending to remove her head. I started sawing through her neck, the blade might have been blunt because I was getting nowhere at all, so I gave it up. If I had cut the head off I was going to leave it somewhere else to make a big mystery out of it. The glass I used was about 3/4 of a pane with the corner missing. I was very frustrated not having found the £5 note, and thinking that my time was up. I remember I kicked her a few times, and I rolled her over before I left her.

'I then drove away realising I should stay looking for the fiver, but I thought I had been there long enough. I got home and went to bed. When I got home I was very surprised to see I had not got much blood on me, just a bit on my shoe and at the bottom of my trousers on one leg, and some on the back of my hand. I washed my hands. I was wearing a pair of casual grey trousers, one of my old pair, the blood wouldn't come off these. I put them in the garage in a cupboard to dispose of later. I was wearing my soft slip on shoes, dark brown. I wiped these clean. I don't think I have got them now. I later burned my trousers with some garden rubbish at the other side of our garden wall on the field.

'I read about the body of Jean Royle being found and sat back waiting for the inevitable, as I had assumed that the line of enquiry about the £5 note would follow. I read about the note being traced to a Shipley bank, I knew Clarks got the wage money from a Shipley bank, and that a local enquiry would be made, and by some miracle I escaped the dragnet.

'I've had at least three hacksaws, I don't know which one it was I took to Manchester. I threw the blade away in the dustbin. One of my hacksaws broke after this and I threw it in the bin.'

Marylyn Moore

Sutcliffe told detectives that two months after murdering Jean, he was 'taken over completely by this urge to kill and I couldn't fight it'. On 14 December 1977, he drove his red Corsair to

Leeds and saw Marylyn walking down Spencer Place. After she had refused to get into someone else's car, he hoped to convince her that he was safer: 'I turned left into Spencer Place, turned first left, and left again into a narrow street, and stopped near the corner of the road I had just been on. It was my intention to get her into my car with the minimum of fuss. I knew she had refused to get in one car, so I got out of my car and walked to the corner. She was only a few yards away walking towards where I was stood. I walked back to my car and as she came into view I shouted, "Bye now, see you later," and, "take care," and I waved towards the houses on my left. I did this to give her reassurance that I was all right.

'I got in and started the engine and opened the passenger window. I asked her if she was doing business. She glanced at the house, said, "Yes," and got in. She told me where to drive. She asked my name, I told her it was Dave. We had some conversation in the car but I cannot remember what I might have said. She directed me to this place which was up a narrow lane and I can only describe it as an oasis of mud. It was an open area with a building to one side. I parked up.

'I suggested she get into the back of the car. She agreed and she got out and she went to the rear passenger door nearside. When she got out, I got out with my hammer, which I had on the floor at my side. I went round the front of my car and up behind her. I took a swing at her with the hammer but I slipped on the mud and lost my balance. I only caught her a glancing blow on the head. She cried out and I hit her again on the head. She was still screaming. After the second blow, she fell down.

'I saw some people walking along about forty yards away on the narrow road at the top. I jumped in my car and started it up. I put my foot down but the back wheels started spinning and I couldn't drive off at first. When the car got a grip I slewed round to the right and I drove away with a lot of wheel spin. I drove straight home. That night I was wearing the old brown car coat, which you've got, and a pair of blue jeans and a pair of brown Doc Martins [sic] boots.'

Yvonne Pearson

Sutcliffe helped his parents move into a new house in Bingley on the evening of 21 January 1978. He waived the offer of a drink with his father and brother Mick in favour of heading instead to Lumb Lane, again in his red Corsair. He recalled: 'A light grey or fawn Mark II Cortina started backing out of Southfield Square on my left as I approached, so I slowed down to let it out. That's when I saw Yvonne Pearson, she was blond and was wearing dark trousers. On reflection it was a very fateful moment for her, me just slowing down as she came along. She stepped straight up to the car as I stopped and tapped on the window. She asked me if I wanted business. This was one time when I was genuinely going home as it happened, but I still had a hammer in the car on the floor, under my seat. I told her to get in.

'She suggested that I turn the car round and she told me where to drive. I drove back along Lumb Lane, past Drummond Mill, turned right down a road onto White Abbey Road, and I was directed to turn by Yvonne left into a street behind Silvios [sic] Bakery. I drove to the very end of this street where there was a large open space like a parking space and parked the car. I asked her how much she wanted. She said, "It depends how much you can afford. A good time £5, more than a good time £10." She had very few words to say after that, the last words she said was, "Shall we get into the back?"'

'We both got out and she went round to the back door of the car on the nearside, she tried to open it but it was locked. I opened the front passenger door, reached in, and opened the rear door catch. As she opened the door, I hit her from behind twice on the head with the hammer. She fell down and started to moan loudly. I dragged her by the feet on her back about 20 yards or so to where there was an old settee lying on its back on some spare land. When I got her to the settee she was still moaning loudly.

'At that moment a car drove up and parked next to my car. I saw there was a blond woman in the car and a man driving. To stop her moaning, I took some filling from the settee, I held her nose and shoved the straw into her mouth, then I shoved it down her throat. I was kneeling behind the settee, hiding from the motor car, keeping hold of her nose. I let go after a while to see if she was still making a noise through her nose, but when I did, she started again, so I took hold of her nose again. The car seemed to be there for ages before it drove away.

'I stayed still, petrified with fear while the car was there. When the car had gone I was seething with rage. Her jeans were nearly off, because she had undone them at the car, and when I was pulling her by the feet I nearly pulled them off. I pulled her jeans right off. I think I kicked her hard to the head and body. I was senseless with rage and I was kicking away furiously at her. After this, I remember acting very strangely, I talked to her and apologised for what I had done, but she was dead. I put the settee on top of her. I was very distraught and I was in tears when I left her. This was the first time I had apologised to someone I had killed. I drove home, I cannot recall the time, but it was after 9pm. I can't remember if Sonia was in the house or not. I remember stopping on the way home and I just sat in the car trying to work out why I had done this killing. My mind was in a turmoil.

'Oh, I've just remembered it might have been a walling hammer that I used on Yvonne, there was two walling hammers in the garage of the house when I moved in. I remember I put one in the car when I threw the other one away at Sharps. It might still be in the garage somewhere.'

Detectives believed Sutcliffe had returned to the crime scene but he denied it, although he admitted checking the newspapers obsessively to find out if Yvonne's body had been discovered: 'I found it incredible to believe that she hadn't been found. I read a story that she had gone to Wolverhampton. I didn't dare go back to where she lay, there was no reason to go back.'

Helen Rytka

Sutcliffe told detectives: 'Before Yvonne was found I had committed another murder in Huddersfield, Helen Rytka. I did not know the Huddersfield red-light area, but one day I had to make a delivery in Huddersfield in the afternoon, I noticed a few girls plying for trade near the market area. Two or three nights later I decided to pay them a visit.'

It was 30 [sic – it was 31] January 1978, ten days after Yvonne's murder: 'The urge inside me to kill girls was now practically uncontrollable, I drove to Huddersfield in my red Corsair one evening. When I got to the red-light area I came across one or two girls walking round the street. I stopped and asked one girl if she was doing business. She said yes, but I'd have to wait, as her regular client was picking her up at any minute. She was a half-caste girl. I drove off, and after going about 50 yards round the corner I saw another half-caste girl. I stopped and asked her and she got in. She told me she shared a flat with her sister, but she was quite willing to have sex in the car. She said it would cost £5.

'She told me where to drive, which was only about eighty to ninety yards away in a timber yard. I drove straight into this yard and parked in an area at the end of the lane that ran between the stack of wood. On the way to the yard we passed the half-caste girl I had tried to pick up. She told me that it was her sister. Afterwards, when I had read about it in the papers, I realised that I had seen these two Rytka sisters in Clayton where they used to live. I must have given her some money, but I can't recall handing it over to her, because she started to undo her jeans and started to pull them down. Then she hesitated and she said it would be better in the back of the car. I agreed thinking that it was what I wanted her to do anyway.

'We both got out, she went to the rear nearside door. I picked up a hammer from under my seat and walked round the front. By the time I got to her she had opened the rear door and was getting in. I hit her on the head with the hammer as she was practically into the car. The hammer struck the edge of the top door sill and diminished the impact with her skull to a mere tap. She jumped back in alarm out of the car, at the same time letting go of her jeans, which fell down around her knees, and she exclaimed, "What was that?" To which I replied, "Just a small sample of one of these," and I hit a furious blow to her head which knocked her down, she just crumpled like a sack. She was making a loud moaning sound, so I hit her a few more times on the head.

'On looking up, I realised that I had done this in full view of two taxi drivers, who were no more that [sic] 35 yards away up the right-hand side of the wood yard. Their cars were parked one behind the other facing me. The drivers were stood talking to each other. I dragged Helen by the hands to the end of the wood yard. I then pulled off her jeans and her knickers and her shoes or boots. She had stopped moaning, but she wasn't dead. I could see her eyes moving. She held up her hand as though to ward off any further attack from me. I told her not to make any more noise, and she would be all right.

'By this time, I was aroused sexually, so I had intercourse with her. I just undid my fly, I spread her legs out, and did it. It only took a few minutes before I ejaculated inside her. Her eyes appeared to be focusing on me when I was doing it, but she just laid there limp, she didn't put anything in to it. When I'd finished, I got up, and she began moaning once again and started to move as well. We were out of sight of the taxi drivers, but I knew they could quite possibly have heard the sounds. I couldn't drive away for obvious reasons, one being that she was still showing signs of life. I was worried sick that I was about to be discovered, and was furious that she could not keep quiet.

'I took my knife from my pocket, I think it was the one with the rosewood handle, which is probably still at home in my knife drawer. I plunged the knife into her ribs and again into her heart, I did this five or six times. Before I did this I had taken all her clothes off, apart her jumper. I threw these over the wall. I dragged her by the arms to where I thought she would not be discovered, which was behind some bushes in a gap between a woodpile and a wall. There wasn't much room, I had to part lift, part pull her in. Then I covered her up with a piece of asbestos sheet.

'I stayed in the wood yard for some minutes and when I looked the taxi drivers had gone. I reversed out of the yard and drove off. The operation had taken about half an hour. I drove straight home. I found that I had some blood on one of my fawn court shoes. I rinsed it off. I had my Levi jeans and I think I had a dark blue pullover on, but I couldn't see any blood on these. I kept the hammer, I'm not sure which one it was, but I don't think it was the walling hammer.'

Sutcliffe later corrected aspects of this statement, telling detectives that he had confused it with Irene's murder: 'From the outset, the one purpose I had in mind was to kill her at the first opportunity, but things were made difficult from the moment I parked the car because Helen unfastened her trousers and seemed prepared to start straight away. It was very awkward for me to find a way of getting her out of the car. We were there five minutes or more, while I was trying to decide which method to use to kill her. Meanwhile, against my wishes, she was in the process of arousing me sexually. I found I did not want to go through with this, so I got out of the car on the pretext of wanting to urinate. I didn't urinate, but I managed to persuade her to get out as well, as we'd be better off in the back of the car.

'As she was attempting to get in, I realised this was my chance, so I hit her from behind on the head with the hammer.

Unfortunately, during the downward swing the hammer caught the top edge of the door frame and gave her a very light tap on her head. She apparently thought I had struck her with my left hand, and she said, "There no need for that, you don't even have to pay." I expected her to immediately shout for help as there were a couple of taxis in view about a distance of forty yards or so. She was obviously very scared. I then pushed her forward onto the ground and she stumbled and fell somewhere in front of the car just out of sight of the taxi drivers. I jumped on top of her and covered her mouth with my hand, it seemed like an eternity and she was struggling. I told her if she kept quiet she would be all right. As she had got me aroused less than a minute previously, I had no alternative than to go ahead with the act of sex as the only means thereby of persuading her to keep quiet, as I had already dropped the hammer several yards away.

'After what seemed like several more minutes, I got up and saw that the cars had gone so I started to grope around looking for the hammer. I found it, and as I was turning towards her she tried to run past between me and the car, this is when I hit her a heavy blow to the head. I then dragged her back in front of the car, and may have hit her again before I dragged her back. I began gathering her belongings and throwing them over a wall. She was obviously still alive then. I took the knife from the front of the car and stabbed her several times in the heart and the lungs. After this, I pulled her to a place a few yards away where I thought she wouldn't be found so quickly, when I got there I covered her with a sheet of asbestos or corrugated metal.'

Vera Millward

Sutcliffe stated that he 'paid another visit to Manchester one evening a few months after Rytka', driving to the city's red-light district on the evening of 16 May 1978: 'When I got there, there was no sign of any girls, so after reaching a night club on a corner in a small labyrinth of terraced houses about three quarters of a mile square, I took the third left after the night club, which was a long street running from one end to the other of this area. I drove down to the bottom end and there I saw a woman obviously waiting to be picked up. It was Vera Millward. I stopped and asked her if she was doing business. She said, "Yes," but it would have to be in the car. The price was £5, she got in and I drove off.

'She told me where to drive and I followed her directions, which led us into a hospital grounds. I stopped the car in an area near a narrow road, from where I could see an archway obviously used by pedestrians. I parked up the car and suggested to her that it would be better in the back. I don't think I'd paid her. She got out of my car and went to the back door. I picked my hammer up from under the seat and walked round the back of the car.

As she was opening the rear door I hit her on the head with the hammer, and she dived backwards past where I was stood. She was on her hands and knees when I hit her again at least once. She fell flat on her face. I pulled her by her wrists over to the edge of the area where there was either a fence or bushes. I took out my knife I was carrying, I think it may have been the same one I used on Rytka, but I'm not sure.

'I pulled her clothes up and slashed her stomach either vertical or diagonal. It opened up her stomach. Then I rolled her over onto her stomach and left her lying there. I drove away. I think I had to reverse out to get back again. I didn't get any blood on me on that occasion. I think I was wearing my brown car coat, which you've got.'

Josephine Whitaker

A year passed between Vera's murder and the death of Josephine Whitaker. On 4 April 1979, Sutcliffe went out drinking with Trevor Birdsall. He dropped his friend home after closing time, then drove to Halifax in his black Sunbeam Rapier, having previously sold the red Corsair. The departure from areas he was more familiar with was due to the police presence in the red-light districts of Bradford and Leeds: 'I'd been driving round aimlessly, the mood was in me, and no woman was safe while I was in this state of mind. Without realising, or without having a particular destination, I arrived in Halifax late at night. I drove along through the centre, passed the Bulls Head, round the roundabout, past the Halifax Building Society.

'I came to a wide road with a sweeping curve to it, I took a right turn and eventually came to a big open grass area. I just kept driving round this grassy area until I came to a row of terrace houses about a quarter of a mile from the grass area. I saw Josephine Whitaker walking up this street. She was wearing a three-quarter length skirt and a jacket. I parked up in this street with terrace houses and started to follow her on foot, and I caught up with her after a couple of minutes.

'I realised she was not a prostitute, but at that time I wasn't bothered, I just wanted to kill a woman.

'When I caught up with her I started talking to her. I asked her if she had far to go. She said, "It's quite a walk." She didn't seem alarmed by my approach. I continued walking alongside her and she started speaking to me about having just left her grandmother's and that she had considered staying there but had decided to walk home. I asked her if she had considered learning to drive, I think she said she rode a horse and that it was a satisfactory form of transport. We were approaching the open grassland area. She told me that she normally took a short cut across the field. I said you don't know who you can trust these days. It sounds a bit evil now, there was I walking along with my hammer and a big Phillips screwdriver in my pocket ready to do the inevitable.

'We both started to walk diagonally across the grass field. We were still talking when we were about 30–40 yards from the main road. I asked her what time it was on the clock tower, which was to our right. She looked at the clock and told me what time it was. I forget the time she said. I said to her she must have good eyesight and I lagged behind her pretending to look at the clock. I took my hammer out of my pocket and hit her on the back of the head twice.

'She fell down and she made a loud groaning sound. To my horror I saw a figure walking along the main road from my right. I took hold of her by the ankles and dragged her face down away from the road further into the field. She was still moaning as I did this. When I thought I was a safe distance from the road, I stopped. Then I heard voices from somewhere behind me to my left. I saw at least two figures walking along the path across the field toward the Huddersfield Road. I forgot to mention that on the way up to the grass we passed a man walking a dog. We were within five feet of him. As these people were walking on the path, she was still moaning loudly.

'I took my screwdriver, I remember I first pulled some of her clothing off. I was working like lightning and it was all a blur. I turned her over and stabbed her numerous times in the chest and stomach with the screwdriver. I was in a frenzy. After I'd stabbed her, she stopped moaning. I left her lying face down. I walked over to the main road, but I thought I saw someone coming up from the bottom, so I went back across the field the way I had come and went to my car.

'I drove home, I don't think I had any blood on me, but my feet were covered in mud. I had my black boots on, which had been worn out and thrown in the bin. I had my old brown coat on that night.' When two police officers interviewed him in 1980, Sutcliffe was wearing the same boots: 'I stayed dead calm, and as I got into the wagon I realised I was standing on the steps, which were mesh, and they could look up and see for themselves that I was wearing those boots. But they didn't. They couldn't see what was in front of their own eyes.'

Barbara Leach

Sutcliffe stated that his 'urge to kill' was so strong that it was 'totally out of my control'. By the time of Barbara Leach's murder, he had exchanged the Sunbeam Rapier for a Rover and wanted to take it out for a spin. He drove towards Bradford university and had just passed the Manville Arms when he spotted Barbara: 'She was walking up the road on my left. I drove past her and turned left into a wide street. I just drove a few yards and stopped on the nearside. I was just going to get out of the car when Miss Leach turned the corner and walked towards the car. She was walking at a very slow pace. She was wearing jeans. She carried on walking past the car.

'I left the car and followed her for several yards. I had my hammer out and I think I had my big screwdriver with me. When she reached an entrance yard to a house, I hit her on the head with the hammer, she fell down. She was moaning. I took hold of her by the wrists, or was it by the ankles, and dragged her up this entrance to the back of the house. She kept making loud moaning noises. There was like a dustbin area at the rear of the house. I remember that I stabbed Barbara with the screwdriver, the same one as Whitaker, and I remember that I put her in the dustbin area and covered her up with something, but I was acting like an automaton and I can't seem to remember the sequence of actions. I think I was wearing my brown coat that night.

'When I left her, I went to my car and drove away and went straight home. I remember I later threw the big screwdriver away over the embankment near the lorry park on the westbound side of Hartshead Service Station.'

Marguerite Walls

Initially, Sutcliffe denied responsibility for Marguerite's murder: 'No, that wasn't me. You have a mystery on your hands with that one. I've only used the rope once on that girl at Headingley [Dr Bandara].'

Eventually he admitted that on 20 August 1980: 'I was on my way to Leeds, with a view to killing a prostitute, when I saw that this woman was walking towards me at a distance of about sixty yards. She disappeared around a corner on my left, so I slowed down and turned into this particular road. I was already in some kind of a rage and it was just unfortunate for her that she was where she was at the time, 'cos I parked the car and got out and followed her along the road.

'Having caught up with her over a distance of three or four hundred yards, I let her have it with a hammer, I hit her on the head, it seems as though there was a voice inside my head saying, "Kill, kill, kill," and as I hit her I shouted, "You filthy prostitute." There was nobody else about, but as she was on the pavement, I dragged her inside a gateway quite a few yards, in what appeared to be someone's garden.

'Round about this time somebody walked past the entrance, I don't know whether they had seen me or not, because they appeared to look in. I didn't have a knife on me this time, but I had a length of cord which I strangled her with. I removed her clothes and I was going to leave her in an obvious position for people to see, but round about this time the road outside started to be quite busy with pedestrians going back and forth. I changed my mind and covered her up with some straw instead.'

Asked where he had left Marguerite's body, he replied: 'In the far corner of the garden near a wall. I was very upset again after this time, I knew I couldn't do anything to prevent myself carrying on killing. The inner torment was unimaginable, because, as strange as it may seem, I never wanted to kill anybody at all, I just had to get rid of all the prostitutes whether I liked it or not.'

Detectives wanted to know why he had denied killing Marguerite. He replied: 'Because when I was questioned initially I knew I was in such deep water through killing through the method I normally use, that this would possibly open completely new lines of enquiry into other murders which could have been committed and which I knew I hadn't done. I thought that maybe it would be better to sort this out at a later date, when I had cleared up all the other matters, and having denied it first, it would have made matters worse at the time if I had changed my mind again. Nothing I would have said could have been taken seriously, this is why I'm making a true account of everything and every detail.'

He gave them an explanation for deviating from his usual method of murder: 'Because the press and the media had attached a stigma to me, I had been known for some time as the Yorkshire Ripper, which to my mind, didn't ring true at all. It was just my way of killing them, but actually I found that the method of strangulation was even more horrible and took longer.'

Upadhya Bandara

Sutcliffe stated that on the evening of 24 September 1980, he 'used the rope on that girl [Dr Bandara]. She was walking slowly along like a prostitute, and I hit her on the head with a hammer. I had looped a rope round her neck. I didn't have any tools with me to finish her off so I used the rope. I dragged her down the road and her shoes were making a scraping noise. I apologized to her and took her shoes off and put them over a wall with her handbag.'

Afterwards, he recalled: 'This is when I decided I couldn't kill people like this. I couldn't bear to go through with it again, as there was something deep inside preventing me.'

Theresa Sykes

Sutcliffe had equally little to say about his attempted murder of sixteen-year-old Theresa on 5 November 1980: 'I saw her walking along the road and followed her down this footpath and hit her a couple of times and knocked her down. But someone started shouting and I ran away and hid in a garden.' He added that he had attacked her simply because 'she was the first person I saw that night. At first, it didn't take me any time to decide which women were prostitutes. I think something clicked because she had on a straight skirt with a slit in it. She crossed the road in front of me.'

Jacqueline Hill

'The last one I did was Jacqueline Hill up at Headingly,' Sutcliffe declared. On Monday 17 November 1980, he drove to Leeds in his Rover, had a quick meal of KFC and then drove around for a while before heading back down Otley Road: 'I was driving slowly when I saw Miss Hill walking on the pavement to my right towards the road I now know is Alma Road. I decided she was a likely victim.

'I drove just past her, turned right into Alma Road, and parked in the near side about five/six yards up and waited for her to pass. I saw her walk up the right-hand side of the road (Alma Road). I got out of the car and followed about three yards behind her. As she drew level with an opening on the right-hand side, I took my hammer out of my pocket and struck her a blow on the head. She fell down. She was making a noise.

'By this time I was again in a world of my own, out of touch with reality. I dragged her, I cannot remember whether by the feet or the hands, into the entrance to the spare land. Just as I got there a car drove into Alma Road from Otley Road with its headlights on. I threw myself to the ground so I wouldn't be seen. The car passed. I can't imagine how I wasn't seen.

'By now Miss Hill was moving about and I think I hit her once again, or maybe twice, on the head. Then I dragged her further onto the spare land out of sight of the road. As I was doing this a girl walked past the entrance, I think she was walking up the road away from Otley Road. I just stopped dead and waited for her to pass. I pulled Miss Hill's clothes off, most of them. I had a screwdriver on me, I think it had a yellow handle and a bent blade. I stabbed her in her lungs. Her eyes were wide open and she seemed to be looking at me with an accusing stare. This shook me up a bit, I jabbed the screwdriver into her eye but they stayed open, and I felt worse than ever. I left her lying on her back with her feet towards the entrance. I think she was dead when I left.

I went to my car and drove up Alma Road to the top and turned round and drove back down to Otley Road. I remember that when I reached about halfway down someone walking indicated to me that I was obviously going the wrong way down a one way street but I carried on into Otley Road and turned left, I turned right at the lights and drove home. The hammer I used on Hill was the one I dumped at Sheffield with the knife I've told you about before.'

Sutcliffe added: 'I am terribly sorry about this tragic loss to her family and friends, I would do anything to alter what has happened. I am glad I have been apprehended because I was totally out of my mind when I committed these acts.'

24

WOMEN ON TRIAL

For those women who had survived Sutcliffe's attacks, news of his capture came as an overwhelming relief. Olive Smelt reflected: 'It meant I could stop looking at friends and neighbours, thinking, "Are you the one who tried to kill me?"'[1] She felt more able to rebuild her life in the knowledge that he was no longer walking the streets: 'It's not going to be easy, but you've got to work at it. I know I've had it pretty bad but we've all got to keep going.'[2] The youngest survivor, Tracy Browne, recalls: 'I was in a pub with some pals when the news came through that Sutcliffe had been caught. I just said, "Thank God for that." But a chill ran through my body when I heard he lived only a mile from me. And when I saw Sutcliffe's photo in the newspaper, I recognized him straight away.'[3] Marylyn Moore felt only anger: 'Him – that bastard – he'll spend the rest of his life in a warm cell with three square meals a day. And me? For as long as I live it will be dreams, dreams, dreams … I'm going to court when Sutcliffe is tried. I want to see him go down. Just to know that he's gone inside forever.'[4]

Relatives of the women Sutcliffe had murdered felt similar relief tempered with a sense of utter desolation. Newly widowed Irene MacDonald recalled: 'We lived for the Ripper to be captured. When we heard the newsflash of his arrest it was just like the end of a war. We all cheered, scarcely able to believe it. I wish Wilf could have been here to see him thrown into prison.'[5] Wilfred MacDonald had passed away on 11 October

1979, only a few weeks after telling a reporter: 'Death is one of the few things I have to look forward to. I have lost my will to live. I think I died, inside me, that dreadful morning in the mortuary.'[6] He was buried in Harehills Cemetery with his beloved daughter.

Victims' children found it hard to comprehend that the killer now had a face and a name; nor did they share Chief Constable Ronald Gregory's sense of being 'absolutely delighted' that Sutcliffe was finally in custody. Wilma McCann's son Richard recalls: 'They were "absolutely delighted". They'd caught him and it was that phrase that stuck in my mind. "Absolutely delighted." Those words, those type of words, I didn't want to hear connected to the death of my mother. Delight? No.'[7] Neil Jackson was taking down Christmas decorations at his aunt's house in Armley when he heard the newsreader mention that his mother's killer was being held in the prison there. He stood on the doorstep in the dusk, staring at the prison opposite and trembling uncontrollably. Across town and in nearby parishes, bells were rung to mark the end of Sutcliffe's reign of terror.

The trial of Peter Sutcliffe opened on 29 April 1981 at the Old Bailey. He stood charged with the murders of thirteen women: Wilma McCann, Emily Jackson, Irene Richardson, Patricia Atkinson, Jayne MacDonald, Jean Jordan, Yvonne Pearson, Helen Rytka, Vera Millward, Josephine Whitaker, Barbara Leach, Marguerite Walls and Jacqueline Hill. He also faced seven counts of attempted murder: Anna Rogulskyj, Olive Smelt, Marcella Claxton, Maureen Long, Marylyn Moore, Upadhya Bandara and Theresa Sykes. Sutcliffe entered a plea of not guilty to murder but guilty of manslaughter on the grounds of diminished responsibility. The prosecution was set to accept that plea, which would have prevented details of the attacks and police errors being made public, but to the surprise of both defence and prosecution, Mr Justice Boreham insisted on a full trial.

Sutcliffe's assertion that 'God encouraged me to kill people called scum who cannot justify themselves to society' was seized upon by the media. No mention was made of the men who used the services of sex workers, or of the fact that for Sutcliffe only prostitutes – rather than child killers and rapists, for example – fitted the category of 'scum'.

In court, the main issue was whether or not Sutcliffe truly believed all his victims were prostitutes and if there was a sexual element to the murders. Sir Michael Havers, leading the prosecution, told him: 'Your story would have gone straight down the drain if you had to say to the doctors that six of them were not prostitutes.' The absence of discussion regarding why he should feel that prostitutes deserved to die implied yet again that there was nothing inherently wrong in that view; his 'madness' only became evident when he harmed women who were not sex workers. *The Times* reported: 'Sometimes after killing women who were not prostitutes he had worried that it might be the voice of the devil [who had failed to make the distinction]. But he was able to tell that they were prostitutes by the way they walked. He knew they were not innocent.'[8] The lack of quotation marks in the report reinforced the implication that his attitude had its own logic.

In truth, there was no need for any examination of Sutcliffe's motives, since he had already made several statements to detectives explaining that his murderous impulses came from a hatred of all women: 'I realised Josephine was not a prostitute but at the time, I wasn't bothered. I just wanted to kill a woman'; 'I realised now I had an urge to kill any woman.'[9] Not those he regarded as 'scum', just 'any woman'.

West Yorkshire Police's updated dossier on his crimes, issued to all forces in the UK during 1979, was a useful tool in supporting his claim that he initially targeted sex workers or women he believed to be soliciting. Sutcliffe's assertion that he had been driven to murder by the actions of a woman who short-changed him when he paid her for sex, was presented in court by Harry Ognall QC on behalf of the prosecution as 'a perfectly sensible reason for harbouring a grudge against prostitutes' and therefore 'a perfectly common-sense motive'. The men in court seemed to be of one mind in affirming that it was 'not hard to see how this cocktail of frustration, guilt and humiliation could lead to fury and the fury to an urge, not just for revenge, but for the satisfaction in spirit, if not in body, of his sexual urge'.[10] Sutcliffe gauged his masculinity against female sexuality by killing women, but could not satisfy that need by a single murder.

The Attorney General, Sir Michael Havers, invited the jury to agree that this contention was quite reasonable and therefore Sutcliffe was sane: 'Was this not a classic case of provocation? God hasn't told him to hate prostitutes or kill them. It was a reason which, you may think, was not altogether surprising, the reaction of a man who had been fleeced and humiliated … The sort of loss of control which you don't have to be mad for a moment to suffer.' Sutcliffe was able to live with himself not *despite* the murders but *because* of them, as Joan Smith points out: 'The common denominator in the attacks is Sutcliffe's obsessional destruction of those parts of the female body which signal gender … he left one of his victim's shoes or boots on her body as a symbol of his power, evidence of the way in which he had trampled his victim underfoot. These are the actions of a man to whom femininity was a threat, who hated and feared it so much that his survival depended on his capacity to locate and annihilate it.'[11]

In legal terms, the dilemma was whether Sutcliffe had been fully aware of his actions and gained sexual satisfaction as a result, or if he had been suffering a delusion in which sexual motivation was absent, thus absolving him of responsibility. Four psychiatrists examined him prior to trial; he told them that God had instructed him to destroy prostitutes. Referring to the murder of Jacqueline Hill, Sutcliffe told Dr Hugo Milne: 'She turned around and looked as if she was adjusting her skirt or her stocking, and this suggested that it was the behaviour of a prostitute. God invested me with the means of killing. He has got me out of trouble and I am in God's hands. He misled police and perhaps God was involved in the tapes so the police would be misled.'[12]

All the psychiatrists gave evidence in court, agreeing that Sutcliffe's 'symptoms' formed a classic manifestation of paranoid schizophrenia. The prosecution disputed this view, pointing out that Sutcliffe had been cunning enough to hide his actions from everyone (with the exception of Trevor Birdsall in the case of Olive Smelt), including those closest to him; that he never made a single reference to hearing voices of any description prior to being apprehended; that he had gone to great lengths to evade capture, even changing his method of killing from stabbing to strangulation in an effort to mislead police; and that he could have used his wife's previous treatment for paranoid schizophrenia as a basis for his depiction of madness, having had ample opportunity to study her symptoms.

After his arrest, Sutcliffe had said nothing to his captors about divine intervention triggering his crimes. By his own admission, he had experienced sexual arousal from the murders, which also showed clear evidence of sexual sadism. Helen Rytka was the only victim with whom Sutcliffe had intercourse and the psychiatrists – all male – appeared to accept that he did so simply to convince other men in the vicinity that no crime was taking place. The fact that Helen was dying in unimaginable agony as he had sex with her did not appear to trouble them, and their acceptance of Sutcliffe's explanation reveals their narrow concept of sexual pleasure; namely, that it was only valid when achieved through penetration.

In their efforts to discredit Sutcliffe's claims of a Godly voice urging him to kill, the prosecution outlined the definition of sexual killing with examples from Sutcliffe's statements and behaviour. The Attorney General referred back to Helen Rytka, saying frankly, 'God didn't tell you to put your penis in that girl's vagina.' He also discussed Sutcliffe's description of Emily Jackson's murder, in which he mentioned lifting her bra and pulling down her pants in order to 'satisfy some sort of sexual revenge on her'. With Sutcliffe in the witness box, Havers told the court that the accused had placed a plank of wood between her legs and asked Sutcliffe whether he had pushed her legs open. He replied, 'No, I don't think so. I may have positioned her to show her as disgusting as she was.'

Referring to the frenzied stabbing of victims' breasts, the repeated insertion of a weapon into the same wounds, and penetrating one victim's vagina with a screwdriver, Havers queried whether this was done to gain sexual gratification. After his arrest, Sutcliffe had taken detectives to a railway embankment near the M1 to locate the screwdriver he had thrown away after using it on his victims. Havers declared that the tool had been sharpened at the tip to create 'one of the most fiendish weapons you have ever seen'.[13] Ognall asked psychiatrist Dr Hugo Milne whether the instance of vaginal stabbing indicated sexual sadism. Dr Milne initially tried to suggest that it might have been accidental, but was forced to retract his remark amid general derision. He then admitted that this action, together with the scratches around another victim's vagina, must have had a sexual element. He also conceded that there were clear indications of a sexual impulse in six of the murders.

The most compelling evidence regarding Sutcliffe's motive was never revealed in court. Nor was it mentioned in Sutcliffe's statements. Had it been made public, his defence of having acted on God's instructions would have been utterly discredited. When Sutcliffe was searched after his arrest, and much later than was normally the case, he was found not to be wearing any underpants. These were tucked inside the lining of his jacket, which was deliberately torn to conceal the weapons he carried. Instead of normal underpants, he wore a self-made garment. Originally a woollen, V-neck sweater, it had been modified with padding halfway down the sleeves. Sutcliffe wore it with his legs inside the sleeves, knees against the padding. He pulled it up to his waist underneath his trousers with the open neck of the jumper leaving his penis exposed when he undid his fly. He could then crouch over his victims while he masturbated, keeping his knees comfortably padded.

The premeditation involved in such a garment left his defence in ruins, and made a complete mockery of the arguments put forward by psychiatrists. In *Wicked Beyond Belief: The Hunt for the Yorkshire Ripper* (2012), author Michael Bilton states that the re-fashioned jumper was 'as important in terms of evidence as the actual weapons he used to murder his victims. It spoke volumes about his sexual motives and his state of mind during his attacks on helpless women.'[14] Yet it was not disclosed at trial, for reasons that have never been explained. Otherwise Ognall's statement on behalf of the prosecution would have had vividly repulsive support: 'This isn't a missionary of God: it is a man who gets sexual pleasure out of killing these women.'

A common thread ran through the court proceedings, with *Spare Rib* asking: 'Who is really on trial at the Old Bailey – Sutcliffe, his wife or the thirteen women he murdered?' Instances of 'victim blaming' were rife, particularly from the Attorney General, who declared that Wilma McCann 'drank too much, was noisy and sexually promiscuous – she distributed her favours widely' and that while some of the victims were prostitutes, 'perhaps the saddest part of this case is that some were not'. The English Collective of Prostitutes held demonstrations outside the Old Bailey, accusing Havers of 'condoning the murder of prostitutes'. Women's groups joined forces to condemn elements of the trial: 'Feminists supported the political agenda of the English Collective of Prostitutes, which demanded a public inquiry into the police handling of the investigation; an end to bias and discrimination by police and the courts; an apology by the Attorney General to the families of prostitute victims; compensation for the victims and their families. The ECP's slogans reminded the public that prostitutes were mothers "fighting to make ends meet" and that the Ripper had orphaned twenty-three children.'[15]

The women in Sutcliffe's life were equally vilified in court and by the world's media in their coverage of the case. Reporters had been forced to adjust their depiction of a 'Jack the Ripper'-type killer who outwitted detectives at every turn when the reality proved numbingly mundane. Writers revised the narrative, turning the case into a gritty northern soap opera which explored Sutcliffe's transformation from someone described by his mates as 'an ordinary bloke' to a mutilator of women. His father John was a sports-mad womanizer who regarded young Peter as a 'mummy's boy' who needed to toughen up. Sutcliffe's relationship with his mother was normal; Kathleen Coonan was a loving and gentle presence in the lives of all her children. But in the media and in court, Kathleen's support was depicted as cosseting, while her affair with a policeman – revealed in public by her husband following his numerous infidelities – was presented as the key to her son's skewed view of female sexuality, despite the incident occurring in 1970, after he had already attacked two women. The family showdown was said to have 'destroyed the saintly vision he had of his mother and intensified his rage against women', leading him to believe that 'women will let you down, women will lie, women will cheat and are not to be respected'.[16] In contrast, his father's adulterous relationships and domestic abuse appear as a mere footnote.

Frustratingly, the emphasis on Sutcliffe's mother has only increased over the years. In 2017, an episode of the CBS series *Murderers and their Mothers* explored the theory and led to headlines in the British press, including: 'Mother's Exposure as Secret Adulteress Set Yorkshire Ripper on Path to Murders'. Asked to address the imbalance between mother and father with regard to their apparently deadly influence, Dr Elizabeth

Yardley stated simply: 'Mothers matter more in the making of murderers because of the inherently gendered nature of society.'[17]

Yet Kathleen Coonan's alleged role in precipitating her son's crimes was minimal compared to that of his wife, Sonia Szurma, whom he began courting in 1967. The media leapt on the details of their marriage as revealed in court, producing innumerable headlines such as 'Sonia's Breakdown', '"Nagging" May Be Link in Tragic Chain', 'Mania of the Ripper's Wife' and 'Ripper Was Hen-Pecked by Wife'. Sonia was deemed to be the more difficult partner in the equation: she had briefly suffered a mental illness and had an affair before they married, prompting Sutcliffe to seek out the sex worker who afterwards short-changed him. Sonia was labelled snobbish, prudish, highly strung and obsessed with cleanliness, refusing to allow her husband to wear his shoes in the house, continually picking specks from the carpets, pulling the plug from the television when he was watching it and 'even banning him from the fridge'.[18]

Prior to the trial, Dr Milne had examined their relationship, explicitly stating that 'Sutcliffe's version of his wife's behaviour accounts for his aggressive behaviour towards women'. While he was never physically violent or aggressive towards her, 'she readily admits that she had been at times temperamental and difficult and freely admits that she has frequently teased and provoked her husband'. The word 'admits' was used to impute blame, implicitly explaining the relevance of her behaviour. In his closing speech on behalf of the prosecution, Sir Michael Havers asked the jury to consider whether Sutcliffe was 'a cold, calculating killer ... or is it because he was having a rough time after his marriage? Was his wife, also because of her own illness, poor soul, behaving impossibly so that he dreaded going home?' Earlier, a 'Ripper Squad' detective had opined: 'When Sutcliffe attacked his twenty victims, he was attacking his wife twenty times in his mind.' Journalist Joan Smith points out that the opposite was true: 'Peter's marriage was not the *cause* of his violence but an attempt to contain it.'[19] His marriage, with its traditional gender roles and sexual intercourse described by both parties as entirely satisfactory, gave him a sense of normality. Together with his job, the relationship with Sonia enabled him to fit into the male, working-class world that his father expected him to eschew.

The trial lasted three weeks. On Friday 22 May 1981, Peter Sutcliffe was found guilty as charged. The jury rejected his defence, having absorbed the evidence of a remand prison officer who had overheard him remark to Sonia: 'I am going to do a long time in prison, thirty years or more, unless I can convince people in here I am mad, and maybe then ten years in the loony bin.' Instead, he was handed twenty concurrent life sentences and dispatched to HMP Parkhurst on the Isle of Wight. Only three years later, he was diagnosed with paranoid schizophrenia and transferred to Broadmoor Hospital, a secure psychiatric facility, where he remained until August 2016. No longer said to be mentally ill, he was returned to HMP Frankland.

Doreen Hill was among those in court to hear the verdict in 1981. Her daughter Jacqueline, Sutcliffe's final victim, should have been celebrating her twenty-first birthday that day. 'I wasn't looking at him,' Doreen recalled. 'I was looking down at the floor. I just wanted to hear the verdict, the right verdict. I felt relief for myself and I thought it was the right verdict for him, to go to a normal prison.'[20] Jayne MacDonald's mother was also present and told waiting reporters that her husband Wilfred had died 'of a broken heart. My daughter's killer also killed my husband and ruined me. If I could get my hands on him, I would kill him now. I wake up in the middle of the night with nightmares about it. I am full of hate.'[21] She had met Barbara Leach's mother for the first time that day. As they left the Old Bailey, Beryl declared through tears of anger: 'I prayed. Oh God, how I prayed for that verdict. I didn't want him to be cosseted in a rest home for the rest of his life. We have lived in a vacuum since Barbara's death two years ago. Our bodies have been alive but our minds have been blank and dead. Now we must start to rethink our lives.'[22] Olive Smelt reflected: 'You sit and look at him and think, how could he do all these horrible things? It's like a sort of horror film that you've been watching. But I'm glad I came. I'm glad it's all over now ... He's gone down for life and that's good.'[23]

Criticism of West Yorkshire Police was widespread and intense in the wake of the trial. The region's Deputy Chief Constable, Colin Sampson, began an internal inquiry on the day that Sutcliffe was sentenced and submitted his report to Ronald Gregory five months later. It consisted of nearly two hundred pages, which Gregory insisted should not be published due to 'operational' reasons. Although there was no attempt to determine individual blame, Sampson's report stated that the last six victims might have been spared had the police been more efficient in managing the evidence. The overall investigation was marred by incompetence, narrow vision, genuine mistakes and administrative bumbling. However, the force had been working well below strength for much of the manhunt and was forced to deal with demands on resources that were 'without precedent'. During 1975 to 1980, in addition to crimes of varying severity, another one hundred and fifty-two murders had been investigated; eight remained unsolved. Sampson made several recommendations for future improvement, including monitoring computer development with a view to taking full advantage of the new technology. Gregory conceded that the organization of the investigation had left much to be desired: 'On four occasions the interviewing officer – or pair of officers, because they usually worked as a team – believed they were questioning Sutcliffe for the first time. Our filing system was in chaos. At times there was a nine-month backlog of reports and statements waiting to be cross-indexed.'[24]

At the request of the government, Lawrence Byford headed an independent inquiry probing deeper into all aspects of the police investigation. He pinpointed considerable errors of judgement and various inefficiencies, particularly in the failure to bring together significant and collaborative documentation. The failure to heed survivors' descriptions of the attacker had been a monumental mistake, along with the credence given to the Sunderland hoaxer. Byford's report was held back from publication due to the inevitable loss of confidence the public would feel in the police force as a whole, and how that would affect officer morale, which was already painfully low. A four-page summary of Byford's main points and recommendations was added to the House of Commons Library. Ronald Gregory stated:

> The findings of this report are similar to those already identified by our internal inquiry and I can say little different to what I have already said. I have already accepted that there were errors of judgement; errors which are not now difficult to see, but when the investigation was current they were much less obvious. The enormity of the Yorkshire Ripper inquiry has left its mark on the West Yorkshire Police, but we will be better equipped in the future. Our methods of investigation and training will be reviewed, and no doubt the police service will learn from our experience.

Sections of the Byford report were released publicly in 2006, revealing a frustratingly unaltered view of the victims and survivors, with pernicious observations such as: 'Whereas most of the earlier victims had been prostitutes or women of loose morals and the attacks had occurred in or near to prostitute areas, Josephine Whitaker was a perfectly respectable young woman who was walking home in a residential area of Halifax not frequented by prostitutes.'

The anger towards police ineptitude remains vivid today among victims' relatives and survivors. Richard McCann asserts: 'I don't want to point the finger but there were definitely some police on the case who were very chauvinistic, real alpha males and who threw out information that came in. We do know that it was a shambles and they got derailed by the hoaxer, and that some of the women who gave accurate descriptions of him not having a Geordie accent were ignored.'[25] Harry Smelt was more direct: 'Olive told the police that it was a Yorkshireman who attacked her but they refused to listen. They were a bunch of idiots.'[26]

The Sunderland letters and tape form a major and very difficult part of people's memories of that time. The hoaxer was eventually brought to trial when, in 2005, DNA taken from a piece of an envelope seal was found to match a sample on the national criminal database. It belonged to John Humble, an alcoholic drifter who had been cautioned for being drunk and disorderly a few years earlier. The Ripper inquiry team had visited the estate where he lived, quizzing his neighbour but not him. Unlike Sutcliffe, Humble did regret his actions, telephoning an incident room in Sunderland on 14 September 1979 in an effort to convince them that none of the material was genuine, but it was too little too late. An attempt at suicide also failed. Humble finally appeared at Leeds Crown Court in January 2006, initially pleading not guilty to conspiring to pervert the course of justice. The following month he admitted the truth and on 21 March 2006, he was sentenced to eight years imprisonment. When questioned about his motivation, he replied that the Ripper case was 'getting on my nerves. It was on the bloody telly all the time. I shouldn't have done it.'[27] He was released in 2009 after serving half his sentence and now lives under an assumed name in the North-East.

'I know Sutcliffe did the murders but I think he [Humble] aided him,' asserts survivor Tracy Browne. 'He helped him along.'[28] Richard McCann agrees and welcomed the prison sentence: 'It feels appropriate to me. I'm not a family member of one of those three women who died towards the end, but yes, it was appropriate. It should have been longer. At the end of the day, the person who did the damage was Peter Sutcliffe. I know that Humble regretted what he'd done almost straight away and phoned the police, then tried to kill himself for this stupid, *stupid* mistake.'[29]

Beryl Leach's daughter Barbara had been murdered by Sutcliffe after Humble wrote his letters and recorded the tape. She reflected on Humble's sentencing from her home in Kettering, where she lived alone following her husband's death and her son Graham's emigration to New Zealand with his wife:

> It was a very wicked thing to do. Some wouldn't have died if he hadn't done that. I think it's possible that Sutcliffe would have been caught sooner ... Without his hoax, there would have been far stronger policing of the Yorkshire area where Peter Sutcliffe was. He'd been through their hands quite a few times, Sutcliffe had, and each time they'd eliminated him because of things that the hoaxer had said. Yes, Barbara might have been alive if John Humble hadn't hoaxed the police. I might have had grandchildren. Might have had a daughter ... But now, it won't happen.[30]

25

RECLAIMING THE NIGHT

In the aftermath of the trial, those women who had survived an encounter with Sutcliffe found the damage done to their reputations among the worst of the consequences.

Anna Rogulskyj declared herself 'fed up with being associated with the list of women killed by this man. I've been afraid to go out much because I feel people are staring and pointing at me. The whole thing is making my life a misery. I sometimes wish I had died in the attack. My main concern is to have my name cleared. Although the police agree I have never been a prostitute, there is a dreadful slur attached to any woman linked with the Ripper's attacks. I am respectable and I want the record put straight.'[1] She bought her home with the £15,000 awarded from the Criminal Injuries Compensation Board, fitting it with a maze of wires and alarms. She became reclusive, trusting only close family and friends, and tending to her beloved cats. Her ex-husband, Roman Rogulskyj, died in March 1989 when a lorry driver lost control of his vehicle in Keighley, ploughing into a car showroom where Roman was talking to the staff.

Anna made a determined effort to put the past behind her, moving to a modest house in Rosemount Walk, Keighley. In a final interview, she insisted:

> I'm not Anna. I will never be Anna again. I'm Joanna now. Anna died that night and I wish I had died with her. I wish I had not had that operation, that there had

just been the blackness and then no more. If I had known what lay ahead for me I would have refused what they term a 'life-saving operation'. My life is ruined. So I've had £15,000 from the Criminal Compensation Board. So what? No amount of money can give me back my anonymity, can give me back my lost boyfriends. No money can remove the stigma of the Ripper.[2]

Suffering from breast cancer and pneumonia, she died in Airedale Hospital in April 2008. Following a well-attended funeral at Oakworth Crematorium, her ashes were returned to Ireland, the country she had left sixty years before, and were buried in the family plot in Kilfeighney Cemetery.

For Olive Smelt, the worst moment of her survival came in 1986, when West Yorkshire Chief Constable Ronald Gregory wrongly described her as a prostitute in his memoirs, which were published in the *Daily Mail*. She recalled:

Of all the things which have happened since Sutcliffe ruined my life, this was without doubt the worst. I was horrified and Harry said he just couldn't take any more, while Linda [their daughter] became very ill with her nerves. All my family just felt as if they couldn't face their friends and workmates while I just wanted to hide. They'll never know how much harm they caused by that libel. Money could never make up for the pain inflicted on us. It just about broke us and I'll never forgive them for it – if anything was guaranteed to make the Ripper stigma stick to me for good, that was it.[3]

Five years after the trial, Olive repeated: 'There's a stigma to being a Ripper victim. It's as if you've been tainted. Somehow, all seven of us who are Ripper survivors seem to have become a part of his depravity. Not the innocent victims of a madman, more like his condemned accomplices.'[4] She had always been an active, feisty lady but 'some days I really don't know why I bother to keep going ... I just don't want to go on. That was never me before all this happened. I was happy-go-lucky and the life and soul of every party. But I'll never be the same old Olive again, never ... Whenever I'm washing myself I can feel the thin ridge of the scar. It's never gone away – it's almost like a kind of curse.'[5] Olive dreaded telling her grandchildren about the attack, but in the end it was forced upon her when her fifteen-year-old granddaughter read about it in a newspaper. 'She was very upset and shocked,' Olive reflected. 'It was like Peter Sutcliffe had been able to affect another generation. I suppose I'm linked to him for ever. I'm resigned to having an obituary that says, "Ripper Victim Dies", like the rest of my life didn't happen.'[6] In December 2004, she suffered three strokes within days of each other and a few weeks later was diagnosed with a serious pancreatic condition. Olive died of pneumonia at the age of eighty-two in Huddersfield Royal Infirmary on 6 April 2011. Her husband Harry passed away four years later.

Marcella Claxton had also applied to the Criminal Injuries Compensation Board for financial aid. Unbelievably, her first application in 1977 was rejected due to West Yorkshire Police's dismissal of her description of the attacker as 'hopelessly inaccurate' on the grounds that her memory was impaired. She was refused again on even more incomprehensible grounds; namely, that she had 'misled the police and clearly provoked the attack'.[7] Following the birth of her son in early 1981, Marcella won an interim award of £3,000 on appeal. She was told that a final decision would be made after she had agreed to a full medical examination. Her solicitor, Dianna Lessing, responded to the Board's statement that they needed to take into account Marcella's 'way of life': 'We do not know what is meant by that. We can only assume that it referred to her walking alone around Chapeltown at night, or possibly to allegations about her being a prostitute.'[8] Miss Lessing said that before the attack Marcella was a pleasant and happy person but afterwards she became withdrawn and angry. Eventually, the Criminal Injuries Compensation Board conceded that there was no question of provocation or of Marcella misleading the police.

In the wake of her attack in Bradford, Maureen Long was plagued by extreme anxiety, day and night: 'I have nightmares about him chasing me round the park, then killing me. I'm afraid to walk through subways on my own and even some TV programmes scare me now.'[9] Her daughter Jacqueline was taken into care while Maureen tried to find some means of coping with the memories of her attack. She found it almost impossible, but for the help of family and friends; her hair turned grey and fell out around a two-inch depression in her skull where the hammer had made its impact. In March 1978, she became unwittingly involved in a fight in Bradford and was struck on the back of the head with an iron bar. Her life was saved a second time by emergency surgery. Later that year she was brought before Bradford Magistrates Court, charged with stealing from three shops in the city centre. The court took into account her background, and the confusion and panic attacks that troubled her daily. She was fined £75. An interim award of £300 from the Criminal Injuries Compensation Board was increased to £1,500 in April 1979 and to £8,500 in 1982 as a result of the psychological damage she had sustained. After Maureen's death, her daughter Denise responded to the news that Sutcliffe was being returned to prison: 'He should never have been in Broadmoor. I am pleased and think it's right he suffers in prison. I try not to talk about it because it still upsets me. He left the scars on my mum and she couldn't get over it. You never forget.'[10]

Tracy Browne had worked hard to overcome the psychological effects of her attack, recalling:

I only suffered a serious degree of panic after a building society worker, Josephine Whitaker, was attacked on her way home from Halifax in 1979. I felt then that he was closing in on me and would come back to finish me off. I started leaving the landing lights on, my door open and curtains apart. I wanted to see him if he was going to break in and get me, I suppose. I began waking in the night in a panic and having cold sweats. I was like this for six months but then my common sense gradually overrode my panic, so in a way I had the upper hand.[11]

She was never offered any outside help or counselling: 'My family helped me get on with things, and I just refused to let him ruin my life. Sutcliffe left me with physical scars but not emotional ones. It didn't affect my personality because I was still growing up when the attack happened. I was young, resilient and with a teenage-type determination to put it all behind me. It didn't affect my relationships with men, perhaps because it wasn't a sexual assault. I grew up and had boyfriends just like any other girl.'[12] In 1992, Sutcliffe admitted the attack on Tracy but the Director of Public Prosecutions ruled that it was not in the public interest to convict him in a further, expensive trial. Tracy felt vindicated nonetheless: 'Although I did know who it was for all those years, there was that element of doubt because it took so long for him to confess to it. It was like sealing it, really, just closing a lid on it.'[13]

Beryl Leach had spoken about rebuilding her family's lives after Sutcliffe's incarceration. But she could not bear to redecorate her daughter's bedroom, leaving it exactly as it was when Barbara left home for university in the summer of 1979. Her favourite teddy bear, Honey, given to her when she was five years old, sat on the bed; her unfinished embroidery lay nearby with the shells she had collected from family holidays. Shortly before his own death, Barbara's father David Leach reflected: 'Although we carried on and lived our lives, I do not think a day passes when we do not think of her, and sometimes speak of her fondly. We seem to feel her loss more acutely as we get older.'[14] Beryl had only one remaining wish regarding her daughter's killer: 'I live in hope that I hear of his death before I die.'[15]

Jacqueline Hill's father passed away six weeks after the end of the trial. He was buried with his daughter, whose gravestone remembers her as 'a gentle and caring person tragically killed 17 November 1980, aged 20 years'. The inscription for her father states that he 'died broken-hearted'. Asked how she managed to carry on living in the wake of such devastating loss, Doreen Hill replied: 'Hatred.'[16] Her primary anger was with Sutcliffe, but it was also directed towards the press who offered large financial incentives for stories from his relatives. She was equally repelled by the news that Ronald Gregory was said to be receiving £50,000 for the serialization of his memoirs, describing it as salt in a wound: 'You cannot get away from the fact that if the West Yorkshire Police had done their job, Jacqueline would still be alive.'[17] She took legal advice on suing Gregory for negligence but was advised to drop her action by a High Court judge, with the Appeal Court upholding the decision. Asked how her family lived with Jacqueline's loss, Mrs Hill answered: 'We do not live with it. You cannot call what we are doing living. We just exist from one day to another.'[18]

The children left motherless as a result of Sutcliffe's actions faced different problems. Neil Jackson was older than most when his mother Emily was murdered in 1976, but the effects were no less profound. He joined the army, then returned home at the bequest of his father, Sydney, who needed him to help take care of his younger brother Chris, whose behaviour was of concern for a time. Over the years, Neil's contact with his father and siblings diminished but his mother's sisters always looked out for him on Emily's behalf. After Sutcliffe's trial, Neil still felt unable to get on with his life 'because my family had been torn apart by him'.[19] His father sold the family home and remarried. When Sydney died, Neil was reunited with his brother and sister at the funeral after years apart, but found it too painful to retain contact. Divorced with children of his own, he only began to find peace of a sort after criminologist Jane Carter Woodrow helped him research his background for a book about his experiences in *After Evil*.

Irene Richardson's son Alan had been adopted by a loving couple in 1970, before his mother's death. They had no idea that she had been murdered and supported his wish to find out about his birth parents, having told him while he was still young that he was adopted. In 2004, now named Geoff Beattie, he contacted the adoption agency and was given a file which had a note attached, stating only that his birth mother had been murdered in 1977. 'It was devastating,' he recalls. 'The first thing it meant was that I was never going to meet her, but to realize she had been killed – that took me a long time to process. In the end though, I wanted to find out as much as I could about her. I wanted to know her.'[20]

He tried searching on the internet first, with no expectations, but then Irene's portrait flashed up on screen, together with the crime scene photographs at Roundhay Park, describing her as the third victim of the Yorkshire Ripper. He is unable to put into words his feelings at that point, but gradually began piecing together his mother's life. He was helped by Richard McCann and made contact with all three of his sisters, who had also been adopted. Now a father himself and happily settled with a partner, he hopes to learn more about his own father, but has very little information – only a name, Jim Brown. 'Apparently he was a Blackpool mechanic,' Geoff states. 'His name isn't on my birth certificate. I found it in my file notes from the social workers. I'd love to know more about him. I might have other brothers and sisters on my father's side, and that would be amazing.'[21] He is equally keen to continue discovering more about the mother he never knew, explaining: 'My mum's immediate extended family runs to one hundred: her kids, grandchildren and others. We've all missed out on her because of his actions. Now my greatest wish is to find my father and learn more about my mother – so I can break the news in a better way to my own three children.'[22]

The latter is a task Wilma McCann's son Richard has recently faced. His route through life was similar to Neil Jackson's at the beginning: he joined the army and was forced to leave, but in his case it was due to all the pent-up emotion from his childhood manifesting itself. Back in Leeds, he experienced one of his lowest points when he began using and then dealing drugs, serving a six-month prison sentence. His sister Sonia had her own problems with drugs and alcohol; she had been in a string of abusive relationships and the daughter she had at seventeen lived with her grandmother. Sonia recalled: 'When I reached the age of 28 – the age [my mother] was when she was killed – I lost hold of the fragile grip I had on my life. I began drinking heavily, unable to hold down a job. I thought, "Why am I alive when my mother isn't?"'[23]

Richard called Sonia one evening and they discussed killing themselves. Later that night, Sonia rang to say she had taken a large quantity of pills with alcohol. It was the turning point in Richard's life: 'I realized I had to be strong and help her to live. Sonia survived, but I realized that I was responsible. I knew I had to do something to sort out the situation or we would go on like this forever until we ended up killing ourselves. Wanting to protect her gave me something to live for.'[24] Sonia recovered and had counselling but her life remained unstable and in 2002, she stabbed a boyfriend in self-defence. Richard had a steady job and income by then, and in an effort to explain how his sister had reached that point, he decided to write a book about their experiences. He became involved with Support after Murder and Manslaughter, had assertiveness training, stopped taking drugs and worked with troubled youths. His books – *Just a Boy* and its sequel *Into the Light* – were bestsellers. He has since gone on to become a hugely successful motivational speaker, and is happily married with children.

Sonia's problems with alcoholism continued. 'Every day I battle with my demons,' she admitted. 'All I want now is to be happy. I haven't been happy since Mum was taken from us. We had our mum and her love. Sutcliffe took that from us.'[25] On 18 December 2007, Sonia texted her sister in a panic, believing there were crocodiles in her room; the following day, she committed suicide, hanging herself in the bathroom of her Armley home. She was thirty-nine; her daughter was twenty-one. Asked later how he had managed to find a way forward from their past when Sonia had not, Richard responded: 'I think she had the burden of being the eldest child. She felt responsible. Mum would leave us with Sonia, so she was like a second mother, almost … She got a worse start than me. Sonia probably would not have done what she did, had he not taken Mum's life. I hate him for what he did. Arguably he killed my sister as well.'[26]

Sonia's death brought Richard closer to his father, Gerry McCann, for the last seven years of Gerry's life. 'When Sonia died I had to break the news to him,' he recalls. 'I did feel for him – I had just had my first child and I was having to tell him that his first child was no longer alive. After that we had a few years where we were closer – not the father and son relationship I would have liked but it was good to have him back in my life. Sadly we lost him in 2014. When I cleared his house out after his death and saw some of the things he'd written down, it became obvious that he had some issues that I wasn't aware of and which explained so much to me.'[27]

Three years ago, Richard and his wife faced the task of telling their children about his mother's murder. 'It wasn't anywhere near as painful as I thought it would be,' he reflects.

> In fact, it wasn't painful at all for them. They knew that my mother had died but they didn't know how. We took advice on how to do this from Winston's Wish, an organization who support families with bereaved

children. The advice they gave me was to tell them as much as you feel you can because children are resilient. It was also a question of keeping our children's trust. If they had found out from their school friends, for example, they might well feel that we had lied to them. So we sat them down and told them. It was a very moving afternoon and the kids were brilliant.[28]

One of the many ventures Richard has been involved with is The Forgiveness Project. He had attended a lecture by Desmond Tutu on forgiveness, which made him realize that he had 'the capacity to change the situation by changing how I felt about what had occurred'.[29] Eight years on, he is clear that forgiveness is not a one-off action, but requires renewed effort:

Forgiveness is a very personal thing and I think generally speaking people seem to think it means befriending someone perhaps, but to me it's not – it's about letting go of the anger that I have or had for Sutcliffe. The forgiveness I felt for my father was completely different because I wanted him in my life. But with Sutcliffe it was a matter of letting go of the anger and the need for revenge. I decided the day I met Tutu to let it go. But sometimes that anger re-emerges and you have to work at it again.[30]

More than any other case of its kind, the murders and attacks committed by Peter Sutcliffe instigated a powerful reaction from women about male violence and how we react to it. The act of 'victim blaming' forced many women to add their voices to those that previously belonged only to radical feminists, bringing the discussion of many issues into the mainstream. We know that not all of Sutcliffe's victims were prostitutes, and that if they were, that had no relevance whatsoever in their murders, except that it made them more vulnerable perhaps. While the perception of sex workers has changed since the 1970s, the risks associated with their job – which involves around eighty thousand women in the UK – remain critical. According to the British Medical Journal, female sex workers have mortality rates six times higher than the general population and are eighteen times more likely to be murdered. The myth of the isolated loner who cannot get a woman to sleep with him otherwise no longer holds true, with research showing that the average man who pays for sex is married, employed and around thirty years old.

How we discuss the Sutcliffe case in general still leaves a great deal to be desired, as Richard McCann explains: 'I try to rise above how the media talk about my mother and the other women who died because of Sutcliffe, but it's difficult. You have the likes of the *Sun* who just refer to her as 'Wilma McCann, hooker' and that really frustrates me. As far as other cases are concerned, I think it's changed, but not enough.'[31]

He refers to the Rochdale sex abuse scandal, in which young girls in the region's care homes were passed from one man to another. Investigations into the case are ongoing but around 1,510 potential victims are believed to be involved and more than one hundred abusers. 'I was at a conference recently,' Richard recalls, 'and one of the speakers talked about what had taken place in Rochdale with those young girls. Those girls were described by the authorities and the police in a very similar way. I think in some ways the police have changed but I'm not sure they have completely in their souls towards women who've suffered like this. It's questionable. There's definitely still some work to do.'[32]

26

UNBROKEN

Author Judith Walkowitz declares one clear difference between Jack the Ripper and his modern namesake: 'Because the Yorkshire Ripper was apprehended and brought to trial, his story achieved a closure absent in the original Ripper story.'[1]

But not quite.

Sutcliffe's first acknowledged attack on a woman occurred in September 1969; the first murder accepted by the authorities as his responsibility took place in October 1975. During the five-year period of the killings, there were long gaps: nine months between the attack on Marcella Claxton in May 1976 and the murder of Irene Richardson in February 1977; almost a year between the murders of Vera Millward in May 1978 and that of Josephine Whitaker in April 1979, and another year between the deaths of Barbara Leach in September 1979 and Marguerite Walls in August 1980. In those periods, no attacks or murders occurred which have been attributed officially to Sutcliffe.

Lawrence Byford made clear his views on the matter in his official report into the investigation: 'It is my firm conclusion that between 1969 and 1980, Sutcliffe was probably responsible for many attacks on unaccompanied women, which he has not yet admitted, not only in the West Yorkshire and Manchester areas but also in other parts of the country. I have arranged for senior operational officers in the forces concerned to ensure that my findings are taken into account in the further interrogation of Sutcliffe after his appeal has been finalized.'

After succeeding Ronald Gregory as West Yorkshire Chief Constable, Colin Sampson instructed Keith Hellawell, later Chief Constable himself, to head a small team of experienced officers examining other crimes that may have been committed by Sutcliffe. Seventy-eight unsolved murders and attempted murders were reduced by a process of elimination to twenty-two possible offences, twelve within their jurisdiction. These were then whittled down by an even more exacting approach to ten 'probables'. The attack on Tracy Browne was top of their list; Hellawell met her and walked the route she and Sutcliffe had taken in summer 1975.

The second probable was the attempted murder of student Ann Rooney on 2 March 1979, who had been attacked from behind while walking through college grounds. She received three blows to her skull, causing a compound depressed fracture. The description of her attacker was similar to Sutcliffe, and the weapon was identified as a hammer. Most compelling was the evidence that a dark-coloured Sunbeam Rapier had been spotted in the area at the relevant time – the type of car Sutcliffe owned then.

The third most likely attempted murder was that of Yvonne Mysliwiec, a twenty-one-year-old newspaper reporter who was attacked from behind on 11 October 1979, after crossing the footbridge near the railway station in Ilkley. Her attacker bore some resemblance to Sutcliffe and her injuries included a compound depressed fracture of the skull and scratch marks on her abdomen. Like Ann Rooney, Yvonne recalled the attack for Hellawell 'with great reluctance'.[2]

Professor David Gee had examined Ann Rooney in hospital and thought her head injuries similar to those inflicted by the Ripper. He consulted another patient in the hospital at the same time: a sixteen-year-old schoolgirl who had been attacked in February 1979 from behind with a blunt object but had not caught sight of her attacker. Gee's report of her head injuries made it clear these were not accidental; incredibly, North

Yorkshire Police decided she had injured herself by slipping on ice. Meanwhile, Oldfield's team dismissed Ann Rooney's attack as being part of the Ripper series due to a different hammer having been used to cause the head injuries.

When Hellawell approached Sutcliffe, he found him uncooperative, insisting he had no more to add to what he had already told the police, although his manner was friendly enough. Eventually he admitted two attempted murders: Tracy Browne and Ann Rooney. Sutcliffe's recollection of both was remarkably vivid; he remembered how, after attacking the young student in Horsforth, he had tried to escape by car but found himself in a dead-end street and had to retrace his route.

All at once, Sutcliffe refused to talk any further. 'Try as I might, and certain as I was that Sutcliffe had committed other crimes, he clammed up,' Hellawell reports. 'He told me that after his two further confessions Sonia remonstrated with him for not telling her. She said he had betrayed her trust.'[3] Hellawell continued to visit Sutcliffe for many months but the killer flatly refused to say more.

Among those women (and possibly men) thought to have been attacked by Sutcliffe is Maureen Lea. Her life was spared only by the intervention of a quick-thinking stranger.

In 1980, Liverpool-born Mo was a twenty-year-old art student at Leeds Polytechnic. On the evening of Saturday 25 October 1980, she spent time with friends in a Headingley pub, discussing plans for her upcoming twenty-first birthday party. 'I loved my course, I was a happy person and naturally outgoing,' she reflects. 'Yes, there were these terrible attacks happening, but it honestly didn't really affect me. I was living in this fantastic bubble, going to gigs, having lots of friends – just enjoying life.'[4] Mo left the pub at 10.30 p.m., walking through the campus to catch her bus home. As she reached the university clock tower, she debated whether to take a left through the town centre which was a long walk but well-lit, or a right turn down Hillary Place, which was poorly lit but a shorter route. She chose the latter, walking at a quick pace until she heard someone call to her.

'He sounded really friendly and I thought it must be someone I knew,' Mo remembers. She walked towards the man, who had his collar turned up. 'I took a good look at him and realized I didn't know him at all. I was terrified. So I began to run. And I could hear him all the time, gaining ground on me. My legs didn't seem to belong to me – I went to jelly. And then I felt this massive, *massive* blow on my head and the ground just came up and hit me.'[5]

Another Leeds University student, Lorna Smith, was also on her way home from the pub with a friend when she spotted something: 'I remember seeing a man's arm raised and I could hear shouts. As we got slightly closer I remember seeing this man running off and then we realized there was somebody lying in the gutter. And when I got even closer I saw just how much blood was there. So much blood.'[6] Lorna and her friend rushed to Mo's aid. They called an ambulance, which took her to Leeds Infirmary.

'When I came round, my jaw was all wired up and I was so groggy,' she recalls. 'I remember these other women on the ward looking at me suspiciously. "What have you done to deserve that then?" was what they wanted to know. And that was my first taste of the attitude that prevented me from talking about it for so long.'[7] Mo had been beaten about the head with a hammer. Her skull and cheekbone were fractured; her jaw had been shattered and her assailant had inserted two screwdrivers into the base of her spine, just missing her spinal cord.

As Mo began the slow process of recovery, a doctor informed her that her injuries were very similar to those he had seen in Ripper victims; he advised her that the police needed to be informed. Mo spoke to detectives: 'They weren't interested. Their attitude wasn't much different to the women on the ward. I was just another woman who had got herself beaten up. They couldn't have cared less.'[8]

Detectives also visited Lorna Smith, who made a statement. She declared: 'What I do remember is the officer saying, "If we do decide to take this incident seriously, we may want to question you again." And that phrase – "if we decide to take this seriously" – just echoed. It took my breath away. I thought, what state do you have to be in for them to take it seriously? I found it just an extraordinary statement.'[9] No firm correlation was made to the Ripper series, despite the nature of Mo's injuries and the site of her attack, which had taken place about two miles from the attempted murder of Dr Uphadhya Bandara one month earlier. The *Yorkshire Evening Post* featured Mo's story on 27 October 1980, adding: 'A police spokesman said it was thought there was no connection between the attack on Miss Lea and other attacks in the area recently.'[10]

Less than a month later, Jacqueline Hill became the last victim of Peter Sutcliffe when she was murdered in Headingley, approximately two and a half miles from where Mo had been attacked. When she heard the news, Mo was aghast: 'I couldn't believe the police didn't make the connection between my attack and Jacqueline Hill's murder. I just couldn't believe they were that stupid.'[11] The young woman who saved her life, Lorna Smith, had a similar reaction: 'I thought, my God, this has got to be the same attacker. It was a Saturday night, a woman student on her own, a hammer was used – I just felt that the two incidents were connected. That phrase kept coming back through my mind: "If we decide to take this seriously …" And I just remember thinking, well, if they had taken it seriously would Jacqueline Hill have had to die?'[12]

Leaving the hospital and returning to the outside world had many challenges, Mo discovered: 'I was very aware of how people looked at me. It was as if they couldn't believe I hadn't done anything to provoke it because it was so vicious, so appalling. My parents really struggled, but they got me through it. My art saved me too – that got me through it, even though it changed. Isn't that strange? Everything was colourless.'[13]

Mo decided to try and paint her pain, hoping that one day the man who had attempted to kill her might see the images and understand what he had done. In one raw image she lies in a hospital bed with her jaw wired up and recalls that work was done 'in a moment of utmost despair and anger, shortly after I was attacked. This is how I felt inside, completely destroyed and mutilated.'[14]

When the news was announced that Peter Sutcliffe had been charged, Mo watched in horror as the face she had seen appeared on screen: 'I recognized him. It floored me. I knew it was him. The police said they weren't sure because I hadn't included a beard in my description of him, but that was because he had his bloody collar turned up, not because my attacker didn't have a beard! But then I felt this other thing – I didn't want to be known as a victim of the Yorkshire Ripper. Or a survivor – I didn't want that connection made because of the way everyone judged the women he attacked. There was no justice for them, not in the way they were discussed. I didn't want that attitude coming back on me.'

Mo finished her degree, staging exhibitions of her work in Harrogate before moving to Birmingham for a Master of Arts course, where she met up with an old boyfriend. They married and divorced and she became a senior university art lecturer in Bedford, settling down with a new partner. In 1996, the police contacted her and she was stunned to learn that her attack had been in their files ever since it took place as one of twenty unsolved crimes for which Sutcliffe was the chief suspect. She met Keith Hellawell, who told her that he had spoken to Sutcliffe about her attack and he had neither confirmed nor denied it, replying only that he could not remember. 'That's playing games,' she states grimly. 'Isn't it? Cat and mouse. He's a coward.'

In 2002, the *Sunday Telegraph* reported that West Yorkshire Police were confident they could bring new charges against

Sutcliffe for the April 1977 murder of Debra Schlesinger and the attempted murder of Mo Lea in October 1980. Those charges have not yet been brought against him, but from time to time the press report that these, and others, are imminent.

Now retired from lecturing, Mo focuses on her artwork with some of the proceeds going to Victim Support. 'I've said a few times that being a victim of Peter Sutcliffe makes you part of a pretty exclusive club,' she reflects. 'One that you don't want to be part of. And it's true. I was diagnosed with post-traumatic stress disorder and there are all sorts of things that I struggle with because of the attack but he didn't break me and he never could. I'm a survivor, not a victim. Nothing can break me. He can't take my art away and he can't destroy who I am. I'm lucky to be here and I want to make the most of it.'[15]

Nonetheless, Mo would like the closure of acknowledgement: 'As long as he doesn't admit it, he has got this hold on me. He didn't kill me, but he has still got me trapped. It's like being stuck under water and not being able to find a hole in the ice. If he admits attacking me, I'll say, "Yes, I knew it was him all along." But if he doesn't, I will have to live the rest of my life in doubt and that is an unbearably painful thought.'[16]

It seems incredible that almost forty years later, the Yorkshire Ripper case should remain relevant in terms of the issues it raises, but stories of sexual violence and abuse towards women have dominated the headlines during the writing of this book. These involve some powerful men, including US President Donald Trump and Hollywood film producer Harvey Weinstein, the latter sparking the #MeToo movement. More recently still, revelations about gross sexual misconduct during Oxfam's 2011 campaign to help earthquake-torn Haiti have severely damaged the charity's image. Meanwhile, the Rochdale scandal, in which ten men were convicted of grooming and trafficking girls between the ages of thirteen to twenty-three, continues to produce further claims of horrific abuse.

One bright ray of light emerged in February 2018, however, when two women attacked by black-cab rapist John Worboys won their claim for compensation from the Metropolitan Police. Worboys was jailed in 2009 for nineteen offences against twelve women. Despite being suspected of attacking a hundred more, in 2017 the Parole Board directed his release. Following the legal action brought by two of his victims, the Supreme Court ruled in the women's favour, finding that detectives had failed to conduct an effective investigation into his crimes.

The decision sets a significant precedent, particularly regarding those attacks for which Sutcliffe has not yet been held legally responsible. At long last, it may now be possible for those forgotten survivors such as Mo Lea to argue their case in court.

ENDNOTES

Introduction

1. Burn, Gordon, *Somebody's Husband, Somebody's Son* (London: Faber & Faber, 2004) p.154.
2. The so-called 'Ripper Squad' was a team of twelve detectives based at Millgarth Police Station and tasked solely with finding the killer.
3. *Guardian*, 'I'm Jack' by Mark Blacklock, Review, Catherine Taylor, 25 June 2015.
4. There is a whole book dedicated to this possibility: *Yorkshire Ripper: Secret Murders* by Chris Clark and Tim Tate (London: John Blake, 2015).

1: Anna

1. Anna's age has always been described as younger, but records clearly show her born in 1933.
2. The surname Rogulskyj is spelled a variety of ways, but this is the spelling that appears on legal documents.
3. Burn, Gordon, *Somebody's Husband, Somebody's Son*, p.172.
4. Ibid, p.172.
5. Ibid, pp.172–174.
6. Ibid, p.131.
7. Ibid, p.130.
8. Ibid, p.132.
9. 'Woman in Hospital After Alley Attack', *Yorkshire Post*, 7 July 1975.
10. Ibid.
11. Cross, Roger, *The Yorkshire Ripper*, p.12.

2: Olive

1. Ibid.
2. 'Happy-go-lucky': 'I'll Always Feel the Ripper's Scars', *News of the World*, 11 May 1986; 'full of energy': Kinsley, Peter and Smyth, Frank, *I'm Jack: The Police Hunt for the Yorkshire Ripper* (London: Pan Books 1980), p.170.
3. 'The Ripper's Bitter Legacy', *Daily Mail*, 1 February 1997.
4. 'Battered Woman Found in Street', *Yorkshire Evening Post*, 16 August 1975.
5. Bilton, Michael, *Wicked Beyond Belief: The Hunt for the Yorkshire Ripper* (London: Harper Press, 2003), p.293.
6. 'The Ripper's Bitter Legacy', *Daily Mail*, 1 February 1997.
7. Ibid.
8. Bilton, Michael, *Wicked*, p.609.
9. 'I'll Always Feel the Ripper's Scars', *News of the World*, 11 May 1986.
10. 'The Ripper's Bitter Legacy', *Daily Mail*, 1 February 1997.

11. Cross, Roger, *The Yorkshire Ripper: The In-Depth Study of a Mass Killer and His Methods* (London: HarperCollins, 1981), p.16.
12. Ibid, p.15.
13. 'I'll Always Feel the Ripper's Scars', *News of the World*, 11 May 1986.
14. 'Police Seek Attacker Who Fled Over Wall', *Yorkshire Evening Post*, 28 August 1975.

3: Tracy

1. *Left for Dead by the Yorkshire Ripper*, BriteSpark Films, 2014.
2. 'He had this beard': *Left for Dead by the Yorkshire Ripper, BriteSpark Films, 2014.*; 'He was about': 'Crime People: I Survived the Ripper', *People*, 16 January 2000.
3. 'Crime People: I Survived the Ripper', *People*, 16 January 2000.
4. Ibid.
5. Ibid.
6. Ibid.
7. 'Legacy of the Yorkshire Ripper', *Daily Mail*, 24 April 1999.
8. 'I thought': 'Ripper Sutcliffe Tells of Hammer Attack on Girl', *Daily Telegraph*, 24 November 1992; 'Her jumper': Bilton, Michael, *Wicked*, p.71.
9. 'Crime People: I Survived the Ripper', *People*, 16 January 2000.
10. 'Girl (14) Brutally Beaten in Lane', *Yorkshire Post*, 28 August 1975.
11. 'Legacy of the Yorkshire Ripper', *Daily Mail*, 24 April 1999.
12. 'Crime People: I Survived the Ripper', *People*, 16 January 2000.
13. 'Legacy of the Yorkshire Ripper', *Daily Mail*, 24 April 1999.

4: Wilma

1. Kinsley, Peter and Smyth, Frank, *I'm Jack: The Police Hunt for the Yorkshire Ripper* (London: Pan Books, 1980), p.16.
2. McCann, Richard, *Just A Boy: The True Story of a Stolen Childhood* (London: Ebury Press, 2004), p.23.
3. McCann, Richard, *The Boy Grows Up* (London: Ebury Press, 2007), p.182.
4. Bilton, Michael, *Wicked*, p.10.
5. McCann, Richard, *Just A Boy*, p.21.
6. 'The Ripper's Final Victim', *Daily Express*, 29 December 2007.
7. BBC Radio 4: *The Choice*, presented by Michael Buerk, 2 September 2008.
8. 'Ripper Is Sure He Will Beat System', *Daily Express*, 20 December 2004.
9. BBC Radio 4: *The Choice*.
10. Wilma's son Richard met with caretaker John Bould years later, who told him that he had responded to the milkman alerting him to something on the playing field; Bould crossed the grass and recognized Wilma immediately. The milkman called the authorities while Bould stayed with Wilma's body. Bould also stated that the dog had been in its kennel that night, yards from where Wilma was found, but had not barked.
11. Beattie, John, *The Yorkshire Ripper Story* (London: Quartet Books Ltd, 1981), p.14.
12. Ibid.
13. McCann, Richard, *Just A Boy*, p.11.
14. Ibid.
15. 'Murder in Fog: Savage and Sadistic Sex Attack on Leeds "Mother in Fear"', *Yorkshire Evening Post*, 30 October 1975.
16. Ibid.
17. Ibid.

18. Ibid.
19. Ibid.
20. 'White Purse is Vital Clue in Hunt for Sex-Killer', *Yorkshire Post*, 31 October 1975.
21. 'The Ripper's Final Victim', *Daily Express*.
22. Ibid.
23. 'Heartbreak Four Are Told "Mummy's Dead"', *Yorkshire Evening Post*, 31 October 1975.
24. Ibid.
25. BBC Radio 4: *The Choice*.
26. McCann, Richard, *Just A Boy*, p.38.
27. Kinsley, Peter and Smyth, Frank, *I'm Jack*, p.16.
28. Richard McCann, The Forgiveness Project website, 29 March 2010. http://theforgivenessproject.com/stories/richard-mccann-england/
29. BBC Radio 4: *The Choice*.
30. Bilton, Michael, *Wicked*, p.16.
31. 'Hunt for Stab Mother's Killer', *Daily Express*, November 1975. Precise date unknown.
32. Kinsley, Peter and Smyth, Frank, *I'm Jack*, p.16.
33. McCann, Richard, *The Boy Grows Up*, p.19.

5: Emily

1. From the autobiography of Emily's son, Neil Jackson, *After Evil* (London, Hodder & Stoughton, 2009), p.260.
2. 'Killer is a Maniac, say Police', *Yorkshire Evening Post*, 23 January 1976.
3. Woodrow, Jane Carter, with Jackson, Neil, *After Evil* (London: Hodder & Stoughton, 2009) p.272.
4. 'Woman Battered: "Killer May Strike Again" Warning', *Yorkshire Evening Post*, 22 January 1976.
5. Woodrow, Jane Carter, with Jackson, Neil, *After Evil*, p.116.
6. Bilton, Michael, *Wicked*, p.26.
7. Ibid.
8. Woodrow, Jane Carter, with Jackson, Neil, *After Evil*, p.124.
9. Yallop, David, *Deliver Us from Evil* (London: Corgi, 1993), p.68.
10. Kinsley, Peter and Smyth, Frank, *I'm Jack*, p.57.
11. Ibid, p.58.
12. 'Husband of Victim Speaks', *Yorkshire Evening Post*, 23 January 1976.
13. 'Killer is a Maniac, say Police', *Yorkshire Evening Post*, 23 January 1976.
14. 'Husband of Victim Speaks', *Yorkshire Evening Post*, 23 January 1976.
15. Kinsley, Peter and Smyth, Frank, *I'm Jack*, p.57.
16. BBC Radio 4: *The Reunion*, presented by Sue MacGregor, 26 August 2016.
17. Kinsley, Peter and Smyth, Frank, *I'm Jack*, p.57.
18. 'Frightened Women Shun City's "Murder Mile"', *Yorkshire Post*, 23 January 1976.
19. 'Square Mile of Fear', *Yorkshire Evening Post*, 23 January 1976.
20. Woodrow, Jane Carter, with Jackson, Neil, *After Evil*, p.212.
21. 'Long Shadow of the Ripper Still Haunts the Children Whose Lives He Tore Apart', *The Yorkshire Post*, 19 July 2009.

6: Marcella

1. Yallop, David, *Deliver Us from Evil* (London: Corgi, 1993), p.68.
2. Bilton, Michael, *Wicked*, p.33.

3. Ibid.
4. Kinsley, Peter and Smyth, Frank, *I'm Jack*, p.57.
5. Ibid.
6. 'Square Mile of Fear', *Yorkshire Evening Post*, 23 January 1976.
7. Woodrow, Jane Carter, with Jackson, Neil, *After Evil*, p.146.
8. Ibid.
9. Cross, Roger, *The Yorkshire Ripper*, p.31.
10. Ibid, p.23.
11. Westwood, Sallie and Williams, John, (eds), *Imagining Cities: Scripts, Signs, Memories* (London: Routledge, 2005), p.114.
12. 'No Woman Safe with Ripper Free, say Police', *Yorkshire Post*, 28 June 1977.
13. Jones, Barbara, *Voices from An Evil God: The True Story of the Yorkshire Ripper and the Woman Who Loved Him* (London: Blake Publishing, 1993), p.119.
14. Ibid.
15. *Manhunt: The Search for the Yorkshire Ripper*, Lysander Productions, Ray Fitzwalter Associates, 1999.
16. Jones, Barbara, *Voices*, p.119.
17. Bilton, Michael, *Wicked*, p.77.
18. Ibid, p.78.
19. 'No Woman Safe with Ripper Free, say Police', *Yorkshire Evening Post*, 28 June 1977.
20. Ibid.

7: Irene

1. 'Murder Victim "Quit Job to Escape Man"', *Yorkshire Evening Post*, 8 February 1977.
2. Kinsley, Peter and Smyth, Frank, *I'm Jack*, p.60.
3. Ibid.
4. 'Lovers' Lane Murder of Mystery Woman', *Yorkshire Evening Post*, 7 February 1977.
5. Bilton, Michael, *Wicked*, p.87.
6. 'Lovers' Lane Murder of Mystery Woman', *Yorkshire Post*, 7 February 1977.
7. Kinsley, Peter and Smyth, Frank, *I'm Jack*, p.62.
8. 'Park Victim Was Young Mother of Two: Link with "Jack the Ripper" Style Deaths? Police Chief Keeps Open Mind', *Yorkshire Evening Post*, 7 February 1977.
9. Ibid.
10. Bilton, Michael, *Wicked*, p.94.
11. 'Park Victim Was Young Mother of Two: Link with "Jack the Ripper" Style Deaths? Police Chief Keeps Open Mind', *Yorkshire Evening Post*, 7 February 1977.
12. 'Murder Victim "Quit Job to Escape Man"', *Yorkshire Post*, 8 February 1977.
13. Ibid.
14. 'Murder: New Clues from Attack Girl', *Yorkshire Evening Post*, 11 February 1977.
15. 'Poster Plea in Hunt for Woman's Killer', *Yorkshire Evening Post*, 14 February 1977.

8: Patricia

1. Bilton, Michael, *Wicked*, p.116.
2. 'Yorks Woman Found Battered: Leeds Link Probe', *Yorkshire Evening Post*, 25 April 1977.
3. Ibid.
4. Ibid.
5. Ibid.
6. Bilton, Michael, *Wicked*, p.113.

9: Jayne

1. 'Jayne's Mother Urges Ripper: Give Up Now', *Yorkshire Post*, 29 June 1977.
2. *Exploring Gender and Fear Retrospectively: Stories of Women's Fear During the "Yorkshire Ripper" Murders*, Louise Wattis, 3 September 2017, paper published online by Taylor & Francis Online. https://www.tandfonline.com/doi/abs/10.1080/0966369X.2017.1372384
3. Debra Sacks, author interview, March 2018.
4. Ibid.
5. Ibid.
6. Ibid.
7. 'Almost bursting': Cross, Roger, *The Yorkshire Ripper*, p.80; 'She was so': 'How Many More Must Die?' *Daily Express*, 17 April 1979.
8. Kinsley, Peter and Smyth, Frank, *I'm Jack*, p.74.
9. Ibid.
10. Ibid.
11. Nicholson, Michael, *The Yorkshire Ripper* (London: Star Books, 1979), p.65.
12. Bilton, Michael, *Wicked*, p.152.
13. BBC Radio News report, presented by Chris Underwood, 22 May 1981.
14. 'How Many More Must Die?' *Daily Express*, 17 April 1979.
15. Bilton, Michael, *Wicked*, p.144.
16. 'Ripper Riddle in Murder of Jayne, 16: Disco Girl Battered in City's Red-Light District', *Yorkshire Post*, 27 June 1977.
17. Ibid.
18. 'Police Find Links', *Yorkshire Evening Post*, 27 June 1977.
19. 'Victims of a Burning Hatred?' *Yorkshire Post*, 27 June 1977.
20. 'Frightened Women Shun City's "Murder Mile"', *Yorkshire Post*, 23 January 1976.
21. 'Police Find Links', *Yorkshire Evening Post*, 27 June 1977.
22. 'Ripper Riddle in Murder of Jayne, 16: Disco Girl Battered in City's Red-Light District', *Yorkshire Post*, 27 June 1977.
23. 'Ripper's Shadow: Jayne, aged 16, Becomes Murder Victim No.5', *Daily Express*, 27 June 1977.
24. 'No Woman Safe with Ripper Free, say Police', *Yorkshire Post*, 28 June 1977.
25. Ibid.
26. 'An Open Message to the Ripper', *Yorkshire Evening Post*, 28 June 1977.
27. *The Times*, 23 May 1981. No further details.
28. *Sunday Mirror*, 10 May 1981. No further details.
29. 'Leeds: Curfew on Men', *Spare Rib,* Issue 83, June 1979.
30. Ibid.
31. Ibid.
32. Woodrow, Jane Carter, with Jackson, Neil, *After Evil*, p.180.
33. BBC Radio 4: *The Choice*.
34. McCann, Richard, *Just A Boy*, p.65.
35. 'How Many More Must Die?' *Daily Express*, 17 April 1979.
36. Debra Sacks, author interview, March 2018.
37. 'The Ripper's Other Victims', *Yorkshire Evening Post*, 30 June 1977.
38. 'Jayne's Mother Urges Ripper: Give Up Now', *Yorkshire Post*, 29 June 1977.
39. 'The Ripper's Other Victims', *Yorkshire Evening Post*, 30 June 1977.
40. 'Police Find Links', *Yorkshire Evening Post*, 27 June 1977.
41. Nicholson, Michael, *The Yorkshire Ripper*, p.30.
42. 'My Years in the Grip of the Ripper', *Bradford Telegraph & Argus*, 17 December 2007.

43. *Left for Dead by the Yorkshire Ripper*, BriteSpark Films, 2014.
44. Kinsley, Peter and Smyth, Frank, *I'm Jack*, p.78.
45. 'No Woman Safe with Ripper Free, say Police', *Yorkshire Post*, 28 June 1977.
46. 'Jayne's Killer May Have Been Heard', *Yorkshire Post*, 30 June 1977.
47. '13,000 Interviews in Hunt for Killer', *Yorkshire Evening Post*, June 1977.
48. 'Ripper Probe Police Reopen Attack File', *Yorkshire Evening Post*, 2 July 1977.
49. Ibid.
50. 'Jayne is Killed – New Fear Stalks Suburb', *Yorkshire Evening Post*, 27 June 1977.
51. Kinsley, Peter and Smyth, Frank, *I'm Jack*, p.83.

10: Maureen

1. Bilton, Michael, *Wicked*, p.153.
2. 'Ripper Police at Woman's Bedside', *Yorkshire Post*, 11 July 1977.
3. Ibid.
4. *Manhunt: The Search for the Yorkshire Ripper*, Lysander Productions, Ray Fitzwalter Associates, 1999.
5. 'Ripper Victim Talks – May Give Vital Clues', *Yorkshire Evening Post*, 11 July 1977.
6. 'Ripper Police at Woman's Bedside', *Yorkshire Post*, 11 July 1977.
7. Ibid
8. 'Ripper Victim Talks – May Give Vital Clues', *Yorkshire Evening Post*, 11 July 1977.
9. 'New Ripper Victim', *Daily Mirror*, 11 July 1977.
10. 'Ripper Victim May Know More', *Yorkshire Evening Post*, 13 July 1977.
11. Kinsley, Peter and Smyth, Frank, *I'm Jack*, p.85.
12. Bilton, Michael, *Wicked*, p.162.
13. Ibid.
14. Byford, Lawrence, *The Yorkshire Ripper Case: Review of the Police Investigation of the Case*: Report to the Secretary of State for the Home Office, Home Office, London, December 1981.

11: Jean

1. Granada Television, *World in Action*: There's No Place Like Hulme, 10 April 1978.
2. Ibid.
3. Ibid.
4. 'What Happened Next?', *Observer*, 7 September 2003.
5. Ibid.
6. Ibid.
7. Glinert, Ed, *The Manchester Compendium: A Street-by-Street History of England's Greatest Industrial City* (London: Penguin, 2009), p.134.
8. Jones, Bruce, *Les Battersby & Me: The Official Autobiography of Bruce Jones* (Brafford: Great Northern Books Ltd.), pp.55–56.
9. Fletcher, Tony, *Memories of Murder: The Great Cases of a Finger-print Expert* (London: Grafton, 1987), p.217.
10. Ibid.
11. 'Who Is She? Body Riddle', *Manchester Evening News*, 11 October 1977.
12. 'Who's This Girl? Murder Riddle', *Manchester Evening News*, 11 October 1977.
13. Kinsley, Peter and Smyth, Frank, *I'm Jack*, pp.88–89.
14. 'Murder Victim Was Mother of Two', *Manchester Evening News*, 12 October 1977.
15. Ibid.
16. 'Maniac's Victim May Be Missing Mother', *Manchester Evening News*, 12 October 1977.

17. Kinsley, Peter and Smyth, Frank, *I'm Jack*, p.89.
18. 'Maniac's Victim May Be Missing Mother', *Manchester Evening News*, 12 October 1977.
19. 'Ghoul Stripped Body', *Manchester Evening News*, 13 October 1977.
20. 'Vice Girls Plea in Murder Hunt', *Manchester Evening News*, 13 October 1977.
21. Fletcher, Tony, *Memories*, p.220.
22. 'Ripper Murder Evidence', *Guardian*, 1 June 1978.
23. Kinsley, Peter and Smyth, Frank, *I'm Jack*, p.90.
24. Ibid.

12: Marylyn

1. 'Leeds: Curfew on Men', *Spare Rib*, Issue 83, June 1979.
2. Kinnell, Hilary, *Violence and Sex Work in Britain* (London: Routledge, 2008), p.19.
3. *Left for Dead by the Yorkshire Ripper*, BriteSpark Films, 2014.
4. Ibid.
5. BBC Radio News report, presented by Chris Underwood, 22 May 1981.
6. Ibid.
7. Beattie, John, *The Yorkshire Ripper Story*, p.53.
8. 'Girl Attacked in Lovers' Lane', *Yorkshire Evening Post*, 15 December 1977.
9. Beattie, John, *The Yorkshire Ripper Story*, p.53.
10. 'Girl Attacked in Lovers' Lane', *Yorkshire Evening Post*, 15 December 1977.
11. Yallop, David, *Deliver Us from Evil*, pp.158–159.
12. 'Girl Attacked in Lovers' Lane', *Yorkshire Evening Post*, 15 December 1977.
13. 'Marilyn: This Man Sought', *Yorkshire Evening Post*, 19 December 1977.
14. Ibid.
15. Sampson, Colin, *The Yorkshire Ripper Case Report*, released 30 June 1983.
16. 'The Ripper File', *Mail on Sunday*, 26 June 1983.
17. *Silent Victims: The Untold Story of the Yorkshire Ripper*, Yorkshire Television, 1996.
18. Ibid.
19. Clark, Chris and Tate, Tim, *Yorkshire Ripper: The Secret Murders* (London: Blake, 2015), p.239.
20. Bilton, Michael, *Wicked*, p.211.
21. 'The Ripper File', *Mail on Sunday*, 26 June 1983.
22. Cross, Roger, *The Yorkshire Ripper*, p.102.
23. Nicholson, Michael, *The Yorkshire Ripper*, p.30.

13: Yvonne

1. Kinsley, Peter and Smyth, Frank, *I'm Jack*, p.124.
2. Beattie, John, *The Yorkshire Ripper Story*, p.64.
3. 'Murdered Girl's Screams Ignored', *Daily Express*, 11 November 1977.
4. Cross, Roger, *The Yorkshire Ripper*, p.109.
5. Bilton, Michael, *Wicked*, p.255.
6. Ibid, p.256.
7. Helen Rytka, whose life and death is the subject of the following chapter.
8. 'My Hell – By Yvonne's Father', *Yorkshire Evening Post*, 7 February 1978.
9. Kinsley, Peter and Smyth, Frank, *I'm Jack*, p.124.
10. 'New Ripper Alert', *Yorkshire Post*, 27 March 1978.

11. Bilton, Michael, *Wicked*, pp.268–269.
12. 'Killer Seeking Notoriety', *Yorkshire Post*, 28 March 1978.
13. Ibid.
14. 'The Terror of a Rival Ripper', *Daily Mirror*, 28 March 1978. Gee believed Yvonne's injuries resembled those inflicted on twenty-year-old Carol Wilkinson, discovered unconscious in a field in October 1977 after being struck with a stone weighing fifty-six pounds. Carol was taken to Bradford Royal Infirmary, where she became the first murder victim to die while on a life-support machine. Twenty years after being convicted of killing her, Anthony Steel was released from prison in one of Britain's gravest miscarriages of justice. He died five years later.
15. 'Killer Seeking Notoriety', *Yorkshire Post*, 28 March 1978.
16. Kinsley, Peter and Smyth, Frank, *I'm Jack*, p.126.

14: Helen

1. Beattie, John, *The Yorkshire Ripper Story*, p.62.
2. 'My Favourite Daughter – By Mother of Ripper Victim', *Yorkshire Post*, 9 February 1978.
3. Ibid.
4. Kinsley, Peter and Smyth, Frank, *I'm Jack*, p.101.
5. 'My Favourite Daughter – By Mother of Ripper Victim', *Yorkshire Post*, 9 February 1978.
6. Ibid.
7. 'The Heartbreak Children', *Yorkshire Post*, 6 May 1974.
8. Ibid.
9. Ibid.
10. 'What Helen Wanted to Do Was to Get Married', *Yorkshire Post*, 8 February 1978.
11. Ibid.
12. Ibid.
13. Ibid.
14. Ibid.
15. Kinsley, Peter and Smyth, Frank, *I'm Jack*, p.104.
16. 'What Helen Wanted to Do Was to Get Married', *Yorkshire Post*, 8 February 1978.
17. Bilton, Michael, *Wicked*, pp.236–237.
18. Yallop, David, *Deliver Us from Evil*, p.176.
19. 'My Favourite Daughter – By Mother of Ripper Victim', *Yorkshire Post*, 9 February 1978.
20. Kinsley, Peter and Smyth, Frank, *I'm Jack*, p.104.
21. Ibid.
22. 'My Favourite Daughter – By Mother of Ripper Victim', *Yorkshire Post*, 9 February 1978.
23. Yallop, David, *Deliver Us from Evil*, p.168.
24. 'The Ripper's Grisly Trail', *Yorkshire Post*, 4 February 1978.
25. 'Ripper Victim?' *Yorkshire Evening Post*, 4 February 1978.
26. 'The Ripper's Grisly Trail', *Yorkshire Post*, 4 February 1978.
27. 'The most tragic': 'The Ripper's Grisly Trail', *Yorkshire Post*, 4 February 1978; 'One of life's losers': 'The Short, Unhappy Life of Helen Rytka', *Yorkshire Post*, 7 February 1978.
28. 'The Short, Unhappy Life of Helen Rytka', *Yorkshire Post*, 7 February 1978.
29. 'Ripper Appeal to Chat Show Wives', *Yorkshire Post*, 10 February 1978.
30. 'My Favourite Daughter – By Mother of Ripper Victim', *Yorkshire Post*, 9 February 1978.

31. 'The Short, Unhappy Life of Helen Rytka', *Yorkshire Post*, 7 February 1978.
32. Bilton, Michael, *Wicked*, p.237.
33. Nicholson, Michael, *The Yorkshire Ripper*, p.71.
34. Ibid.
35. Ibid.
36. 'Police in Row as Ripper Victim's Sister is Gagged', *Yorkshire Post*, 13 February 1978.
37. Ibid.
38. 'Shadows of the Ripper', *Yorkshire Evening Post*, 13 February 1978.
39. Beattie, John, *The Yorkshire Ripper Story*, p.62.
40. Nicholson, Michael, *The Yorkshire Ripper*, p.75.

15: Vera

1. Nicholson, Michael, *The Yorkshire Ripper*, p.79.
2. Jackson, Louisa A., Bartie, Angela, *Policing Youth: Britain 1945–70* (Oxford: Oxford University Press, 2014), p.125.
3. 'It's Going to be a Lean Night for Anyone with a Geordie Accent', *Daily Express*, 28 June 1989.
4. Nicholson, Michael, *The Yorkshire Ripper*, p.79.
5. 'Ripper May Have Given Victim Lift', *Manchester Evening News*, 19 May 1978.
6. Ibid.
7. Kinnell, Hilary, *Violence*, pp.11–12.
8. Fletcher, Tony, *Memories*, p.223.
9. Kinsley, Peter and Smyth, Frank, *I'm Jack*, p.129.
10. Fletcher, Tony, *Memories*, p.225.
11. 'Patients Quizzed for Ripper Clues', *Manchester Evening News*, 18 May 1978.
12. 'The Ripper Victim's Client Did Not Turn Up', *Manchester Evening News*, 19 May 1978.
13. 'There Will Be No Justice for My Joan', *Lancashire Evening Post*, 11 February 2011.
14. Kinsley, Peter and Smyth, Frank, *I'm Jack*, p.170.
15. Cross, Roger, *The Yorkshire Ripper*, p.16.
16. Kinsley, Peter and Smyth, Frank, *I'm Jack*, p.170.
17. 'Lost interest': 'I'll Always Feel the Ripper's Scars', *News of the World*, 11 May 1986; 'I could not': Cross, Roger, *The Yorkshire Ripper*, p.15.
18. 'I'll Finish You Off This Time, Said Voice: Amazing Escape of Olive Smelt', 1981. No further details of this newspaper clipping.
19. Christa Ackroyd, author interview, 13 March 2018.
20. Ibid.
21. Ibid.
22. The Forgiveness Project.
23. BBC Radio 4: *The Choice*.
24. Bilton, Michael, *Wicked*, p.296.

16: Josephine

1. Denise Cavanagh, author interview, February 2018.
2. Kinsley, Peter and Smyth, Frank, *I'm Jack*, p.23.
3. Ibid.
4. Kinnell, Hilary, *Violence*, pp.12–13.
5. Ibid.

6. Kinsley, Peter and Smyth, Frank, *I'm Jack*, pp.20–21.
7. Ibid, p.25.
8. Ibid, p.140.
9. Ibid.
10. Ibid.
11. Bilton, Michael, *Wicked*, p.326.
12. Sir Michael Havers, trial testimony, May 1981.
13. Kinsley, Peter and Smyth, Frank, *I'm Jack*, p.136.
14. Ibid, p.138.
15. '"Terrible Mistake" Fear in New Ripper Hunt', *Yorkshire Post*, 6 April 1979.
16. 'Every Woman in Danger', *Yorkshire Post*, 7 April 1979.
17. Ibid.
18. 'Fatal Error of the Ripper', *Daily Express*, 7 April 1979.
19. 'Pray for the Ripper', *Daily Express*, 9 April 1979.
20. Kinsley, Peter and Smyth, Frank, *I'm Jack*, p.29.
21. Ibid, pp.142–143.
22. 'That's the Man: Photofit Ties In, says Ripper Victim Who Lived', *Yorkshire Evening Post*, 10 April 1979.
23. 'She was a tall': 'Fatal Error of the Ripper', *Daily Express*, 7 April 1979; 'I don't hate': 'Watch Girl's Deadly Rush', *Yorkshire Evening Post*, 7 April 1979.
24. Kinsley, Peter and Smyth, Frank, *I'm Jack*, p.140.
25. 'Pray for the Ripper', *Daily Express*, 9 April 1979.
26. Kinsley, Peter and Smyth, Frank, *I'm Jack*, p.142.
27. 'A Leeds Mother's Prayer … This Monster Must Be Caught', *Yorkshire Evening Post*, 10 April 1979.
28. 'How Many More Must Die?' *Daily Express*, 17 April 1979.

17: Barbara

1. Bilton, Michael, *Wicked*, p.346.
2. Ibid, p.347.
3. 'Ripper Hunt: Attack Girl Is Sought', *Yorkshire Evening Post*, 10 February 1977.
4. Smith, Joan, *Misogynies*, p.181.
5. 'Police Probe Ripper Writing', *Daily Mirror*, 25 February 1979.
6. *The Real Story with Fiona Bruce: Ripper Hoaxer*, BBC1, 2006.
7. *Left for Dead by the Yorkshire Ripper*, BriteSpark Films, 2014.
8. *Martin Kemp's Murder Files: The Yorkshire Ripper*, Discovery Networks/IWC Media 2016.
9. *The Real Story with Fiona Bruce: Ripper Hoaxer*.
10. Smith, Joan, *Misogynies*, p.185.
11. Ibid, p.184.
12. Ibid, p.171.
13. Ibid, p.170.
14. Kinsley, Peter and Smyth, Frank, *I'm Jack*, p.167.
15. Ibid, p.154.
16. 'The Ripper's New Trail of Grief', *Daily Express*, 6 September 1979.
17. *The Real Story with Fiona Bruce: Ripper Hoaxer*.
18. Ibid.
19. 'The Ripper's New Trail of Grief', *Daily Express*, 6 September 1979.
20. 'Victim of a Monster', *Daily Express*, 5 September 1979.
21. Ibid.
22. 'Tragedy of the Girl Who Loved Horses', *Yorkshire Post*, 6 September 1979.

23. Ibid.
24. *The Real Story with Fiona Bruce: Ripper Hoaxer.*
25. 'Victim of a Monster', *Daily Express*, 5 September 1979.
26. Kinsley, Peter and Smyth, Frank, *I'm Jack*, p.159.
27. *The Real Story with Fiona Bruce: Ripper Hoaxer.*
28. 'The Rendezvous Ripper Victim Barbara Couldn't Keep', *Yorkshire Evening Post*, 7 September 1979.
29. 'Victim of a Monster', *Daily Express*, 5 September 1979.
30. *The Real Story with Fiona Bruce: Ripper Hoaxer.*
31. 'Girl's Murder Starts Major Ripper Alert', *Yorkshire Post*, 4 September 1979.
32. 'The Ripper Claims His 12th Victim', *Yorkshire Evening Post*, 4 September 1979.
33. 'Ripper Police Wait for Killer's Message', *Yorkshire Post*, 5 September 1979.
34. Ibid.
35. 'Barbara's Mystery Walk into a Maniac's Clutches', *Yorkshire Post*, 5 September 1979.
36. Ibid.
37. Ibid.
38. 'Killing Rekindles Hate for "Evil Monster"', *Yorkshire Post*, 5 September 1979.
39. 'Everyone Was Special to Barbara', *Yorkshire Post*, 5 September 1979.
40. Kinsley, Peter and Smyth, Frank, *I'm Jack*, p.161.
41. 'The Rendezvous Ripper Victim Barbara Couldn't Keep', *Yorkshire Evening Post*, 7 September 1979.
42. Editorial, *Yorkshire Post*, 5 September 1979.
43. Beattie, John, *The Yorkshire Ripper Story*, p.85.
44. Christa Ackroyd, author interview, 13 March 2018.
45. 'Ripper Police Believe Net is Closing', *Yorkshire Evening Post*, 6 September 1979.
46. Cross, Roger, *The Yorkshire Ripper*, p.177.
47. 'Next Spot for Murder Named in New Letter', *Yorkshire Evening Post*, 7 September 1979.

18: Marguerite

1. 'An obvious': Smith, Joan, *Misogynies*, p.174; 'dissimilar to': Smith, Joan, *Misogynies*, p.172.
2. Ibid, p.178.
3. Ibid, p.172.
4. Ibid, p.174.
5. Ibid.
6. 'Legacy of the Yorkshire Ripper', *Daily Mail*, 24 April 1999.
7. Ibid.
8. Smith, Joan, *Misogynies*, p.181.
9. Ibid, p.179.
10. Ibid, pp.176–177.
11. Ibid, p.175.
12. Byford, Lawrence, The Yorkshire Ripper Case.
13. 'Checklist for Survival', *Sunday Mirror*, 15 April 1979.
14. 'A Fear Which Had Claimed the Night', *Guardian*, 17 December 1979.
15. Ibid.
16. McSmith, Andy, *No Such Thing as Society: A History of Britain in the 1980s* (London: Constable & Robinson, 2011), p.37.
17. Walkowitz, Judith R., *City of Dreadful Delight: Narratives of Sexual Danger in Late Victorian London* (Chicago: University of Chicago Press, 1992), p.4.
18. Ibid.

19. *Sunday Mirror*, 10 May 1981. (No further details.)
20. Walkowitz, Judith R., *City of Dreadful Delight*, p.4.
21. Ibid.
22. Ibid.
23. 'Good Girls, Bad Girls', *Guardian*, 2 October 1979.
24. 'Prostitutes Are Just Easy Pickings', *Spare Rib*, quotation taken from British Library website: Spare Rib online: https://www.bl.uk/spare-rib
25. 'Sex Killer Victim', *Yorkshire Evening Post*, 22 August 1980.
26. Bilton, Michael, *Wicked*, pp.427–428.
27. 'A New Ripper at Large, Fear Police', *Yorkshire Post*, 22 August 1980.
28. 'Sex Killer Victim', *Yorkshire Evening Post*, 22 August 1980.
29. Ibid.
30. Ibid.
31. 'Police Comb Margo Diaries', *Yorkshire Evening Post*, 23 August 1980.
32. 'How Margot Walked to Her Death', *Daily Mirror*, 23 August 1980.
33. 'Did Margo Have Secret Lover?' *Yorkshire Evening Post*, 25 August 1980.
34. 'Opinion: Don't Walk Alone', *Keighley News*, 28 November 1980.

19: Upadhya

1. 'Alley Attack on Leeds Woman, 34', *Yorkshire Evening Post*, 25 September 1980.
2. Ibid.
3. Ibid.
4. Ibid.
5. 'Fairground Quiz Over Attack on Woman', *Yorkshire Evening Post*, 26 September 1980.
6. 'Doctor Kept Ripper Attack a Secret for Four Months', *The Straits Times*, 24 May 1981.
7. Ibid.
8. Beattie, John, *The Yorkshire Ripper Story*, p.89.
9. 'Doctor Kept Ripper Attack a Secret for Four Months', *The Straits Times*, 24 May 1981.
10. Ibid.
11. BBC 2: *Newsnight*, 27 November 1980.
12. Ibid.
13. Ibid.
14. Ibid.
15. Ibid.
16. Ibid.
17. Ibid.
18. Ibid.
19. Jones, Barbara, *Voices*, p.209.
20. Kinsley, Peter and Smyth, Frank, *I'm Jack*, p.145.
21. 'I'll Finish You Off This Time, Said Voice: Amazing Escape of Olive Smelt', 1981. No further details.
22. 'The Ripper's Bitter Legacy', *Daily Mail*, 1 February 1997.
23. *Spare Rib*, quotation taken from British Library website: Spare Rib online: https://www.bl.uk/spare-rib
24. McSmith, Andy, *No Such Thing*, pp.34–35.
25. Ibid, p.37.
26. 'Girls in Ripper Riot Fury', *Daily Mirror*, 23 November 1980.
27. *The Times*, Mary Whitehouse to the Editor, 9 December 1980.

20: Theresa

1. BBC News online, 'Ripper Victim: "He Shouldn't Be Let Out at All"', 16 July 2010. http://www.bbc.co.uk/news/uk-10657170
2. BBC News online, 'Yorkshire Ripper Victim: I'll Never Forget That Face', 16 July 2010. http://www.bbc.co.uk/news/av/uk-10654188/yorkshire-ripper-victim-i-ll-never-forget-that-face
3. BBC News online, 'Ripper Victim: "He Shouldn't Be Let Out at All"'.
4. BBC News online, 'Yorkshire Ripper Victim: I'll Never Forget That Face'.
5. ITN News clip, 30 November 1980.
6. 'Ripper Chase Riddle', *Daily Express*, 1 December 1980.
7. ITN News, 30 November 1980.
8. Bilton, Michael, *Wicked*, pp.430–432.
9. 'Ripper Chase Riddle', *Daily Express*, 1 December 1980.
10. 'I Am Sure It Was the Ripper', *Daily Express*, 2 December 1980.
11. Ibid.
12. Cross, Roger, *The Yorkshire Ripper*, p.189.
13. *Manhunt: The Search for the Yorkshire Ripper*.
14. Cross, Roger, *The Yorkshire Ripper*, p.190.

21: Jacqueline

1. 'The Girl Who Died …' *Daily Express*, 6 January 1981.
2. 'My Friend and Her Fellow Victims are Worth More Than Crimes That Shook the World', *Radio Times*, 28 March 2013.
3. Jones, Barbara, *Voices*, p.201.
4. 'When the Friday Phone Calls Stopped for Mrs Doreen Hill', *Sunday Express*, 10 May 1981.
5. Cross, Roger, *The Yorkshire Ripper*, p.192.
6. 'Don't Shield This Maniac', *Daily Mirror*, 21 November 1980.
7. Beattie, John, *The Yorkshire Ripper Story*, p.147.
8. 'Ripper Police Stay Tight-Lipped', *Guardian*, 21 November 1980.
9. 'My Friend and Her Fellow Victims', *Radio Times*, 28 March 2013.
10. 'Another Maniac At Large', *Yorkshire Post*, 19 November 1980.
11. Ibid.
12. 'Police Start Inquiry', *Yorkshire Post*, 22 November 1980.
13. 'Ripper Police Stay Tight-Lipped', *Guardian*, 21 November 1980.
14. 'It's the Ripper', *Yorkshire Evening Post*, 19 November 1980.
15. 'Terrified Women Say: We're Under Curfew', *Yorkshire Evening Post*, 20 November 1980.
16. *Exploring Gender and Fear Retrospectively: Stories of Women's Fear During the "Yorkshire Ripper" Murders*, Louise Wattis, 3 September 2017, paper published online by Taylor & Francis Online. https://www.tandfonline.com/doi/abs/10.1080/0966369X.2017.1372384
17. Ibid.
18. 'Why Can They Not Catch the Ripper?', *Yorkshire Post*, 20 November 1980.
19. 'Ripper Riddle of the Bloodstained Handbag', *Yorkshire Evening Post*, 21 November 1980.
20. Ibid.
21. *Yorkshire Post*, 21 November 1980. No further details.
22. 'Angry Women', *Yorkshire Post*, 24 November 1980.

23. McSmith, Andy, *No Such Thing*, p.41.
24. Bilton, Michael, *Wicked*, p.443.
25. McSmith, Andy, *No Such Thing*, p.41.
26. Ibid.
27. Ibid.
28. '"Help Trap Ripper", Pleads Girl's Mother', *Yorkshire Post*, 25 November 1980.
29. BBC Radio News report, presented by Chris Underwood, 22 May 1981.

22: Olivia

1. 'Olivia Reivers Has Reason to Wonder', *People*, 26 January 1981.
2. 'The Luckiest Escape', *Yorkshire Post*, 19 May 1981.
3. 'Olivia Reivers Has Reason to Wonder', *People*, 26 January 1981.
4. McSmith, Andy, *No Such Thing*, p.41.
5. Ring, Robert, report on the arrest, January 1981, read at court, May 1981.
6. Beattie, John, *The Yorkshire Ripper Story*, p8.
7. Peter Sutcliffe, witness statement, January 1981. Unless otherwise stated, all quotations from Sutcliffe are taken from his witness statements of January 1981.
8. BBC Radio 4: *The Reunion*.
9. Beattie, John, *The Yorkshire Ripper Story*, p.8.
10. Ibid.
11. 'Terror of £10 Vice Girl in Ripper Hunt', *Daily Star*, 6 January 1981.

23: 'An Inner Compulsion to Kill'

1. Trevor Birdsall, trial testimony, May 1981.

24: Women on Trial

1. 'The Ripper's Bitter Legacy', *Daily Mail*, 1 February 1997.
2. 'I'll Finish You Off This Time, Said Voice: Amazing Escape of Olive Smelt', 1981. No further details.
3. 'Crime People: I Survived The Ripper', *People*, 16 January 2000.
4. Beattie, John, *The Yorkshire Ripper Story*, p.54.
5. Ibid, p.146.
6. Ibid, p.40.
7. *Silent Victims: The Untold Story of the Yorkshire Ripper*.
8. *The Times*, 7 May 1981. No further details.
9. Ibid.
10. *Observer*, 7 May 1981. No further details.
11. Smith, Joan, *Misogynies*, p.193.
12. Peter Sutcliffe, pre-trial testimony to Dr Hugo Milne, read in court.
13. Josephine Whitaker's injuries included a small puncture wound to her left breast, which caused some disagreement between experts regarding its cause; had detectives been able to state with conviction that it was a bite mark, it would have been considered a sexual component. There was no mention of it during the trial, but afterwards *The Sunday Times* described it as a bite mark, although Sutcliffe had categorically denied it.
14. Bilton, Michael, *Wicked*, pp.493–494.
15. Walkowitz, Judith R., *City of Dreadful Delight*, p.4.

16. 'Mother's Exposure as Secret Adulteress Set Yorkshire Ripper on Path to Murders', *Daily Express*, 3 September 2017.
17. 'Anti-Mothers, Uber-Mothers, Passive Mothers and the Making of Murderers', *Huffington Post*, 13 May 2016.
18. *Spare Rib*, 1981.
19. Smith, Joan, *Misogynies*, p.200.
20. *The Yorkshire Ripper Investigation*, ITN, 1988.
21. 'I'd Like to Hang Him', *Daily Express*, 23 May 1981.
22. 'Evil Coward', *Daily Mirror*, 23 May 1981.
23. 'You sit': *The Yorkshire Ripper Investigation*, ITN 1988; 'He's gone': 'I Was Just Praying For A Verdict of Murder', *Yorkshire Post*, 19 May 1981.
24. 'Chief Says Police Let Ripper Slip', 27 June 1983, United Press International website, https://www.upi.com/Archives/1983/06/27/Chief-says-police-let-Ripper-slip/1086425534400/
25. Richard McCann, author interview, February 2018.
26. 'Suspect Admits to Wearside Jack Hoax', 24 February 2006.
27. 'Wearside Jack', *Independent*, 21 March 2006.
28. *The Real Story with Fiona Bruce: Ripper Hoaxer.*
29. Richard McCann, author interview, February 2018.
30. *The Real Story with Fiona Bruce: Ripper Hoaxer.*

25: Reclaiming the Night

1. Jones, Barbara, *Voices*, pp.102–103.
2. Yallop, David, *Deliver Us from Evil*, p.7.
3. 'I'll Always Feel the Ripper's Scars', *News of the World*, 11 May 1986.
4. Ibid.
5. Ibid.
6. 'The Ripper's Bitter Legacy', *Daily Mail*, 1 February 1997.
7. 'Ripper Victim Wins Fight for Compensation', *Guardian*, 2 December 1981.
8. Ibid.
9. Nicholson, Michael, *The Yorkshire Ripper*, p.92.
10. 'Ripper Was Never Mad, Just Pure Evil', *Daily Mail,* 13 August 2016.
11. 'Crime People: I Survived The Ripper', *People*, 16 January 2000.
12. Ibid.
13. *Silent Victims: The Untold Story of the Yorkshire Ripper.*
14. 'Parents of Yorkshire Ripper Victim Say Her Killer Must Die in Jail', *Northamptonshire Telegraph*, 27 March 2010.
15. '£10 Million for Keeping the Ripper in Comfort', *Daily Mail*, 29 November 2015.
16. 'When the Friday Phone Calls Stopped for Mrs Doreen Hill', *Sunday Express*, 10 May 1981.
17. 'Victim's Mother May Sue Over Ripper Articles', *Guardian*, 24 June 1983.
18. 'When the Friday Phone Calls Stopped for Mrs Doreen Hill', *Sunday Express*, 10 May 1981.
19. 'Long Shadow of the Ripper Still Haunts the Children Whose Lives He Tore Apart', *Yorkshire Post,* 19 July 2009.
20. Geoff Beattie, author interview, March 2017.
21. Ibid.
22. 'Son's Search for Answers', *Blackpool Gazette*, 23 May 2012.
23. 'The Ripper's Final Victim', *Daily Express*, 29 December 2007.
24. Ibid.
25. Ibid.

26. BBC Radio 4: *The Choice*.
27. Richard McCann, author interview, February 2018.
28. Ibid.
29. The Forgiveness Project.
30. Richard McCann, author interview, February 2018.
31. Ibid.
32. Ibid.

26: Unbroken

1. Walkowitz, Judith R., *City of Dreadful Delight*, p.4.
2. Keith Hellawell, *The Outsider: The Autobiography of One of Britain's Most Controversial Policemen* (London: HarperCollins, 2002), p.164.
3. Ibid.
4. Mo Lea, author interview, March 2018.
5. Ibid.
6. *Silent Victims: The Untold Story of the Yorkshire Ripper*, Yorkshire Television, 1996.
7. Mo Lea, author interview, March 2018.
8. Ibid.
9. Ibid.
10. 'Leeds Hunt after Girl Student Attacked', *Yorkshire Evening Post*, 27 October 1980.
11. Mo Lea, author interview, March 2018.
12. *Silent Victims: The Untold Story of the Yorkshire Ripper*.
13. Mo Lea, author interview, March 2018.
14. *Silent Victims: The Untold Story of the Yorkshire Ripper*.
15. Ibid.
16. 'The Ripper Scarred Me For Life', *Daily Telegraph*, Catherine O'Brien, 5 December 1996.

PICTURE CREDITS

Page 1: Map by Claire Cater

Page 2: Simon Wilkinson / REX / Shutterstock (top); Phillip Jackson / *Daily Mail* / REX / Shutterstock.

Page 3: Mirrorpix (top left and right); Steve Bent / *Mail on Sunday* / REX / Shutterstock (bottom).

Page 4: *Yorkshire Post* (top); Simon Wilkinson / REX / Shutterstock (bottom).

Page 5: Associated Newspapers / REX / Shutterstock (top left); Topfoto (top right); Simon Wilkinson / REX / Shutterstock (bottom left); PA/Topfoto (bottom right).

Page 6: Simon Wilkinson / REX / Shutterstock (both).

Page 7: David Muscroft / REX / Shutterstock (top); Photofusion / REX / Shutterstock (bottom).

Page 8: © Simon Wilkinson / SWpix.com (top); Mirrorpix (centre); © Mo Lea (bottom).

INDEX

accents 11, 111
Geordie 173, 174, 189, 234
Yorkshire 12, 17, 18, 48, 174, 281
Ackroyd, Christa ix–x, 154, 186–7
Atkinson, Patricia 62–8, 116, 118,
120, 126, 195
murder scene 65–6
Sutcliffe's confession 244–6

Bandara, Dr Upadhya 202–5, 298
Sutcliffe's confession 266
Beattie, Geoff (Alan Richardson)
289–90
Bilton, Michael 275
Birdsall, Trevor 232, 233, 234–5,
237, 261, 273
Birkett, Cy 146–7, 150, 151, 152
blood groups 32, 153, 172, 189
non-secretors 32, 58
Bolton, John 57
Bould, John 26
Bould, Margaret 26–7
Bradford
Barbara Leach case 176–88
Maureen Long case 86–93
Mecca Ballroom 86, 87, 91, 92
Patricia Atkinson case 62–8
prostitution 126, 157, 194
Yvonne Pearson case 115–26
Bransberg, Jack and Pat 71–2, 77,
82–3
Bray, Steven 55, 60, 61
Browne, Nora 14, 16–17, 113–14
Browne, Tony 14, 114
Browne, Tracy 14–19, 48, 82,

113–14, 174, 190–1, 234, 269,
281, 286–7, 295, 296
Byford, Lawrence 226, 280
Byford Report 93, 106, 112, 144–5,
151, 152, 163, 205, 216, 223,
280, 294

cars
descriptions of 18, 25, 38, 43, 51,
61, 88, 90, 109, 111, 112, 140,
142, 165–6, 183, 229, 295
surveillance operations 91, 104,
112, 148, 156
tyre tracks 59, 91, 112, 150, 151
Cavanagh, WPC Denise 100, 150,
156
Claxton, Marcella 49–53, 56, 60–1,
114, 285–6
Sutcliffe's confession 242–3
Clelland, Melvyn 137–8
climate of fear 156, 186, 192–3,
222, 224, 225–6
Coonan, Kathleen 276, 277
copycat killers 123–4
Criminal Injuries Compensation
Board 50, 283, 285, 286

De Mattia, Bernardina 127, 128–9,
134, 135, 142–3, 145
denigration of victims 1, 2, 20,
22–3, 32–3, 79–80, 92, 192,
275, 284, 292
Domaille, Det. Chief Supt. John
head of Ripper investigation
squad 126, 148